LOBEL'S MEAT *and* WINE

# LOBEL'S

## MEAT and WINE

### GREAT RECIPES FOR COOKING AND PAIRING

*by* Stanley, Leon, Evan, Mark, and David Lobel

with Mary Goodbody and David Whiteman

Photographs by James Baigrie

CHRONICLE BOOKS

SAN FRANCISCO

Library of Congress Cataloging-in-Publication Data
available.

ISBN-10: 0-8118-4732-2
ISBN-13: 978-0-8118-4732-2

Manufactured in China.

DESIGNED BY Jacob T. Gardner
PROP STYLING BY Alison Attenborough
FOOD STYLING BY Barbara Fritz
TYPESETTING BY Blue Friday

Distributed in Canada by Raincoast Books
9050 Shaughnessy Street
Vancouver, British Columbia V6P 6E5

10 9 8 7 6 5 4 3 2 1

Chronicle Books LLC
85 Second Street
San Francisco, California 94105

www.chroniclebooks.com

*Writing this book has been enormously rewarding and would not have been possible without the help of many people. Thanks to Mary Goodbody and David Whiteman, whose collaboration with us made this book possible. Thank you to our agent Jane Dystel, who saw the project through from start to finish, and to Bill LeBlond, Amy Treadwell, and the rest of the team at Chronicle who turned our manuscript into a beautiful book. The book would be far less rich were it not for the keen palates that participated in our occasionally formidable wine and food tastings. We are especially grateful to Melissa Delvecchio, Patty Pulliam, and Sergei Boyce. We also benefited from the advice of a number of excellent wine merchants in both New York and Connecticut, and we're expressly thankful for the unflagging help of the entire staff at Nancy's Wines for Food in Manhattan. And a very special thanks to Professor Everett Bandman at the University of California at Davis, whose insight into the science of meat and wine cookery helped shape our thinking in chapter two. We also thank our employees, customers, and friends who make practicing the art of butchery an everyday joy for each of us. And nothing we do would be as gratifying as it is without the loving support of our families.*

# CONTENTS

# Foreword

We in the English-speaking world are blessed in our culinary literature. Our bookstores and libraries are filled with wonderful cookbooks, and wonderfully enlightening books about food. Every year, in my estimation, brings at least half a dozen new, top-flight titles that immediately go to the head of this class—and I'm delighted to predict that food-lovers will install *Lobel's Meat and Wine* there, embracing it as one of the very best new collections of recipes that has been published in a long time.

Compelling as that is, however, there is another reason for the signal importance of this groundbreaking book. Yes, our literature is rich in culinary information—but when it comes to books that intelligently and accurately discuss the pleasures of food and wine together, our storehouse of published knowledge is meager.

And that's why I'm particularly excited. *Lobel's Meat and Wine* is that extremely rare book that will actually teach you how to think about popping corks any time you're setting forks.

Why is there such a paucity of good advice on this subject?

The reason, I submit, is a simple one: Arbiters of taste, when it comes to these oeno-gastronomic matters, have been lazy. By and large, they accept the standard body of advice that has come down as "wisdom" and direct most of their efforts to applying that advice to various contemporary foods—to ethnic cuisines that have come into vogue, to new types of ingredients that have become accessible and popular, to creative innovations of chefs that need wine matches.

In precious few cases have these "arbiters" questioned the standard body of advice itself, or put in the hard work required to intelligently challenge it.

Consequently, most Americans with a newborn interest in pairing wine with food are taught the oversimplified rules of color-coding: white wine goes with fish, and red wine goes with meat. For many, there is no access to thought more sophisticated than this, and so color-coding endures as the chief criterion of wine selection.

When intrepid gastronomes want to dig a little deeper into this subject, they hit another kind of wall in the literature—the oft-repeated, classic belief that matching food and wine is based on matching a main ingredient with a grape variety. "What should I drink with lobster?" goes the query. "Chardonnay!" comes the knee-jerk answer. Forget the fact that "Chardonnay" can be the grape variety in a thin, acidic wine from a cold summer in northern Burgundy that lands on your palate like a squeeze of lemon juice, or that Chardonnay can be the basis of the thick, almost-sweet, high-alcohol juice produced in a sweltering California Central Valley summer that lands on your palate like a Mack truck. And let's not even consider how many different kinds of dishes, with different kinds of wine demands, can contain lobster as a main ingredient.

When wine lovers realize the absurdity of this strategy, they usually graduate to another, one that gets considerable play in the literature: matching flavors in food and wine. Unfortunately, this too is antediluvian thinking that needs considerable freshening. Distressingly, there are many matchmakers who get the ball rolling by determining a chief flavor in a dish—say, the flavor of raspberries in a salad dressed with a raspberry vinaigrette. Then they set out to find a wine that makes wine tasters say, "Oooh! Nuances of raspberry!" I don't deny that sometimes a flavor correspondence pays off in a small way—but looking for it, in my opinion, should never be the primary path in the search for a good match.

One of the initial joys of *Lobel's Meat and Wine* is that none of this old-fashioned, unquestioned nonsense is rehearsed again for the millionth stale time. The Lobels have crashed through to the only prescriptive system for food-and-wine matching that I think makes any sense: an anticipation of the ways in which the very basic food-flavor components of sourness, sweetness, bitterness, and saltiness interact with wine. With the help of David Whiteman, their terrific food-and-wine consultant, they add to this an equally logical view of the way in which the basic wine components of alcohol, tannin, oak, and fruitiness play with food. They present it all in one of the most well organized, clearly written, and logically argued discussions of matching wine with food—in this case wine with meat— that I've ever seen in a major cookbook, in an essay that is alone worth the book's cover price.

Then they do something that most authors on this subject never do—they get empirical. I mean highly empirical. At the time of recipe development, the Lobels, in addition to cooking up a storm, also opened myriad bottles of wine with each dish, testing their hunches, rolling the dice on long shots, and restlessly looking to prove their principles with specific, real-world wine choices . . . or overturn them entirely. They did find a few surprises, but, generally speaking, the principles articulated early in the book indeed held very well—and we are the beneficiaries, because we come away with a wealth of very specific, scrupulously tested and quite wonderful wine choices to go with the book's marvelous recipes for meat and poultry. To gild the lily, there are choices that teach, choices from which we can learn something, expressed in language that facilitates learning.

Listen to the way they discuss wine choices for a Catalan-style veal stew made with prunes and potatoes (page 84): "Because veal itself is fairly neutral . . . we looked to the ingredients that surround it. Here, the ripe sweetness of prunes . . . steered our choices. As we've stated elsewhere, when there's sweetness in a dish—even just a little—it usually tastes better with a white wine that has a touch of sweetness itself or a red that has a rich core of fruit flavors . . . In either case, what you don't want are wines that are bone-dry, austere, or, for reds, tannic."

When the Lobels go on to recommend two Spanish whites, a California Chenin Blanc, an unusual red from the Costers del Segre in Spain, and a Napa Valley Cabernet-Merlot blend—specific bottles of them—you just know you're in good hands. And if you've read the introductory material at the front of the book, you know exactly why. You're even on your way to needing no wine recommendations at all, since they guide us in how to apply the logic ourselves.

Another good example of this process—and note how the Lobels' savviness about meat and the art of cooking it has a beneficial impact on their thinking—is the discussion of the wine choices for the Tuscan roast loin of pork with rosemary, sage, and garlic (page 111): "Though boldly flavored on the outside with herbs and garlic, this pork loin roast still presents, in the end, a very delicate mouthful of pork. Although most of the Sangiovese-based Tuscan wine favorites would work quite well with this classic dish, some are better than others. It is not the particular flavors of these wines that matter; it's their relative weights and textures. Among the many sub-regions of Chianti itself, we found that the regular, *normale*, bottlings harmonize best. These are medium-to-medium-full-bodied wines with warmly tart black cherry flavors; their tannins offer support and no more. Wines like this should go down without a catch; bigger wines will breathe too much of their alcoholic fire into the delicate pork."

And then come the specific bottles recommended, which I am, of course, completely ready to honor.

One benefit of this close, dish-by-dish analysis in *Lobel's Meat and Wine* is that you get a lot of details focusing on ingredients beyond meat alone. I loved the book's discussion of wine and cream in the recommendations for a venison stew with grappa-herb cream (page 189): "When it comes to wine, cream is a strange thing . . . Wines with too much tannin, too much acidity, and too much body clash with the soft richness of this creamy stew. This is a question of degree because a lightly tannic, lightly acidic, and moderately rich wine works just fine with this great venison stew."

How nuanced the thought . . . and how true the words!

Another type of discussion that sometimes occurs in the dish-by-dish analysis is also of great value: a look at the food matching attitudes of some modern wine drinkers, attitudes which impede the acceptance of appropriate matches. In a consideration of wine choices for Creamy Chicken Livers with Vin Santo (page 205), the authors comment:

"Though wine gods and taste-meisters may hurl lightning bolts, we found that a glass of chilled, sweet, nutty Vin Santo, Tuscany's distinctive dessert wine, tastes best with this. Yes, a number of Tuscan dry reds and whites are quite good, too, so drink them if the thought of consuming liver with a sweet wine makes you squirm . . . Overall, we find that truly great wine and food matches are rare. It's much more fun to play along when a match like this presents itself, a match that, it should be said, wouldn't have struck anybody as strange as recently as a hundred years ago when restaurants and dinner hosts frequently matched meat and sweet wine."

Finally—as valuable as all of this material is—there is one section of the book that absolutely veers into virgin food-and-wine territory, an area of ossified assumptions about cooking with wine that no one, in my experience, has ever had the gumption to question. But the Lobels do—and the result is a series of revelations about meat and wine that should appear as headlines in every responsible gastronomic publication.

In the second chapter, entitled "Cooking with Meat and Wine in Today's Kitchen," the Lobels report on a series of very elaborate, highly controlled experiments that tested the old truths about marinating meat in wine and selecting wine for cooking.

To give you some idea of the ambitious completeness of these tests: In the marinade experiments, they began with a two-fold division—long marinating and short marinating. For the long marinating, five different kinds of wine marinades were used (among the variables were raw wine versus cooked wine and salted wine versus unsalted wine). In the short-marinating experiment (included because chefs might use short marinating for a higher-quality cut of beef), the authors juggled such factors as the reduction of wine or the inclusion of shallots, and also prepared a nonmarinated piece of meat as a quality-and-comparison control.

The discoveries they made, to say the least, were significant, enough to warrant your complete attention before you ever dip a piece of meat again in a wine marinade.

But it went further still. The Lobels then set out to gain some insights—and challenge some mindsets—about the general selection of wine for cooking. They chose eight wines that were all over the stylistic playing field, four whites and four reds. They oversaw a series of tests, divided into long-cooking tests and short-cooking tests, to see how wine performs in different cooking contexts. In their carefully documented report, the reader is privy along the way to all kinds of insights concerning the selection of wine for cooking, as well as the science behind it. In the end, happily, the results are ringingly clear, anything but random or arbitrary: a list of eight principles emerges, gleaned from all the experiments, that you are well advised to consult before you ever again choose a wine to go into your cooking pots.

I loved reading about these experiments for many reasons—experiments so indicative of the Lobels' spirit, a spirit that infuses this book. They are people who know a great deal about food and wine, but, invitingly, they seem here to be saying, "We don't know anything at all—until we meticulously test what we thought we knew." In *Lobel's Meat and Wine,* you can share in this joyful testing by reading the first chapters—and then you can enjoy its aftermath in the recipe chapters, with page after page of learned, sensible, accurate commentary on specific wines with specific recipes.

With all the insights that this cookbook provides, it comes almost as a bonus that you can turn to it again and again to prepare incredible food to make yourself, your family, and your friends extremely happy.

And you don't have to think twice about what to pour.

— David Rosengarten

# Introduction

We represent five generations of butchers, three generations of whom have been selling meat to New Yorkers since the 1930s. Today, Lobel's, our small shop on the Upper East Side of Manhattan, has an international reputation for selling the best meat available. We also have an extremely loyal local clientele.

We come by these accolades with hard work, dedication to the best, and a commitment to our customers, regardless of where they live. We spend our days helping the world's most discerning cooks buy the exact cuts of meat they want. We are passionate about treating our customers fairly and graciously and sharing our expertise when they have any questions, big or small. And, believe us, they have questions! Most are about meat, many are about cooking, and as we've noticed in recent years, an increasing number are about meat and wine.

In our last book, *Lobel's Prime Cuts,* our goal was to help our readers learn to buy meat and poultry with confidence and to provide recipes for these cuts in keeping with contemporary tastes: healthful, simple dishes that incorporate fresh flavors, pairing the best meat available with complementary vegetables, grains, and legumes that integrate the entire meal in a deliciously symbiotic fashion.

With *Lobel's Meat and Wine,* our goal is to demystify an area of the culinary world wherein inexperienced and seasoned home cooks alike may feel doubt. This time we tackle the issue of bringing a knowledgeable eye to choosing wines for cooking and serving with home-cooked meals.

## The Appreciation of Wine

Americans have a mixed and sometimes curious relationship with wine. In a culture where soft drinks and beer are ubiquitous, the regard for wine ranges from casual libation to educated enthusiasm and expertise. In strong contrast to much of Europe, where corked bottles of local "fresh" table wine are part of daily existence and fine cellars are taken for granted as regional treasures, many people in the United States do not encounter the notion of wine appreciation until they are adults.

In recent decades, however, an increased populist interest in fine cooking and wine appreciation has grown out of the proliferation of relaxed, welcoming top-quality restaurants and of sources on the subject on television and the Internet, in lifestyle publications such as custom cookbooks and more accessible wine journals, and in cooking classes and wine tastings for amateurs. As a result there is a much greater awareness of the world of wine and the wealth of information and potential experience within it.

Unfortunately, this positive movement can be derailed by overkill. The old intimidation joined by all the new information may blur into anxiety-producing vagaries on the subject for many of us. There are too many choices, too many ways for us to make a mistake, and so our curiosity may end with a few tried-and-true favorites, or we rely on wine merchants, sommeliers, and dinner guests to make our decisions.

With *Lobel's Meat and Wine,* we hope to provide an entry point to a better understanding of wine and how best to enjoy it, in command of your own kitchen and in the comfort of your own home. As opposed to an approach to wine where prized bottles are put on pedestals, our goal here is to capture and celebrate the less fussy European outlook, where the most important thing about wine is how it is enjoyed as part of a meal.

At Lobel's we sell only aged prime beef and veal and the highest-quality lamb, pork, and poultry. We never compromise on quality, and while it's not always easy to find prime beef and veal, we never fail. Prime beef and veal account for less than 2 percent of the total beef sold in the nation. Beef is America's favorite meat and clearly our biggest seller. With so much beef on the market and because the price for best quality is high, we think it's crucial you know what you're buying and that you buy the right cut. In a number of the recipes for beef braises that follow, we call for chuck. You can read more about selecting meat for slow cooking on page 21, where we emphasize that substituting a more expensive cut, such as sirloin, for the chuck will not yield a better dish. If you want a simple grilled steak, you have a good number of delectable options, but do not use chuck.

We age our beef for the same reason some wine makers age wine: It tastes better. Therefore, it stands to reason that wine lovers should employ the same enthusiasm when buying beef as when buying wine. On these pages, we hope your passion for meat and wine will come to match ours.

Over the years, we have tasted very fine wines with extraordinary beef and have found that the beef enhanced the flavor of the wine. In other words, when the beef has been of the highest quality, its flavor stands out and the wine behaves as an accent. This realization encouraged us to write this book. We want our readers to benefit from top-quality beef, lamb, and pork for their own virtues as well as for how they elevate excellent wine.

We decided to think regionally and study wines on their original European turf for this book. This allowed us to understand the wines in their cultural context as a product of the people who grow, produce, and drink them and, most important, to consider wines alongside local cuisine. We think understanding where wines come from and tasting them with food helps you to better remember flavors and recall the wines you've enjoyed, while the broad exposure is likely to make you more comfortable and adventurous at the wine shop. We chose the wines and the recipes in these pages to showcase the European traditions in marrying food and wine and, of course, their influences as carried out in the thriving food and wine culture in this country. We hope this book restores or reinforces the simple notion that wine adds immensely to the pleasure of a good meal and to the joy of cooking.

Wining and Dining

In the next two chapters, we offer our explanation of what makes a wine "food friendly," tips for how to choose wine for the dining table, and a separate investigation of what qualities distinguish the best wines for cooking with. In the recipe chapters that follow, you will find our adaptations of traditional dishes from Europe's wine country chosen not only because they incorporate a wide variety of favorite and special cuts of meat, but because each features wine as a component of the dish itself. Each recipe is accompanied by a brief, informative wine note offering a glimpse of each region's wine culture and providing a few suggestions for bottles. The source of these notes is different from that of suggestions you might find in other cookbooks: Rather than have a wine expert assess a recipe and write a wine suggestion based on past experience and intuition, for *Lobel's Meat and Wine*, each dish was sampled in the company of five to eight regional wines.

These tastings were overseen by David Whiteman, an experienced chef and wine professional, and they included from one to four other tasters with varying levels of wine knowledge and past tasting experience. These notes are entirely subjective, reflecting the actual experience of the meal, and they are designed to help you discover a rich and varied selection of wines that accompany food with grace and uniqueness—but also to serve as an informed starting point for your own foray into matching foods with wine and to spark the spirit of adventure.

-Chapter 1-

# How to Choose Food-Friendly Wines

If there are twenty wines on display at a wine tasting, typically the ones that stir attention will be those that speak loudest. Too often these are the wines that impress us, soloing from the swirled glass with their sheer scale and power and, in the process, eclipsing the quieter virtues of the other wines tasted alongside. However, we feel it is important to understand that complex, compelling, and even spectacular wines that shine at the tasting counter may not fare well when brought to the dining table. Not all great wines are great with food, and by the same token, a wine that seems underwhelming on its own can deliver immense pleasure and refreshment as an accompaniment to a meal. The Portuguese wine Vinho Verde, for example, is a pale, light, tart, low-alcohol white wine that gets modest marks in wine reviews. But this wine's qualities give it an outstanding ability to wash down any number of foods with the flavors of both in beautiful balance. Is it a complex or compelling wine? Hardly. But that's not what it offers. What it does offer is rarely captured in a comparative tasting or by a well-intentioned rating system. So when it comes to choosing a wine for your meal, it is not as simple as reaching for the fullest-bodied and -flavored Cabernet to match a beef stew or other rich dish; it may well overpower rather than enhance the food you've worked so hard to prepare.

There are, though, a few simple guidelines that will make the search for your own favorite food-friendly wines easy, and we recommend finding a good fine-wine merchant to make the process even more informative and fun.

Most cooks have a general sense of when to serve red or white, but here is a summary:

- Most beef dishes prefer red wines.
- Lamb generally prefers red but also takes to white, particularly richer Sauvignon Blanc–based wines.
- Veal, pork, chicken, rabbit, and turkey can go either way. Let the intensity of the sauce or the method of preparation be your guide.
- The natural affinity between white wines and fish and seafood dishes is well known and appreciated. Many lighter reds are delicious with all but the most delicate fish dishes.

When it comes to the specific dish, logic applies: Match the intensity of the wine with the intensity of the food, paying particular attention to more intense food flavors that may need special attention—spicy, highly acid, or very sweet, for example. Light-bodied dishes should be served with light-bodied wines, full-bodied dishes with full-bodied wines. And as you'll see in the discussion of wine components that follows (and in the wine notes that accompany each recipe), it's important to think about the sauce, too. Its role can be more central to the flavor experience than the main ingredient itself.

Wine selection can be tackled from another direction, an approach that puts less emphasis on the menu and more on the wines themselves—especially on the qualities that make specific wines compatible with various foods. The strategy in a "wine first" approach begins with understanding that there are some wines that accompany a huge range of foods and cuisines (what we call "food-friendly" wines) and others whose usefulness at the table is undeniably narrow. The first task is to learn something about the components that exist in all wines and that account for these differences; the next is to become familiar with the wines that embody the particular virtues of food friendliness and to use that knowledge to explore their versatility. This is the approach that informs the remainder of this chapter and most of the wine notes in the recipe chapters that follow.

You will find that food-friendly wines greatly increase

the odds of a happy match at the table, especially when faced with a complex multicourse (or multiethnic) meal. You can call on your recognition of these wines not only when selecting a bottle to accompany your own home cooking but at restaurants, too, where, as it often happens, everyone around the table has ordered an entirely different dish, seeming to defy any one wine choice. Armed with an awareness of the few basic principles guiding this book, you can begin the relaxed style of cooking and pouring we support.

When we plan a meal, we usually first consider how the meat will be cooked and then consider the wine. We determine the cut of beef, veal, lamb, or pork, which largely depends on how long the dish is cooked. For braises and stews, we generally recommend less expensive cuts. A great lamb stew should be made with meat from the shoulder, not from the leg. For beef braises, we use the chuck rather than bottom or top round. It simply holds up better and has better flavor. You can always make something tender with long cooking, but unless the cut of meat can withstand this cooking technique, you will lose flavor and texture.

Many of our recipes require long cooking, or braising, a technique that we've observed intimidates some of our customers. They are sometimes wary of using less expensive and often less familiar cuts of meat, and they may have reservations about the time the dish requires. But, as we hear in the shop, once they try a braised dish and have rejoiced in its full flavor, they feel like they've found buried treasure!

We agree that long cooking is not always easy for a busy family, but for the most part, these dishes can be made ahead of time and actually taste better the next day, even two or three days later. Frankly, we can't think of a more satisfying way to spend a chilly weekend than preparing a braise. The kitchen fills with warm, rich aromas, and everyone has a sense of well-being, knowing that when the dark of night falls, they will be eating a filling full-flavored meal.

Most of our recipes can be frozen for up to two months. Freeze them after they have cooled and be sure to include the sauce (or other cooking liquid) with the meat. Let the braise defrost in the refrigerator and then reheat it gently, adding a little broth or water if needed to return it to the desired consistency.

## Components in Wine for Food Friendliness

We isolated six components or characteristics that we feel determine a wine's flexibility and food friendliness: acidity, alcohol content, sweetness, tannin, fruitiness, and oak. Although we all have different thresholds for these components, they are, to a large degree, not subjective. They are players in the chemistry that happens in our mouths with every bite and every sip.

ACIDITY: The presence of good levels of acidity may be the single most important factor in making a wine pair well with a range of foods. Acidity is what gives wine its pleasing tang, or sourness, and brings it to life. You do not want, of course, an acidity that is invasive or too sharp: Balance is always the goal.

All wines are reliant on their acidities for achieving a good match at the table, white wines especially so. Additionally, good levels of acidity seem to act as a carrier of food flavors, which suggests that crisply acidic wines are not only refreshing and flexible at the table, but are also able to intensify the experience of eating itself.

Perhaps surprisingly, not only is a good level of acidity essential to the makeup of most food-friendly wines, but it is also your biggest ally when confronting food that itself has an acidic element—always a stumbling block for "low acid" wines. For instance, a lower-acid Merlot-based wine grown in a warmer climate, though delicious on its own, would have a terrible time accompanying the recipe for Chicken with Vinegar Sauce on page 153. This effect is more easily tasted than described, but it's sufficient to say that the vinegar takes a huge "bite" out of a wine like this, robbing it of whatever attractively soft and full-fruited quality it had and emphasizes instead a thinned-out, fruitlike alcohol component. By contrast, the two red wines and one white we enjoyed with the very same chicken dish were positively spectacular (you can read more about these wines on the recipe page itself). What they shared was an abundant natural acidity that stood up to (or mated with) the intense tanginess of the vinegar sauce surrounding the crisp chicken. In this way, acidity provides the first example of a bit of very useful advice: "Like goes with like." That is, when the major ingredient of a dish is acidic (a vinaigrette or a fruit-based sauce, say), it is best paired with a wine that offers good levels of acidity, too. We'll revisit the notion of "like goes with like" in the wine component discussions that follow and throughout the wine notes in the book.

Certain varieties of grapes are naturally higher in acids and thus yield wines with correspondingly higher acidity levels, but the levels of acidity still vary depending on where the grapes are grown. In general, warm climates produce wines with less acidity, while cool climates produce wines with more. Thus, levels of acidity—like so many other wine traits—are forged by the complex relationship between climate and the grape variety itself. Major varieties with the highest natural acidities are, among whites, Riesling, Chenin Blanc, Sauvignon Blanc, Grüner Veltliner, and some cool-climate Chardonnays; and among reds, Pinot Noir, Gamay, Barbera, Sangiovese, and some cool-climate Cabernet Francs. This list is hardly exhaustive; there are many lesser-known varieties and regional wines that display these high-acid traits, many of which you'll meet in the wine notes ahead.

ALCOHOL CONTENT: Alcohol is not present in grapes but is a by-product of fermentation, produced by yeasts acting on the sugars present in grapes, which in turn convert the sugars into alcohol. The more sugar in the grapes, the higher the potential alcohol. Alcohol is what largely determines a wine's weight, or "body": The more alcohol, the greater the feeling of weight in your mouth. So while alcohol is essential to the structure of the wine itself, excessive alcohol levels can make a wine taste "hot," or too heavy to flatter the food it is drunk with. High-alcohol wines tend to come from the same warm climates that produce lower-acid wine because as grape sugars continue to accumulate in ripening grapes (increasing the potential alcohol), the acidity continues to drop—another reason higher-alcohol wines tend to be less compatible with food. Generally speaking, the lower the alcohol, the more food friendly and flexible the wine.

Most wines at or below 13 percent alcohol are good candidates for serving with the widest range of dishes, and the choice of possible food partners begins to drop as wines approach 14 percent and move beyond. Again, this is not to say that a wine containing 14.5 percent alcohol won't nicely accompany a meal; many do, especially those that are well balanced (that is, display a certain harmony among parts) and contain good levels of acidity. You'll find, however, that many of the wines discussed in this book range between 8 and 13 percent alcohol by volume. Although law does not require producers to record these figures with precision, the indication of alcohol content on a wine label can be used as a general tool to help you select wines lower in alcohol.

SWEETNESS: The discussion of sweetness applies more to white wine than red (most reds are dry wines), as a greater percentage of whites rely on a light sweetness to balance them. (We're speaking here of table wines, not fully sweet dessert wines.) Most of us display a conflicted view toward sweetness in our wines. When asked, many Americans will say they prefer totally dry wines, when in fact, a number of the wines they regularly enjoy contain a measured amount of sweetness. (An obvious example of this can be found in the popularity of California Chardonnays; truly "bone-dry" white wines, like Sancerre from France's Loire Valley, are rare on the West Coast and in other warm-climate wine zones.) Along with acidity (and like fruitiness in reds; see page 24), a slight sweetness should be thought of as an aid to the pairing of food and wine. And again, this raises the notion of "like goes with like," in this case suggesting that when we're confronted with a dish that displays some sweetness within it—say, one that features apples or prunes—a good response is to pair it with a wine that itself employs some sweetness.

It's important to emphasize that sweetness as a component in wine does not mean *sweet*; it is a nuance within the flavor profile and one that does its best work when accompanied by brisk levels of acidity. Too-sweet wines short on acidity are actually sugary, flat, and hardly worth drinking. Nor are they very flexible with food. A balanced combination of a keen, food-friendly acidity with a light degree of sweetness results in a wine that really sings with a meal. Excellent examples are the pleasingly sweet-tart German Rieslings and Loire Valley Chenin Blanc wines, which partner with dishes of all kinds.

We don't want to suggest that sweetness in a wine is essential to all wine and food pairings; rather, think of it more like a tool you can choose to employ when the time is right. Truly dry white wines, for example, have among their ranks some of the most food-friendly wines, too; like slightly sweet wines, these are reliant on their vibrant acidities for this status. The use for true dry wines with food can differ enormously from their sweetish counterparts. For instance, imagine a lightly sweet-tart German Riesling next to a plate of pork and apples, and then, in contrast, imagine a steely-dry and crackling-crisp glass of France's Muscadet next to a plate of briny oysters, and you can get a sense of the different strategies at work with each of these two food-friendly wines. But here's a twist: It turns out that the same German Riesling is quite delicious with the plate of oysters, too (acidity again)—just one reason why you shouldn't think of this overview as a set of rules to be doggedly applied but, rather, as a set of food and wine "tendencies" that are best used to jump-start your own palate and instincts when selecting wines.

TANNIN: Tannin is a bitter substance present in the skins, seeds, and stems of grapes used to make red wines, imparted to a greater or lesser degree during fermentation. As a wine extracts color and flavor from grape skins, it picks up tannin as well. Tannin is also found in wood and so can be imparted by aging in oak barrels, particularly new ones. While it acts as a preservative and helps some red wines to age, it also accounts for a certain texture and feel of many of these wines when young. The effect of tannin on your mouth is a drying, astringent, sandpapery texture and is mostly to blame for any bitterness in a wine. As wine ages, its tannin softens and eventually disappears. Some grape varieties are far more tannic than others.

Although moderately tannic wines don't do too much harm, a high degree of tannin can compromise the flexibility of a wine with food. If a wine tastes powerfully tannic to you, it will probably prove troublesome at the table. Instead, save these wines for drinking on their own or perhaps with a prime steak simply prepared over a wood fire. In general, steer away from the major varietals high in tannin when they are young unless the food particularly suits them or experience suggests a bottle is less tannic than the norm. Examples of these are Cabernet Sauvignon, Nebbiolo, Aglianico, and sometimes Cabernet Franc. Exceptions are a few categories of food that can pair happily with high-tannin wines: fatty foods, which seem to absorb the tannins, and those made bitter by the cooking techniques, such as charcoal grilling.

FRUITINESS: This component is an elusive one for analysis. Since most red table wines are essentially dry wines, it is their fruitiness that plays out in the palate the way sweetness does for whites. It's an admittedly vague description that for some wines may suggest a rich, lush "plumpness" or "roundness"; in others, you might say there's no more than a wafer-thin "cushion" of fruit. In both examples the word "ripeness" might be used, too. These wines are, as they say in the trade, "fruit-forward," suggesting that some of their other traits—most notably tannin—have taken a backseat.

Elusiveness aside, fruitiness in red wines—assuming the wine isn't strongly tannic or high in alcohol—is clearly a very food-friendly trait. It's *such* a helpful trait that some reds with only moderate levels of acidity still manage to accommodate a wide range of foods. One example, southern Italy's brooding, darkly fruity Montepulciano d'Abruzzo is put to good use alongside a number of dishes in this book—particularly with dishes that feature the "fruitiness" of tomato sauce. (Note that many wines smell of fruit when inhaled from a swirling glass; these aromas may or may not signal a fruity wine in the way we're defining it. The significant effect of fruitiness is more tactile—a round, juicy impression in your mouth.)

When fruitiness in a red wine is aligned with a good dose of tongue-tingling acidity, you're onto one of the most food-friendly combinations around. The undisputed champion in this category is Beaujolais. This and other fruity, high-acid red wines will accompany almost anything you can throw at them, from tangy salads to pork smothered with sweet prunes to a grilled N.Y. strip steak. There's no disputing that wines like these are important because they taste so good with such a wide variety of things, offering a delicious flexibility that every cook and wine enthusiast should take advantage of.

Fruitiness in white wines is a slightly different story. To describe fruitiness in whites, the same adjectives apply as for reds: in the mouth there is a tactile impression of plumpness, roundness, ripeness, and so on. But because white table wines present a wider gamut from dry to lightly sweet, their fruitiness is a more unpredictable factor. Simply put, the food friendliness of fruity white wines—dry or sweet—rises or falls on good levels of acidity. Without good acidity, fruitiness in white wines can interfere with food flavors, rather than mingle with them, as fruity reds (which are mostly dry wines) tend to. This undesirable effect can be somewhat like drinking a piece of fruit with your food instead of a wine. Some low-acid fruity wines come from warmer wine zones such as in California and Southern France and Italy and, therefore, also often contain a fairly high level of alcohol, another trait that tends to make them less food friendly. However, when acidity levels are good, these fruity wines—especially the lightly sweet bottles—are some of the best wines in the world, with all kinds of food. Again, German Riesling and the Chenin Blanc–based wines of France's Loire Valley (such as Vouvray) are the finest examples.

Like acidity and sweetness, fruitiness in a wine is a component that can be useful in the concept of "like goes with like." If a fruity component strongly marks a dish (a fruit-based sauce is again a good example), the fruitiness of a wine should be part of your strategy for selecting the pairing.

OAK: Some of the world's great wines are placed in new oak barrels for fermentation or aging, or both. Traditionally this technique was reserved for full-bodied wines to help harmonize their flavors. Increasingly, these barrels are used with far lighter wines as a kind of seasoning whose chief characteristic, an enticing vanilla-like aroma, signals, in effect, "Look here, this is a quality wine." Thoughtfully applied, this approach can result in a wine as graceful as any at the table, but when used in excess, it marks a wine strongly and masks its distinctive flavors with an oaky astringency jarring to food. By contrast, fermenting or aging wine in more neutral, older oak barrels—a practice common in many of the world's wine regions—has little or no impact on a particular wine's flexibility with food. When it comes to sorting out the oak-aging regimens of various wines, a good wine merchant is a valuable friend indeed.

### Top Food-Friendly Wines

Those marked with an asterisk (*) are place names; all others are grape names, except for Vinho Verde, which is neither.

*Whites*
Riesling (dry and off dry)/Germany
Riesling and Grüner Veltliner/Austria
Riesling and Pinot Blanc/Alsace, France
Champagne*/Champagne, France
Sauvignon Blanc/Friuli and Alto Adige, Italy

Sauvignon Blanc (Sancerre, Pouilly-Fumé, etc.)/East Loire Valley, France
Sauvignon Blanc/New Zealand
Chenin Blanc (dry and off-dry Vouvray, etc.)/Loire Valley, France
Chablis*/North Burgundy, France
Mâcon-Villages*/South Burgundy, France
Muscadet/West Loire Valley France
Prosecco (sparkling)/Veneto, Italy
Soave*/Veneto, Italy
Albariño/Galicia, Spain
Vinho Verde/Minho, Portugal
Verdicchio/Marches, Italy

REDS
Barbera (with little or no new-oak aging)/Piedmont, Italy
Cabernet Franc (Chinon, Bourgueil, etc.)/Loire Valley, France
Valpolicella, Bardolino*/Veneto, Italy
Rioja* (all *Joven*, traditional-style *Crianza*, *Reserva*, and *Gran Reserva*)/Rioja, Spain
Lambrusco/Emilia-Romagna, Italy
Merlot/Friuli, Italy
Burgundy* (Côte d'Or, Côte Chalonnaise)/Burgundy, France
Beaujolais*/South Burgundy, France
Chianti* (*Normale* not Riserva)/Tuscany, Italy
Montepulciano d'Abruzzo/Abruzzi, Italy
Pinot Noir (lighter)/Oregon and California, United States
Pinot Noir (lighter)/New Zealand and Australia
Shiraz (fruitier)/Australia

-Chapter 2-

# Cooking with Meat and Wine in Today's Kitchen

When writing *Lobel's Meat and Wine*, we were interested in how wine and food interact in the kitchen as well as at the table. After all, this is a cookbook, and we are most concerned with great-tasting dishes.

We decided to take a scientific approach to the questions with the end goal of providing a digest of simple, practical advice on cooking with wine for the home cook. To confirm prior experience and expand our knowledge, we devoted four days to a series of tests designed to answer some of our questions. Four tasters (a food and wine professional, two food professionals, and one "civilian") evaluated dozens of food samples prepared with various techniques and wines. Though the tests were imperfect and incomplete (we performed just a fraction of the tests we would have liked to have completed, had time and money permitted), every attempt was made to simulate a laboratory environment in our farmhouse kitchen.

We performed four tests. The first two focused on the effects of different techniques for marinating tougher cuts of meat overnight and for marinating tender cuts for shorter periods of time. The second two tests focused on how wines with very distinctive styles compare to one another when used in two kinds of dishes, a slow-cooked stew and a quick pan sauce.

We used thermometers and digital clocks to determine temperature and time, both before and after cooking. In any given test, we cooked all samples side by side under the same conditions. We evaluated all samples using detailed tasting sheets. While exacting, the process was fun, with many surprises along the way.

## Marinating

In days gone by, meat was marinated for simple reasons: to preserve it, tenderize it, or both. Thanks to refrigeration, very little of the food we now buy requires us to preserve it to extend its edible life. So, if we eat beef jerky or prepare sauerbraten it's because we like the way these things taste. It's also true that the meat and poultry in our markets is much more tender today than it once was. Given the quality of today's meats, even tougher parts of the animal, it appears the tradition of marinating in wine carries on for one reason: flavor. When developing recipes for this book, we found ourselves questioning this age-old technique—even the flavor aspect—and decided to explore it further.

We set some ground rules. First, we decided to limit the tests to beef, America's favorite meat, and a perennial candidate for marinades in our cuisine. Secondly, we used only red wine for the marinades, as it is more fully flavored than white and this more readily exhibited its effects (whites were evaluated next).

As you will see, some of the results influenced the recipes in this book and in fact forever changed the way we look at cooking with wine. Read on.

## Long Marinating for Tougher Cuts of Beef

We had two general objectives here. First, we wanted to compare a beef stew made without first marinating the beef to several for which the meat was marinated overnight before going in the pot. Second, for the latter, we compared the differences between four different marinating techniques.

We made five stews, each using 8 ounces of beef chuck (shoulder) cut into cubes. For the first stew, the beef was not marinated; for the other four, it was marinated for fourteen hours, and each stew used a different approach to the marinade itself. At cooking time, the beef for each sample was browned (except for sample 5, which was browned prior to marinating; see facing page) and then simmered gently with ¼ cup of finely chopped vegetables (onion, carrot, and celery) and 1 cup of homemade chicken stock for four hours in the oven. The stews were then uncovered and reduced until slightly thickened. After a rest of twenty minutes, the samples were evaluated.

Here's the breakdown of the samples for the test:

1. The meat was *not* immersed in a wine marinade, but 1 cup of dry red wine was included in the stew.

2. The meat was marinated in 1 cup of plain, unheated dry red wine.

3. The meat was marinated in 1 cup of unheated dry red wine mixed with 2 teaspoons kosher salt.

4. The meat was marinated in 1 cup of plain, dry red wine simmered until reduced by one-third and allowed to cool.

5. This sample added a new dimension: We heated 2 tablespoons vegetable oil in a skillet, sprinkled the beef with 2 teaspoons kosher salt, and browned it deeply on two sides before removing it from the skillet. We then added 1 cup red wine to the skillet and cooked it until reduced by one-third. The flavorful browned bits on the bottom of the skillet were scraped up and stirred into the marinade. While still warm, the marinade was poured over the beef and set to marinate like the others.

### The Results

When the results were in, no one was prepared for the disparity between these five stews—and no one had expected the relative failure of the one technique we had used most often for years. Nor did we expect an unorthodox method to walk away with best in show.

The unmarinated red wine stew was very good. Its taste and texture were everything you'd expect in a long, gently cooked stew of beef, red wine, and vegetables. In contrast to other samples, the flavor of meat stood out in this stew, its beefiness emphasized. While the flavors of the wine had mellowed, some tasters felt the sauce more "acidic" than the two best samples. And compared to these two, it was "not quite as interesting or complex" but very fine nevertheless. Because it was not marinated, this method of course produced the quickest stew by far.

The stew with beef marinated in plain, unheated wine got low marks, with complaints of an unappetizing "livery" taste and a "jarring, sour wine" flavor, as well as a dry texture. This was the most surprising result in this round of tests because it's the technique that most cooks have long relied on when marinating in wine. The third stew, with the small addition of salt to the marinade, made a poor dish worse, actually diminishing the intensity and harmony of the meat and wine flavors. This time the texture of the meat was described as "gummy" and "mushy."

The marinade with simple reduced wine performed better. Everyone felt it helped to integrate the flavors and give the stew a classic complexity.

To our surprise, it was the marinade combined with browned meat and the deglazed pan drippings that was the unanimous winner. It was the "most complete" and "most harmonious," with a sauce that was more interesting and richly flavored than any of the others. Here the mellow, tangy wine flavors seemed in near-perfect balance with the beefy flavors of the meat. This marinade has the added advantages of not requiring straining, and the meat does not need to be patted dry before browning it, as it is browned before marinating.

We feel that this last technique should be explored by any cook interested in marinating meat in wine. It seems conclusive to us that when a high proportion of wine is called for in a marinade, superior results will be gotten when the wine is first reduced.

Regardless of the technique employed, it is also clear to us that the choice to marinate or not comes down to two issues. The first involves the nature of the changes that occur in meat during marinating. As much as we loved the samples 4 and 5, there was no question that the extended marinating time had, to some extent, altered the texture and flavor of the beef itself. This was evident simply by comparing the four marinated samples to the one using unmarinated beef. Our results suggest that marinating is a "stylistic" choice, whose chief contribution is to help drive the flavor of the wine and other marinade ingredients into the meat, thereby resulting in a more complex and harmonious-tasting stew. Cooks should remember, however, that there may be instances where the more straightforward, natural flavor and texture of the meat we so enjoyed in the first sample may well be the result they are looking for.

The second is a question of time. Marinating meats destined for long cooking usually requires a minimum of six hours and often much more to achieve the desired effect. Thus, the additional time required may be reason enough for a cook to choose a quicker route.

It is largely due to this last reason that we opted not to marinate the meats in a number of this book's recipes. However, there were a handful we felt justified the extra time, particularly those dishes whose character depends on long marinating, such as the classic sauerbraten recipe, Marinated Beef Pot Roast with Vinegar and Riesling, page 69.

### Short Marinating for Tender, Quick-Cooking Steaks

When recipes call for relatively thin cuts of meat, they frequently suggest that these cuts marinate for a brief time. Usually, these meats are then pan-fried, broiled, or grilled. We wanted to compare the effect of distinct methods of marinating thin, tender steaks and so used exceptionally high-quality tender, well-marbled prime strip steaks. Once marinated for two hours, the steaks were blotted dry and pan-fried for three minutes on each side for medium rare.

The four different techniques used were as follows:

1. The steak was not marinated but was simply salted and then tasted alongside the other samples. We felt this would help us better evaluate the effects of a wine marinade on "perfect steak" and act as a control.

2. The meat was marinated in ⅓ cup of unheated dry red wine mixed with 2 tablespoons of minced shallot.

3. The meat was marinated in ⅔ cup of dry red wine simmered until reduced by one-half, cooled, and mixed with 2 tablespoons of minced shallot.

4. The meat was marinated in ⅔ cup of dry red wine simmered until reduced by one-half, cooled, and mixed with 2 tablespoons of minced shallot and 2 teaspoons of kosher salt.

### The Results

We discovered that yet another timeworn technique was called into question, and we were encouraged to rethink the way we compose wine marinades for steak. The excellence of the unmarinated steak reinforced an important truth: When simply salted and pan-fried, top-quality prime steak needs no other help and has no peer. That said, some cooks like to marinate any cut of meat for the extra flavor punch and because, let's face it, it's fun to mix the ingredients and smell the gorgeous aromas of garlic, olive oil, and fresh herbs mingling with a good red wine.

This is especially true for the less prized cuts such as flank steaks, skirt steaks, and others, whose toothsome texture can really benefit from a marinade.

Again, the marinade made with unheated wine demonstrated serious drawbacks. It seemed to concentrate a "sharply winy" flavor on the exterior surface only, leaving the delicious meat as a completely isolated and separate taste on the inside, as if it had been "dipped" or coated in wine, yet with no harmony between the wine and the meat.

As with the stews, reducing the wine for the marinade produced decidedly winning results. The brief cooking to concentrate the wine has the effect of melding its flavor to the steak like a well-integrated seasoning.

The reduced salted-wine method produced the strangest creature in the entire four days of experiments. Completely disjointed in effect, the salt flavor tasted as though it was floating all over our mouths but had not been driven into the steak itself. The steak was also tougher.

After our experiments, we happily decided we could abandon some old assumptions about marinating and were able to compile some prevailing old and some new wisdom into a list of marinating guidelines:

- Marinating techniques differ enormously in their effects.
- Marinating often changes the character of a piece of meat or poultry and the nature of the finished dish; that is, marinating can make a dish taste more complex, but it may diminish some of the characteristic flavors and textures of meat. The trade-off points to different advantages for different dishes.
- When opting to use a marinade with a high proportion of wine, superior marinated dishes result from using wine marinades cooked until reduced by one-third or one-half. (Note: we did find that the use of wine straight from the bottle for marinades is fine when the wine represents a small proportion of the marinade.)
- Avoid putting salt in a wine marinade for meat. (Although brining, a different process all together, can be great for pork and poultry.)

## Cooking with Wine

In our next pair of tests, we undertook the question of how different wines of very different styles compare when added directly to the pot or saucepan. Are the differences noticeable, if there are any, in the finished dish? Or do all wines behave in pretty much the same way?

We performed two tests, one for a slow-cooked stew and the other for a quick pan sauce, with eight vastly different wines. While all of the wines were top-flight representatives of their types, each represented a classic style of table wine that would, in a very broad sense, represent the kinds of wines we drink or cook with every day. We used four styles each of red and white wine.

WHITES

1. Medium-light-bodied, simple, thin, neutral (Orvieto/Italy)
2. Medium-bodied, aromatic, lightly sweet-tart and fruity (off-dry Riesling/Germany)
3. Medium-bodied, crisp, concentrated, dry (Sauvignon Blanc/New Zealand)
4. Full-bodied, rich, fruity, oaky (Chardonnay/California)

REDS

5. Medium-light-bodied, delicate, tangy, balanced (Red Burgundy/France)

6. Medium-bodied, moderately concentrated, spicy (Côtes du Rhône/France)

7. Full-bodied, ripe, rich, soft (Primitivo/Italy)

8. Very full-bodied, powerful, concentrated, oaky, moderately tannic (Cabernet Sauvignon/California)

**Using Wines for Slow Cooking**

In the first test, eight beef stews were prepared without marinating the beef beforehand. The meat was browned and then stewed with vegetables, wine, chicken stock, and salt.

**The Results**

1. The mild-mannered Orvieto, included to represent the kind of well-made, neutral wine that could be a prototype for the sort commonly used in cooking, produced a surprisingly dismal stew. We found it had sharp, winy flavors that were not integrated.

2. All agreed the stew made with the Riesling was excellent but odd. The excellence resulted from the concentration of the high-quality fruit and mineral "extract" that define this as a quality wine. The oddness resulted from the concentration of two other distinctive components: its high acidity and its slight sweetness. After four hours of stewing, the acidity and sweetness had distilled into an "unfamiliar but interesting taste" when combined with the flavors of beef, flavors that seemed a bit diminished by the sweet-tart effect. The verdict: Off-dry Riesling is an excellent cooking wine but with very particular traits. Use it discriminatingly to achieve a sweet-tart effect in dishes that will benefit from it, especially pork and game (see Pork Cutlets with Apples, Onions, and Marjoram, page 103). (Note: Dry Rieslings are a bit more flexible and also make excellent cooking wines. We call for their use in Marinated Beef Pot Roast with Vinegar and Riesling, page 69; Chicken in Creamy Riesling Sauce, page 156; and Alsatian-Style Chicken with Crayfish, page 160, to name a few.)

3. The Sauvignon Blanc was our winner, hands down. The stew was balanced, with distinctive, harmonious flavors that let the beef flavor emerge. This wine showed that concentrated wines without excessive fruitiness, sweetness, or oaky flavors make the best all-purpose white cooking wine. Although crisp, concentrated, unoaked Sauvignon Blanc performed well in these tests, there are a number of wines—many less crisp and acidic than this one—that make equally good cooking wines due to their quality and concentration.

4. The Chardonnay was entirely different in character from the others. The stew was rich with beefy flavor, but was marked by the concentration of "creamy vanilla flavors" and "woodiness." In spite of these distractions (which made the stew taste "weird"), there was good wine flavor and harmony.

5. The red Burgundy split the panel. What was "mild-mannered and delicate" with good beef flavor for some was bland and uninteresting to others. The pale, slightly tart red Burgundy we used was of excellent quality, which suggests that this style of wine may generally pose problems in cooking, especially if poorer-quality wines are used. So, pale, acidic red wines can yield sharp, imbalanced dishes, especially if a lot of wine is used in the dish. This does not, however, condemn all Pinot Noir–based wines. The finest and more concentrated red Burgundies that were once affordable enough to be used in cooking (famously, in Classsic Chicken in Red Wine, page 158, and Beef in the Style of Burgundy, page 62) were probably excellent cooking wines in their day. The smoother, richer Pinot Noirs from California, Oregon, New Zealand, and Australia are usually very

fine cooking wines. The problem with these wines is that most are too expensive to cook with, except for a special dish or occasion.

6. As hoped, the Côtes du Rhône was a good all-around cooking wine, producing a well-balanced stew with a nice intensity in color and flavor. Alongside the previous sample, this yielded a simple lesson: All else equal, the more concentrated the wine, the richer the flavor of the dish.

7. All four tasters were of one mind: The Primitivo produced the best stew—"full and earthy with no rough edges"—among the red wines. The deep, meaty flavor was in harmony with the warm, ripe, balanced flavors of the wine. This wine reinforced the lessons from the previous two: Wines of good quality and high in dry extract (see sidebar, page 36) yield the best-quality dishes. In addition, this wine was fairly soft and "flabby," that is, low in acidity and tannin, which may have been partly responsible for the rich and mellow taste we praised.

8. The Cabernet Sauvignon provided more proof that the style of a cooking wine leaves its mark on the finished dish. The intensity, weight, and concentration of the wine was easy to identify. But, as with the Chardonnay, the stew couldn't escape the "strange woody tastes" contributed by new oak barrels. We all tasted a "bitter astringency," too. Whether this was caused by the concentrated tannins or oak was difficult to tell. All of this was a shame because these flavors obscured the otherwise excellent intensity, richness, and complexity of the stew.

## Using Wines for Quick Cooking

In the second test, a quick pan sauce was made with each of the wines and some minced vegetables and then reduced heavily before being finished with a tablespoon of salted butter.

## The Results

1. The pan sauce made with the Orvieto was as disappointing as the stew, with a "hollow, incomplete" character. Whatever made this wine pleasant enough to drink on its own was undone in the cooking. "Undone" may be the wrong word, because in time, we began to see that the wine had not lost anything at all. It never had the right stuff to begin with.

2. The pan sauce made with the Riesling emphasized the wine's positive traits and showed a sweet-tart flavor and texture. The quality of the sauce was "excellent and gently fruity" and "without astringency." As with the stew, its distinctive Riesling traits remained identifiable, underscoring the need to use this wine with ingredients tailored to its flavors; here it unanimously made the second best sauce of the four.

3. As with the stew, the Sauvignon Blanc was the winner among whites for the pan sauce. The sauce was "smooth and delicious, with the balanced, green appley–herbal flavors apparent in the finished sauce," and it was cleaner tasting and less sweet than the very good Riesling sauce.

4. Though the Chardonnay made for an odd but fairly good-flavored stew, the wine's worst traits became magnified in the pan sauce. It was "the most intense and awkward in the group" as well as the "least appealing." Most tasters were bothered by the "intense flavor of oak" that was outright "astringent." This sauce showed that wines marked by the invasive taste of new oak barrels make middling cooking wines. While some may display concentrated, high-quality wine flavor in slow cooking, the oak is unpalatable in a highly reduced pan sauce.

5. Again the red Burgundy/Pinot Noir split the panel, emphasizing that wines made in a light, acidic style can produce unbalanced results.

6. The Côtes du Rhône produced just as pleasing results in the pan sauce as in slow cooking. The sauce was well balanced and reflected some of the "spicy," "zippy," "gently fruity" flavors of the wine itself.

7. The Primitivo was again the winner among the reds, producing an outstanding pan sauce. The rich, soft, fruit-filled quality of the wine seemed to have been partly responsible for the rich and mellow taste we praised in both preparations.

8. As with the stew, the Cabernet was problematic, with bitterness and distracting wood flavor. The lesson: Excellent-quality Cabernet Sauvignon (and other wines like it) is capable of producing an intense, complex stew or sauce, but avoid wines that feature the flavors and textures of new oak barrels and choose those with moderate to low levels of tannin.

As with the marinating tests, it was instructive for our laypeople and experts alike to revisit the particulars of cooking with wine. We concurred that the oft-repeated credo "Don't cook with a wine you wouldn't drink" is still good advice, but we found a corollary: Only some wines good enough to drink make good cooking wines. While some excellent wines are equally excellent for cooking, others can actually damage a dish. This is especially important when the wine makes up a large percentage of the ingredients in a dish or is to be featured in a particular preparation. In addition, good cooking wine or bad, the character and style of a particular wine will leave their altered but strongly related "imprint" on a dish in spite of the fact that most of the wine's delicate aromas are destroyed by cooking.

It was interesting to note that some wines appear to perform better in long cooking than in shorter preparations (see the Chardonnay) or vice versa and that some wines with potentially overly assertive flavors can yield a delightful dish (as with the Riesling). But ultimately our results defined a set of principles that we can apply to cooking with wine in general:

- The best cooking wines are high in dry extract (see sidebar, pages 35–36), concentrated, and full of flavor, although they are not necessarily heavy wines. The opposite is also true: Thin, less-concentrated, more-diluted, watery wines can cook poorly.
- Some good-quality, less-concentrated, delicate wines produce good but lighter-tasting sauces and stews.
- The balance and tang that acidity provides are central to the character of wine-based dishes, and the more acidity, the greater the effect.
- Red wine tends to mark a dish more strongly than white with its character as well as its color. White wines are also usually lighter in flavor than reds and therefore sometimes a more subtle addition to a dish; they may require more reduction to concentrate them in certain preparations where wine is a major feature of the dish.
- Avoid excessively tannic wines in cooking.
- Avoid excessively oaky-tasting wines in cooking.
- To aid in the evaporation of alcohol, give cooking wines a "jump start" for a few minutes by simmering them without other liquid ingredients in the pot (see facing page).

In the recipes that follow, we usually do not call for a specific wine but instead refer to a particular style of wine in those dishes where we felt such a wine would enhance the outcome. By and large, we call for dry red wines and dry or off-dry white wines. Should you choose to take some of our cooking wine "discoveries" to heart, we hope you'll have a clearer understanding of what to look for. That said, we encourage you to wear our advice lightly, for we strongly believe that a thoughtful and passionate cook in the kitchen can do far more to enhance the goodness of a dish than any bottle of wine ever will.

## What Happens to Wine When It's Heated?

When wine is cooked or reduced, various chemical changes take place. Some components dissipate while others concentrate.

Of the major components in wine, alcohol is among the most heat sensitive and dissipates quickly when cooked. Normally between 8 and 16 percent by volume, just 20 to 40 percent of this remains in a finished pan sauce. And after a stew simmers for four hours, about 5 percent of the alcohol remains. Contrary to conventional wisdom, alcohol is never entirely eliminated by cooking. When warmed, raw alcohol tastes "coarse" and "hot" and upsets the balance of a dish. Partial evaporation is desirable, and the original alcoholic content of a wine doesn't much matter as long as it has had time to evaporate sufficiently. But the alcohol remaining in a dish may have its benefits. For instance, it is said to act as a carrier for the other aromas and flavors in a dish to make it more interesting and appetizing.

The complex aromatic compounds responsible for making wine the compelling drink that it is also dissipate during cooking. These are the fine details of a wine, and though we may hope to transfer their nuances to a dish, we can't prevent losing some to the heating process. Cooking more gently has been said to help retain more of them. (Insofar as the mellowing of these compounds accounts for the major differences between wine that has been cooked and wine that hasn't, it may also sometimes be advantageous; see Marinating, page 28.)

The other major components in wine concentrate when cooked. Acidity is one of the most noticeable of these because it gives wine its pleasing tartness and refreshing backbone. As a major feature in any dish that includes wine, acidity works as a ballast that counterbalances the fats and proteins in meats. Acid can be overly concentrated to a bitter sharpness, so wine should not be reduced beyond a certain point. It's best to taste often as you cook. Sugar also concentrates in those wines that contain it. This includes not only dessert wines but many dry and off-dry table wines. Obviously tasting is important here to determine how much sweetness is present. A wine or wine sauce that seems overly sweet in the dish can benefit from a few drops of vinegar or lemon.

Tannin, the mouth-drying, slightly bitter component in all red wines (see page 23) also concentrates during cooking. Tannin can accumulate to bitter effect in sauces, which is why we recommend low-tannin wines for cooking. Note, though, that the effects of tannins in cooking are offset by whatever proteins are present in a dish. In other words, a dish high in meat and protein-rich stock is more immune to the effects of tannin than one without.

The flavors of new oak barrels also concentrate during cooking. Whether these flavors are picked up by barrel aging or by the use of oak chips or oak extract used to flavor less-expensive wines, there are nevertheless lots of overly oaky wines on the market. Any good wine merchant can steer you away from these when choosing a wine for cooking.

If you could remove all the above-mentioned components from a glass of wine (alcohol, acidity, sweetness, tannin, and oak), you'd be left with a glass of purple water. Remove the water, and you'd be left with a small pile of purple powder, or "dry extract," at the bottom of the glass (pale for whites, dark for reds). The amount of this powder, representing the essence of the grapes, is largely responsible for the quality and concentration of a wine's flavor. Good levels of dry extract are associated with low-yielding vines, strict grape selection, certain grape varieties, and warm climates (and good vintages in cooler climates). A high amount of dry extract is the wine component most responsible for the quality and success of dishes prepared with wine. Wines high in dry extract tend to be concentrated, not with alcohol, tannin, or oak, but with what is best described as a concentrated "sappiness" of the grape itself. We're not suggesting you walk into your wine shop and ask for a cooking wine high in dry extract—a subject of interest mainly to wine makers—but, along with the suggestions in this chapter, it will bring you closer to an understanding of the qualities that make a good cooking wine.

*-Chapter 3-*

# BEEF

# Beaujolais-Style Hanger Steak with Red Wine Sauce

### Onglet Sauce Beaujolaise

**Serves 2**

A perfectly browned hanger steak is the centerpiece of this straightforward and delicious bistro-style dish. It's embellished with an intense wine sauce that relies more on wine than stock, so it's important to use both a good wine and a good-quality stock, preferably homemade, to balance it and mellow the sauce. That said, we have used canned beef broth with very good results. But a word of caution: If you use canned broth, it's especially important to add the juices that accumulate under the resting steak to give the sauce the beefy flavor it needs. Don't let them escape! Serve this with any type of potato and a salad of bitter greens, crumbled bacon, and vinaigrette.

**Butcher's Note:** In the old days, butchers were said to keep this especially flavorful cut of steak for themselves. They knew how outstanding it was, but because the hanger is an unattractive, lumpy-looking steak, it was not as easy to sell as a thick sirloin or plump roast. Recently home cooks and chefs have discovered hanger steaks and, predictably, fallen in love with their full flavor and toothsome texture. Hangers "hang" between the rib cage and loin cage, and so are not cut from a larger portion of meat. This means nearly all are about the same size and weight. We suggest you ask the butcher to remove the tough center vein to leave you with two pieces. Neither is of uniform thickness but both are absolutely delicious.

**Wine Note:** This dish is as good with the fruity simplicity of Beaujolais nouveau as with the richer *cru* Beaujolais wines. The nouveau, served cool, refreshes without interfering with the flavors and textures of the steak. The more serious and pricier choices offer more concentrated flavors, somewhat like the food itself: solid and meaty. Both wines are exceptional mates for the hanger steak—testimony to the flexibility of this family of Gamay-based wines. Some favorites for nouveau are Jean Paul Brun "L'Ancien" Beaujolais Nouveau, Terres Dorées; for cru Beaujolais, Jean Foillard Morgon "Côtes du Py"; and for an American choice that is a bit fruitier in taste but no less flexible with food, the Beringer Gamay Beaujolais from California.

---

*5½ tablespoons unsalted butter*

*2 ounces white mushrooms, thinly sliced*

*3 tablespoons finely chopped shallot*

*1 large clove garlic, minced*

*Kosher salt*

*1 tablespoon all-purpose flour*

*1 cup dry red wine*

*¾ cup Veal Stock (page 213), Beef Stock (page 212), or canned low-sodium beef broth*

*1 large sprig fresh thyme, plus 2 teaspoons finely chopped thyme for garnish*

*Freshly ground black pepper*

*One 1¾-pound hanger steak, trimmed of excess fat and center vein removed, cut into 4 equal rectangular steaks*

*3 tablespoons vegetable oil*

---

1. In a skillet, melt 3 tablespoons of the butter over medium heat and cook the mushrooms, stirring occasionally, until pale gold at the edges, about 3 minutes. Stir in 1 more tablespoon of the butter, the shallot, garlic, and a generous pinch of salt. Reduce the heat to low and cook, stirring occasionally, until the shallot is softened but without color, about 5 minutes.

2. Sprinkle the flour over the vegetables and cook for about 1 minute, stirring. Add the wine, stock, thyme sprig, and ⅛ teaspoon salt. Raise the heat and simmer until the liquid is reduced by half (to about ¾ cup), about 5 minutes (you will have about 1 cup including solids as well). Pass the mixture through a fine-mesh strainer into a cup or small bowl, pushing firmly on the vegetables until all of the liquid has been extracted. Discard the solids and set the wine mixture aside.

3. Generously salt and pepper both sides of the steaks.

4. In another skillet, heat the oil over medium-high heat. When hot, swirl the oil to coat the bottom of the skillet and cook the steaks until dark brown and crusty, reducing the heat if the steaks threaten to burn, 4 to 6 minutes per side for medium-rare. If the steaks are much thicker than 1 inch, reduce the heat and cook a little longer. Transfer to a plate, tent loosely with aluminum foil, and let rest in a very low (200°F) oven.

5. Let the skillet cool slightly and return to medium-low heat. Add the reserved wine mixture and bring to a bare simmer, scraping the bottom of the skillet to loosen any browned bits. Simmer until reduced by one-fourth.

6. Reduce the heat to low and whisk in the remaining 1½ tablespoons butter. Stir in any accumulated juices from the plate holding the steaks. Taste and adjust the seasonings. Let the sauce reduce for a few moments more over low heat to concentrate the flavors, if necessary.

7. Divide the steaks between warmed serving plates, leaning one piece attractively against the other. Pour the sauce over each pair of steaks, garnish with chopped thyme, and serve.

**Make-Ahead Tip:** You can make the sauce through the point of reducing and straining the wine mixture up to 1 day ahead and store, covered, in the refrigerator. Bring to room temperature before cooking the steaks and finishing the sauce.

# Marinated and Breaded Sicilian-Style Steaks

### Bistecche Impanate

**Serves 2**

The trick to this tasty dish from Sicily is to get the skillets hot but not smoking before cooking the thin breaded steaks so that the crust turns golden brown but never burns. If you want to double the recipe, we suggest using four strip steaks instead of porterhouse or T-bone because they are easier to handle and will fit in two skillets. Serve with a salad of bitter greens and tomatoes dressed with lemon juice and olive oil.

In this dish we disregard our own advice to briefly cook wine marinades before use (see page 31). The reason? There are a lot of other flavors and textures in the preparation, from the lemon juice to the breadcrumb crust, and so the role of the wine isn't central. If you prefer, begin with ⅔ cup wine, cook to reduce it to ⅓ cup, let cool slightly, and proceed with the recipe.

**Wine Note:** Here's a case where thinking "steak" means "big, tannic red wine" can get you in trouble. From our tasting, a big wine is out of place here because these steaks are fried with a bread-crumb crust. We found two medium-weight Sicilian wines, typical of the distinctive wines that keep flowing from the island of Sicily, that perfectly reflect the spirit of this dish. One favorite with the golden-crusted steak was Abbazia Santa Anastasia Nero d'Avola, made from the indigenous grape variety of the same name, whose gently refreshing, berrylike fruit is worth the attention of any wine lover. Another favorite was the Planeta "Segreta" Rosso, made with a refined blend of local and international varieties (Nero d'Avola, Merlot, and Syrah). Serve these slightly cool in the summer. From the United States, try Joseph Phelps's "Le Mistral," a wine modeled on the wines of France's Rhône Valley that nevertheless has a real southern European feel—just right for the Sicilan-style steak.

*⅓ cup dry white wine*

*2 tablespoons fresh lemon juice*

*4 large cloves garlic, crushed*

*2 tablespoons finely chopped flat-leaf parsley*

*2 tablespoons finely chopped fresh marjoram or oregano or 2 teaspoons dried*

*Freshly ground black pepper*

*Two ¾-pound porterhouse or T-bone steaks, each about ⅝ inch thick, trimmed of excess fat*

*1 cup fine dried bread crumbs, preferably homemade (see Note)*

*Kosher salt*

*⅔ cup olive oil*

1. In a glass, ceramic, or other nonreactive dish just large enough to hold the steaks, stir together the wine, lemon juice, garlic, parsley, 1 tablespoon of marjoram, and a few grindings of pepper. Add the steaks, turn to coat, and marinate for 2 hours at room temperature, turning and basting the steaks once or twice. Refrigerate if marinating any longer than this.

2. On a large plate, mix together the bread crumbs, ½ tablespoon salt, a few grindings of pepper, and the remaining 1 tablespoon marjoram. Lift the steaks from the marinade, letting the marinade drip back into the dish. Evenly salt the steaks on both sides. Coat the steak with the seasoned bread crumbs on both sides, pressing to form a fairly thick layer of crumbs. Set aside.

3. Preheat two medium skillets over medium-high heat for a few minutes and divide the olive oil between them. Add the steaks and cook for 3 to 3½ minutes per side for medium-rare, reducing the heat if they threaten to burn. Towards the end of cooking, cut a small corner of a steak to check for doneness. Transfer to warmed serving plates and serve immediately.

**Note:** To make fresh bread crumbs, trim the crusts from 2 slices of day-old French or other good-quality white bread. Tear the bread into pieces and pulse in a food processor or blender into fine crumbs. This will yield about 1 cup fresh bread crumbs. For dried bread crumbs, dry the bread slices in a 200°F oven for about 1 hour before processing as directed above.

# Seared Strip Steaks with Horseradish-Raisin Sauce and Red Cabbage

Bistecche al Rafano con Verza

**Serves 2**

There's a strong Austrian influence in this unusual and delicious recipe from the Trentino-Alto Adige in the Italian Alps, where onions, horseradish, raisins, and sweet wine flavor a roux to make a sauce that, odd as it may sound, is surprisingly delicious and probably unlike any steak sauce you've ever had. Sweet amber-colored Vin Santo, while commonly associated with Tuscany, exists as a wine tradition in these northern parts, too. Since you're unlikely to find Northern Italian bottles in the States, go ahead and substitute Tuscan Vin Santo (see page 205) or any golden dessert wine. Serve with roasted baby potatoes alongside.

**Wine Note:** The sauce for the seared steak is slightly sweet and sour, made pungent with horseradish and punctuated with raisins—at a glance not the most wine-friendly concoction. But a warmly flavored five-year-old bottle of Peter Dipoli "Fihl" Merlot-Cabernet from the Alto Adige was the favorite among a range of excellent local specialties (including Lagrein, Teroldego, and Marzemino). For those who enjoy Merlot- and Cabernet-based wines (and maybe more so for those who think they do not), the versions from this mountainous, Austrian-inflected part of Italy are rewardingly worthy of note. Here, when the climate cooperates, the best wines feel more vibrant than many Bordeaux wines of similar composition and price. So, too, are these Alto Adige reds lighter in weight and less fruity than most Merlot and Cabernet (Sauvignon and Franc) made by American and Australian wineries. Are the wines better? Not necessarily, but they are special: Alto Adige–grown Cabernet Sauvignon, Cabernet Franc, and Merlot (bottled together or alone) display a clear, cool intensity of flavor that distinguish them from all others. As in many cool-climate regions, the particular vintage can make a difference in these wines, so ask your merchant. Interestingly, there is one producer in California bottling a grape variety indigenous to this part of Italy: Il Podere dell'Olivos (a label of Au Bon Climat Winery in Santa Barbara) makes a delicious Teroldego that's worth looking for.

½ cup Vin Santo or sweet Marsala wine

⅓ cup raisins

5 to 8 tablespoons vegetable oil

½ head red cabbage, halved again, cored, and very thinly sliced

Kosher salt

3 tablespoons unsalted butter

3 tablespoons very finely chopped yellow onion

2 tablespoons all-purpose flour

1½ cups Beef Stock (page 212) or canned low-sodium beef broth, plus more as needed

Freshly ground black pepper

1 teaspoon sugar

2 teaspoons red wine vinegar

5 tablespoons grated fresh horseradish (see Note), plus more for serving, if desired

Two 10- to 11-ounce strip or T-bone steaks, each about ¾ inch thick, trimmed of excess fat

1 tablespoon finely chopped fresh chives

1. In a small bowl, combine the wine and raisins, and set aside.

2. In a large skillet, heat 3 tablespoons of the oil over medium-high heat and cook the cabbage, tossing to coat with the oil, until it begins to shrink, 2 to 3 minutes. Reduce the heat to medium and continue cooking until the cabbage softens slightly but is still quite crisp and bright in color, 4 to 6 minutes. Salt to taste and toss again. Let cool slightly, transfer to a saucepan, and set aside.

3. In a skillet, melt the butter over medium heat and cook the onion, stirring occasionally, until softened but without color, about 5 minutes. Sprinkle the flour over the onion and whisk to incorporate. Reduce the heat to medium-low and cook until the mixture is pale brown and smooth, 2 to 3 minutes.

4. Gradually whisk in the stock, ¼ teaspoon salt, and a few grindings of pepper and whisk until smooth. Bring to a bare simmer and cook, whisking and scraping the sides with a rubber spatula every so often, until the mixture is very thick but still just pourable, about 15 minutes. Stir in the wine-raisin mixture, the sugar, the vinegar, and 3 tablespoons of the horseradish. Bring to a bare simmer and cook for 5 minutes longer. The mixture should be thick but still easily pourable (it will thicken a bit when served). Taste and stir in more salt, sugar, or vinegar as needed to achieve a lightly sweet-and-sour flavor. Set aside.

5. Generously salt the steaks on both sides. Turn on the stove vent if you have one.

6. In 1 large or 2 smaller skillets just large enough to hold the steaks, heat the remaining 2 to 5 tablespoons oil over medium-high heat until it begins to smoke. Swirl the oil to evenly coat the bottom of the skillet(s) and cook the steaks until nicely browned on both sides,

about 3 minutes per side for medium-rare. Transfer to a plate and set aside.

7. Meanwhile, gently reheat the cabbage and the sauce, thinning the sauce with a little stock or water if it has gotten too thick as it cooled.

8. Spoon a mound of cabbage on one side of each serving plate and lean the steaks attractively against it. Ladle the sauce over the steaks and the plates. Sprinkle with the remaining 2 tablespoons horseradish and the chives and serve right away, passing more horseradish at the table, if you like.

**Note:** To grate the horseradish, peel with a vegetable peeler or small, sharp knife, then grate using the small holes of a box grater.

**Make-Ahead Tip:** You can make the cabbage and the sauce up to 3 hours ahead.

# Grilled Rib Steaks with Red Wine and Marrow Sauce

Entrecôte à la Bordelaise

**Serves 2**

We prefer these steaks grilled, but you can also cook them in a very hot skillet with a few tablespoons of vegetable oil. If you like to grill over wood, you are in luck here: The steak is outstanding cooked over a smoldering wood fire, even better if you have vine cuttings to toss on top of the wood. Don't let the marrow scare you off from trying this dish; it's easy to work with and adds rich flavor. We find the flavor of the rib or strip steaks to be equally good whether on or off the bone. Rather than insisting on steak that has a bone, just look for well-marbled, light cherry red beef with creamy white outer fat.

**Butcher's Note:** Beef marrowbones are taken from the hind or forelegs of the animal and are usually cut in crosswise sections to expose the marrow. Depending on exactly where along the length of the leg they're cut from, the diameter of the marrow within can vary from about ¾ inch to 2 inches. Marrow should be firm and off-white; if it feels soft or is yellowed, avoid it. For this recipe, six to eight bones cut about 1 to 1½ inches long with the interior marrow measuring about 1 inch in diameter will give you all the marrow you need. Keep the bones chilled so the marrow is firm and thus easily removed.

To extract the marrow, hold a chilled bone in both hands and then push the marrow out with your thumb or forefinger. Work from side to side where the marrow is narrowest. Pry or scrape any remaining marrow from the bone with the blade of a small knife, but try to keep it in the largest possible pieces.

Some recipes call for marrow to be soaked overnight in cold water to rid it of traces of blood, which reduces any discoloration during cooking. Here the marrow is blanched and then folded into a red wine sauce, so this step isn't necessary.

**Wine Note:** This is a dish that suits the top Bordeaux reds, even young, fairly tannic ones; the blackened, savory, and slightly bitter char produced by cooking over fire seems to soften any potential overenthusiasm of these young wines. The classically proportioned Château Grand-Puy-Lacoste from Pauillac, at just five years old, was a standout in our tasting, but let your merchant be your guide. A word of caution: While most tannic wines respond well to grilled beef, be careful you don't overdo it; really blackened steaks can have the opposite effect, clashing horribly with the tannic wine's edge. Any number of American wines would do well here, but for a preparation that shows off a classic Bordeaux red wine so well, we'd pour the Napa Valley equivalent: the refined Chateau Montelena Napa Valley Cabernet Sauvignon.

*6 to 8 marrowbones, each 1 to 1½ inches long (see Butcher's Note)*

*4 cups water*

*Kosher salt*

*2 cups Veal Stock (page 213), Beef Stock (page 212), or canned low-sodium beef broth*

*2 cups red Bordeaux wine*

*⅔ cup finely chopped shallots*

*1 clove garlic, lightly crushed*

*1 large sprig fresh thyme*

*½ bay leaf*

*½ teaspoon sugar*

*Generous pinch of freshly grated nutmeg*

*Freshly ground black pepper*

*2 tablespoons cold unsalted butter, cut into small pieces*

*Two 10- to 11-ounce rib or strip steaks (on or off the bone), each about ¾ inch thick, trimmed of excess fat*

*Vegetable oil for brushing*

*1 tablespoon finely chopped fresh flat-leaf parsley*

1. Extract the marrow from the bones as instructed in the Butcher's Note.

2. In a small saucepan, bring the water and 1 tablespoon salt to a boil. Add the marrow and reduce the heat so that the marrow simmers gently until cooked through, about 5 minutes for smaller pieces (less than ¾ inch) and up to 15 minutes for the largest (about 2 inches). As each piece is finished cooking, transfer it with a slotted spoon to a cutting board. Coarsely chop the marrow,

transfer to a small bowl, cover with plastic wrap, and set aside.

3.  In a saucepan, bring the stock to a boil over medium-high heat and cook until reduced to about 3 tablespoons, about 15 minutes. Add the wine, shallots, garlic, thyme, bay leaf, sugar, nutmeg, and a few grindings of pepper. Bring to a boil, reduce the heat to medium, and simmer until the liquid and solids together measure about ⅔ cup, about 10 to 15 minutes more. Discard the garlic, thyme, and bay leaf.

4.  Remove from the heat and whisk in the butter 1 piece at a time. Stir in a generous pinch of salt, or to taste. Set aside in a warm place.

5.  Let the steaks come to room temperature. Meanwhile, prepare a fire in a charcoal or wood grill or preheat a gas grill to medium-high.

6.  Brush the steaks lightly with vegetable oil and salt them generously on both sides. Grill to the desired doneness, about 3 minutes per side for medium-rare. Transfer to warmed serving plates and tent loosely with aluminum foil or place in a very low (200°F) oven.

7.  Return the sauce to a simmer, stir in the reserved marrow, and cook until just heated through. Spoon the sauce over the steaks, sprinkle with the parsley, and serve immediately.

# The Pizza Maker's Wife's Pan-Fried Steaks

Bistecca alla Pizzaiola

**Serves 2**

Bathing a tender, well-browned steak in tomato sauce may strike some as odd, but with this classic dish from Campania, Italy, the results are delicious.

The oregano-scented tomato sauce is prepared separately and, if you like, can be prepared up to two days earlier and refrigerated. Besides using good-quality steaks and canned tomatoes, the trick to getting this simple dish just right is to brown the steaks deeply in a very hot skillet while leaving them slightly undone in the center so they finish cooking in the tomato sauce. Try this steak with sautéed zucchini or eggplant—alone or in combination—served on the side. Together, these flavors evoke the direct and exceptional cooking of Naples.

**Wine Note:** Tomato sauces can be tough on wine because of the tomato's two main characteristics: acidity and fruitiness, in both taste and texture (they are, after all, a fruit). These qualities concentrate even more when cooked into a rich tomato sauce. Acid and fruit: You'd think we were talking wine, no? It turns out that tomato sauces have as much or more of these two key components than are present in many wines we may choose to drink alongside them, which is what can knock the stuffing out of some wines. The most sympathetic wines for tomato sauce are found by following one of the principles given in chapter one: "Like goes with like." That is, since tomato sauce is acidic and fruity, your wine choice should be either nicely acidic, somewhat fruity, or both. For us, that means two standbys when it comes to central and southern Italian food with tomato sauce: You can match the acidity of the sauce by serving a simple, tangy (acidic) Chianti or match its fruitiness by serving warm, darkly fruity Montepulciano d'Abruzzo. Two favorites: Fattoria di Lucignano Chianti Colli Fiorentini and Barone Cornacchia Montepulciano d'Abruzzo. Tuscany's Sangiovese hasn't taken off in California as some had predicted, but there are a few producers who make inspired versions. One favorite is Long Vineyards Sangiovese (selected from Seghesio Vineyards in Sonoma's Alexander Valley).

*Two 10- to 11-ounce strip steaks (on or off the bone),
each about 1 inch thick, trimmed of excess fat*

*5 tablespoons extra-virgin olive oil*

*4 large cloves garlic, finely chopped*

*One 28-ounce can peeled whole tomatoes,
drained, with ¾ cup juice reserved,
and finely chopped (see Note)*

*Kosher salt*

*Generous pinch of crushed red pepper flakes*

*1 ½ teaspoons finely chopped fresh oregano
or ½ teaspoon dried*

*Freshly ground black pepper*

*½ cup dry white wine*

*1 tablespoon finely chopped fresh flat-leaf parsley*

1. Let the steaks come to room temperature while you make the tomato sauce.

2. In a saucepan, heat 3 tablespoons of the olive oil and cook the garlic over medium-low heat until pale golden at the edges, 3 to 4 minutes.

3. Add the tomatoes and reserved juice, raise the heat, and bring to a simmer. Stir in ½ teaspoon salt and the crushed red pepper flakes and simmer gently for 20 minutes.

4. Stir in the oregano and a few generous grindings of black pepper and simmer until the sauce has thickened but is still somewhat fluid, about 5 to 10 minutes longer. Remove from the heat and set aside.

5. Generously salt the steaks on both sides. Turn on the stove vent if you have one.

6. In a large, heavy skillet, heat the remaining 2 tablespoons olive oil over medium-high heat. When it just begins to smoke, swirl the oil to coat the bottom of the skillet and cook the steaks until nicely browned on both sides but still a good deal rarer in the middle than you prefer to eat them (that is, slightly raw), 2½ to 3½ minutes per side. Transfer to a plate and set aside.

7. Let the skillet cool slightly and then place over medium heat. Add the wine and simmer until reduced by half, scraping the bottom of the skillet to loosen any browned bits, 2 to 3 minutes.

8. Gently reheat the tomato sauce and add it to the skillet with the reduced wine, along with any accumulated juices from the plate holding the steaks. Stir to incorporate.

9. Return the steaks to the skillet and spoon enough sauce over them to cover. Simmer gently until the steaks are cooked to your liking, 3 to 4 minutes for medium-rare.

10. Transfer the steaks to warmed serving plates. The sauce should be thickened but still a little fluid. If necessary, simmer the sauce for a few moments more to thicken, or thin it with 1 or 2 tablespoons water. Top the steaks with tomato sauce, garnish with the parsley, and serve.

**Note:** Use the best-quality canned tomatoes you can locate, because they make a difference in this dish. If imported San Marzano tomatoes (a variety from the region in Italy and widely considered one of the best cooking tomatoes in the world) are available, use them. Muir Glen organic tomatoes—whole or whole plum tomatoes—are also excellent. Both can be found in well-stocked supermarkets or specialty food stores.

# Marinated Rib Steaks with Garlic-Parsley Butter

### Steak Chalonnais

**Serves 2**

Rich, full-flavored garlic-parsley butter is a favorite in Burgundy and for very good reason: How else could the French have convinced so many people from all corners of the globe to devour snails? It's equally lovely spooned over rib steaks, which, cut from the rib section, are a little fattier and have bolder beef flavor than steaks cut from the loin.

**Wine Note:** We found that any medium-bodied Pinot Noir from the Côte Chalonnais that isn't too marked by the flavors of new oak barrels is spot-on with this dish, and all of them tasted particularly good when served cool or at cool room temperature. Paul Jacqueson's Rully 1er Cru "Les Clous" was a standout in our tasting, but there's an abundance of food-friendly wine produced in the Côte Chalonnais, wines usually a little lighter on their feet than the region's more famous cousin, the Côte d'Or, to the north. Also look for wines from Mercurey, Givry, and Montagny or serve a good-quality Bourgogne rouge. From the New World wine regions, look for producers of lighter-weight and more delicate Pinot Noir, whether from Oregon, California, New Zealand, or elsewhere. One regionally chauvinistic favorite: Millbrook Pinot Noir from New York's Hudson Valley.

*1 cup medium-bodied Pinot Noir*
*(see page 32 for notes on cooking with Pinot Noir)*

*1 large shallot, thinly sliced*

*Freshly ground black pepper*

*6 tablespoons vegetable oil*

*Two 10- or 11-ounce rib or strip steaks*
*(on or off the bone), each about ¾ inch thick,*
*trimmed of excess fat*

*¼ cup unsalted butter, at room temperature*

*½ teaspoon minced garlic*

*2 tablespoons finely chopped fresh flat-leaf parsley*

*1 teaspoon all-purpose flour*

*Kosher salt*

1. In a small saucepan, bring the wine to a boil over medium-high heat. Reduce the heat to medium and simmer until reduced by one-fourth (to ¾ cup), about 4 minutes. Let cool slightly.

2. In a glass, ceramic, or other nonreactive dish just large enough to hold the steaks, whisk together the reduced wine, the shallot, and a few generous grindings of pepper. Whisk in 3 tablespoons of the oil. Add the steaks and turn a few times to coat. Marinate at room temperature for 1 to 2 hours, turning and basting every so often. Refrigerate if marinating any longer than this.

3. Meanwhile, in a small bowl, mash together the butter, garlic, parsley, flour, a pinch of salt, and a few grindings of pepper until well combined. Shape into 4 tablespoon-sized rounds, put on a small plate, cover, and refrigerate.

4. Remove the steaks from the marinade, reserving the marinade. Blot the steaks lightly with a paper towel to remove excess moisture and sprinkle generously with salt.

5. Preheat a heavy skillet over medium-high heat until almost smoking. Carefully add the remaining 3 table-spoons oil and swirl the oil to coat the bottom of the skillet. Add the steaks and cook for about 3 minutes per side for medium-rare.

6. Transfer the steaks to serving plates and pour off any fat in the skillet. Keep the steaks warm in a very low (200°F) oven.

7. Pour off excess fat and let the skillet cool for about 30 seconds and then place over medium heat. Add the reserved marinade and cook until reduced by half, scraping the bottom of the skillet to loosen any browned bits. Remove from the heat and whisk in the garlic-parsley butter, 1 piece at a time, until smooth. Spoon the sauce over the steaks and serve immediately.

# Beef Fillet as Rossini Might Have Liked It

Filetto di Manzo alla Rossini

**Serves 4**

This is not so much a traditional Italian dish as it is reportedly the quirky, delicious invention of Gioacchino Rossini, the great Italian composer—or perhaps a dish conceived in his memory. As well as composing magnificent operas, Rossini, a longtime resident of Paris, was an accomplished and unusu-ally experimental cook. Both his adopted home and his sense of culinary adventure influenced this

dish. This is sometimes confused with *tournedos Rossini,* which it resembles insofar as both perch a filet mignon on top of a toast round, although that dish sports a small slab of foie gras instead of the ham and cheese used here. This version and some variations of it are occasionally found in the Marches, the Italian coastal region where Rossini was born in 1792 and where *filetto di manzo alla Rossini* continues to be served as homage to the composer. The combination of flavors and textures is elegant and satisfying.

**Wine Note:** In this dish, a round of fillet beef is accompanied by lots of other things: some béchamel sauce, a slice of cured ham and another of cheese, all surrounded by a flavorful Madeira sauce. While these components aren't overtly sweet, they have a richness that suggests a *kind* of sweetness. And sweetness in food is a signal that you'll need either a slight sweetness in your white wine (the principle of "like with like") or a slight fruitiness in your red wine, which plays the role of sugar absent in most reds. We serve red wine with this dish, so we've learned to avoid the unfruity—the very dry and the very tannic, which almost invariably clash. Rosso Cònero, the best-known red of Rossini's homeland, the Italian region of the Marches, fits the bill splendidly. Made mostly from the Montepulciano grape, the same variety that makes the better-known Montepulciano d'Abruzzo wines to the south, it shares some of the fruit-filled warmth of these wines. Yet good Rosso Cònero is a firmer, usually more elegant wine than Montepulciano d'Abruzzo (whose wines were nonetheless also really good with the dish—see pages 46 and 137 for some favorites). Many producers make more than one red: A basic Rosso Cònero is the entry-level wine, typically followed by a fancier bottling that showcases a wine maker's best grapes. These often are distinguished by a proprietary name on the label. Often we found the basic (and less expensive) wines to be more flexible with food, but in this tasting, the sweet-fruited intensity of the premium selections were just delicious with the beef. One favorite: Lanari Rosso Cònero "Fibbio." A great choice from the United States is Shafer Vineyards "Firebreak," one of a handful of really good Sangiovese-based wines from California.

---

*1 cup Beef Stock (page 212), Chicken Stock (page 215), or canned low-sodium beef or chicken broth*

*¾ cup dry Madeira*

*4 slices high-quality white bread such as French, Italian, or Pullman, cut about ⅔ inch thick*

*7 tablespoons unsalted butter at room temperature*

*1 heaping teaspoon anchovy paste or 2 anchovy fillets, drained and mashed*

*Four 5- to 6-ounce filet mignon steaks, each 1¼ to 1½ inches thick*

*Kosher salt and freshly ground black pepper*

*2 tablespoons olive oil*

*1 small black truffle, shaved (optional)*

*2 tablespoons finely chopped fresh flat-leaf parsley*

*4 very thin slices prosciutto di Parma or similar cured ham, each cut about 3 inches square (see Note)*

*4 thin slices Gruyère cheese, each cut about 3 inches square (see Note)*

*Scant ½ cup Béchamel Sauce (page 52)*

---

1. In a small saucepan, simmer the stock and Madeira over medium heat until reduced by half, about 10 minutes. Set aside.

2. Using a 3-inch ring mold (or a similar-sized clean, empty tuna can or glass jar), cut circles from the bread slices and discard the trimmings. Toast the bread circles in a toaster until very crisp and golden brown, and set aside.

3. Mash together 3 tablespoons of the butter and the anchovy paste, mixing well. Set aside.

4. Generously season the beef on both sides with salt and pepper.

5. In a skillet, heat the olive oil over medium-high heat. When hot, cook the steaks for 4 to 5 minutes on each side for medium-rare. Reduce the heat slightly if the steaks threaten to burn. Transfer to a shallow, flameproof baking dish and keep warm in a very low (200°F) oven.

6. Preheat the broiler.

7. Return the skillet to medium-high heat and add the reduced Madeira mixture. Stir in half of the truffle, if using. Bring to a boil, reduce the heat, and simmer, scraping the bottom of the skillet to loosen any browned bits, for about 10 minutes, or until the liquid is again reduced by half (to a little less than ½ cup). Reduce further to concentrate the flavors, if necessary, and stir in any juices that have accumulated in the dish holding the steaks.

8. Reduce the heat to very low and whisk the remaining 4 tablespoons butter, 1 tablespoon at a time, into the Madeira sauce to thicken. Season to taste with salt and keep warm.

9. Coat one side and the cut edge of each of the toasts with the anchovy butter. Roll the edges of the toasts in the parsley to coat. Place a toast, buttered side up, in the center of each of 4 serving plates and set aside.

10. Remove the dish holding the fillets from the oven and top each with a slice of ham. Top the ham with a slice of cheese and then 1 heaping tablespoon of the Béchamel Sauce. Slip under the broiler and broil briefly, until the cheese melts and the béchamel just bubbles. Center the fillets on the toasts and top each with the remaining black truffle, if using. Surround with the Madeira sauce and serve.

**Note:** Depending on how precise you want to be, you can cut the ham and cheese with a knife or use the same ring mold as for the bread.

## Béchamel Sauce

**Makes about 1 cup**

*1½ tablespoons unsalted butter*

*1½ tablespoons all-purpose flour*

*1 to 1¾ cups warm milk*

*Generous pinch of freshly grated nutmeg*

*Generous pinch of kosher salt*

1. First, make a roux: In a small saucepan over medium-low heat, melt the butter. As the butter melts, sprinkle the flour over it and cook, stirring, for about 1 minute. Gradually add the milk, whisking to prevent lumps.

2. Add the nutmeg and salt and continue to cook for 1 to 2 minutes, or until the roux thickens but is still slightly fluid—neither thick and pasty nor runny. If not thick enough, cook for a few more minutes, or if too thin, add a little more milk. Set aside, covered with plastic wrap, until needed. Thin with a little milk before using, if necessary.

**Note:** Béchamel, once made, is usually kept warm over simmering water until ready to use, but for this dish it can be made an hour or so in advance, covered with plastic wrap, and kept at room temperature. Although this recipe makes more than needed for the Beef Fillet as Rossini Might Have Liked It, it's difficult to make less. Discard what you don't use, or save it for another use.

# Oven-Braised Beef Short Ribs with Black Pepper and Chianti

Peposo

**Serves 4**

Much has been made of the story of how this peppery dish prompted the first labor strike in Florence, in the early fifteenth century. Italian architect Filippo Brunelleschi was so fond of the long-cooking stew called *peposo,* which he first tasted in a small town outside his home city of Florence, that he instructed his own cooks to make it regularly in his residence. He even had them carry it up the scaffolding to workers laying tile on the Duomo, also known as the cathedral of Santa Maria del Fiore. He may have had good intentions, but it didn't take the Florentine workers long to realize that this robbed them of their lunch hour, and they went on strike to restore the midday break. This elemental dish of beef, garlic, pepper, and good Chianti requires hours to cook, but is well worth the wait—or a climb up to or down from the Duomo.

**Butcher's Note:** Until recently, it was mainly people of our grandparents' generation who bought short ribs from Lobel's; when they came into the shop, we would chat about how flavorful the ribs are and reminisce about old-time recipes. Times are changing, of course, and now more of our customers than ever before are buying short ribs for their great flavor. Compared to other cuts of beef, they are also economical and, like many economical cuts, require long, slow cooking so that the meat becomes tender, nearly to the point of falling from the bone.

One cut of short ribs is called flanken style, typically thick strips of the rib section cut across the bone to yield short pieces of bone anchoring the length of the meat. You or the butcher can cut right between the bones to make single riblets, or small pieces of flanken for use in this dish.

Another popular cut is lengthwise along the bone. It is from the latter that large or small pieces of boneless ribs are obtained for Beef Stew with Cumin and Horseradish (see page 64). For boneless ribs, it is easiest to have your butcher cut the meat from the bone for you, but if you prefer, you can do it yourself by putting a very sharp boning or chef's knife between the meat and the bone, and pressing the blade toward the bone, working your way down it to separate the meat from the bone.

**Wine Note:** For this classic Tuscan dish, serve that region's reds made with the Sangiovese grape: Young, fresh, simple, good-quality Chianti such as Lilliano Chianti Classico is excellent, and a more muscular, traditionally made, young Rosso di Montalcino is better still. A standout in our tasting was the Livio Sassetti Rosso di Montalcino. Compared to the lighter Chianti, the somewhat more alcoholic Montalcino wines underwent an unusual but delicious effect as the dish coaxed out their fruit flavors. Avoid wines aged in sweet, new oak, which throws off the balance of the dish; the wood flavors become exaggerated, and the experience gets a lot less enjoyable. Compared to Tuscany's way with Sangiovese, there just aren't many substitutes in the wine regions of the New World, so, as with the recipe for beef fillet (page 50), we looked to California's Rhône-style specialists to get a taste of southern European sunshine. One favorite is Tablas Creek Vineyard "Côtes de Tablas" red wine from Paso Robles.

*4 pounds flanken-style beef short ribs, cut between the sections of bone into approximately 2-inch chunks*

*1 tablespoon plus 1 teaspoon kosher salt*

*1¼ cups dry red wine, preferably good-quality Chianti*

*1¼ cups Beef Stock (page 212) or canned low-sodium beef broth*

*1¼ cups water*

*1 generous tablespoon tomato paste*

*Cloves of 1 large head garlic, peeled*

*2 teaspoons freshly ground black pepper*

*4 large slices good-quality country-style bread*

*Extra-virgin olive oil for drizzling*

1. Preheat the oven to 350°F.

2. Put the beef in a 15-by-10-inch flameproof glass, ceramic, or earthenware dish. Sprinkle evenly with the salt, tossing to coat all the surfaces of the meat.

3. In a saucepan, combine the wine, stock, and water and bring to a boil. Reduce the heat to medium and simmer for 3 minutes.

4. Ladle a few tablespoons of the hot liquid from the saucepan into a small bowl. Add the tomato paste and stir to dissolve. Return to the saucepan. Set aside

1 garlic clove and stir the rest into the saucepan along with 1 teaspoon of the pepper. Pour over the meat.

5. Cover the dish tightly with aluminum foil and place on the stove top over 2 burners. Bring just to a boil over medium heat. Transfer to the oven and cook for 20 minutes. Reduce the oven temperature to 250°F and continue cooking until the meat is quite tender but not yet falling off the bone, 2½ to 3 hours. Check the stew every so often to ensure that it's just barely simmering. Adjust the oven temperature as needed.

6. Remove the meat from the oven and remove the foil. Make a new foil top to fit the perimeter of the dish but about 1 inch smaller all around. Lay the foil centered on top of the meat and return the dish to the oven. Cook, again adjusting the heat as needed to maintain a gentle simmer, until the meat is very tender and the liquid has been reduced to 1 to 1½ cups, 30 to 45 minutes more. As the liquid begins to thicken slightly, turn the pieces of meat in the dish every now and then to bathe them. If the liquid seems to be evaporating too quickly, add small amounts of stock, water, or wine, or a combination of all three. Remove from the oven.

7. Meanwhile, grill or toast the bread until golden brown. Cut the reserved garlic clove in half and rub each toast with the cut side of the garlic. Drizzle generously with olive oil and place a toast in each of 4 shallow serving bowls.

8. Add the remaining 1 teaspoon pepper to the meat and reheat gently on the stove top over 2 burners set on medium heat, uncovered. Again, turn the meat to bathe it in the reduced sauce. When the sauce has thickened so that there is about ⅔ cup in the dish, divide the meat among the serving bowls. Spoon the remaining sauce (including any separated cooking fat) over the meat and garlic toasts. Serve at once.

# Hungarian Beef Goulash with Paprika and Hand-Pinched Dumplings

Bogrács Gulyás

**Serves 4**

This dish, laced with more than ¼ cup of sweet paprika as befits one with the word "Hungarian" in its title, falls somewhere between a soup and a stew. The goulash contains a relatively small amount of meat and an abundance of intensely flavored liquid made satiny with the abundant collagen in the beef shank. To exploit its juiciness, the dish is completed with dumplings, a classic accompaniment. While the hand-pinched style here may not match your usual idea of a dumpling, they are far better with home-made goulash than any store-bought product such as egg noodles. You can cook the dumplings the day before serving, if you like.

If you want to make and serve the goulash the same day, try to allow time to let it cool so you can more easily skim the fat from it. Even better, refrigerate the goulash overnight and lift off the congealed fat the next day.

**Butcher's Note:** Bigger and heavier than veal shanks, beef shanks may be harder to find, but don't be tempted to substitute veal here. As they are becoming more popular in recent years, beef shanks may be on hand, or you can special order them from the butcher or supermarket meat counter. We prefer beef foreshanks, slightly smaller than hind shanks, because they tend to be a little more flavorful and moist.

**Wine Note:** For this dish, we tasted both Hungarian and Austrian wines and found in the goulash another beef dish that is friendly to white wine. In fact, white is often the choice in Hungarian homes and restaurants. Because so little dry Hungarian white wine is imported into the United States (most common are the famous Tokaij dessert wines, although this is changing), we only considered Austrian whites. Grüner Veltliner made in a more richly textured style (whether by virtue of vineyard, house style, or a warm vintage) is great with goulash. One favorite is Schloss Gobelsburg Grüner Veltliner "Steinsetz."

Reds are excellent, too. An "old-school" choice from Hungary is a medium-weight blended wine called Egri Bikaver, which is usually soft, pleasing, and just right for the goulash when not fancied up excessively by new oak barrels. One of our favorites is Vitavin Egri Bikaver. A more modern-styled Austrian choice (and maybe the most dynamic pairing) was the Glatzer "Riedencuvee," an addictively gulpable blend of the sappy Zweigelt grape refined with a little St. Laurent. These two increasingly important varieties, along with the their local stablemate, Blaufrankisch, are the source of a number of high-quality, food-friendly wines in a country best known for whites. From California, a mouthwatering Zinfandel is a great choice with the paprika-laced goulash. Always good is the Sausal Winery Zinfandel from the Alexander Valley in Sonoma.

---

*¼ cup vegetable oil*

*2½ to 3 pounds bone-in beef shank meat cut by the butcher as for osso buco (see Butcher's Note page 89), then cut into 1-inch cubes to yield 1½ pounds of meat with marrowbones reserved*

*2 yellow onions, halved and thinly sliced*

*4 garlic cloves, crushed*

*5 tablespoons best-quality Hungarian sweet paprika*

*¼ teaspoon cayenne*

*¼ teaspoon ground caraway seed*

*¾ cup dry white wine*

*3½ cups Beef Stock (page 212) or canned low-sodium beef broth*

*1½ cups water*

*1½ teaspoons kosher salt*

*½ pound potatoes, peeled and cut into ½-inch dice*

*1 green bell pepper, seeded and cut into pieces about ½ inch long and ¼ inch wide*

*1 batch Hungarian Hand-Pinched Dumplings (page 58)*

*2 teaspoons finely chopped fresh marjoram (optional)*

*4 tablespoons sour cream (optional)*

---

1. Preheat the oven to 350°F.

2. In a 6-quart flameproof casserole or Dutch oven with a tight-fitting lid, heat the oil over medium-high heat until hot. Working in batches if necessary, cook the beef until deeply browned on two sides, about 5 minutes per side. Transfer to a plate and set aside.

3. Reduce the heat to medium-low and add the onions and garlic. Cook gently, stirring occasionally, until softened but without color, about 10 minutes. Stir in 4 tablespoons of the paprika, the cayenne, and the caraway. Add the wine, bring to a simmer, and cook, scraping the bottom of the pot to loosen any browned bits, for 3 minutes. Add the stock, water, salt, marrowbones, and the browned meat, along with any accumulated juices.

4. Stir well, cover, and place in the oven for 20 minutes. Reduce the oven temperature to 250°F and continue cooking, stirring once or twice, until the meat is tender, about 3½ hours, adjusting the oven temperature as needed to maintain a very low simmer. Remove from the oven and let cool slightly. Use a slotted spoon to remove the marrowbones from the casserole; they will be empty by now. Discard the bones. Let the casserole cool completely, cover, and refrigerate for at least 3 hours or up to overnight.

5. Skim off most or all of the orange-colored fat and save it for another use (such as frying potatoes). Place the casserole over medium-low heat and bring to a gentle simmer. Stir in the potatoes, cover, and simmer gently until the potatoes are nearly tender, about 20 minutes.

6. Stir in the bell pepper and the remaining 1 tablespoon paprika. Cover and cook for 15 minutes more. At this point the goulash should be richly flavored, with a consistency somewhere between a soup and a stew. Add salt to taste, if necessary, and simmer briefly, uncovered, to concentrate the flavors. If it's too thick, add a little stock or water.

7. To serve, bring a large pot of lightly salted water to a boil, add the dumplings, and cook briefly just to reheat. Drain and divide the dumplings among wide, shallow bowls. Ladle the goulash over the dumplings. Sprinkle with marjoram and top with sour cream (if using) and serve immediately.

# Hungarian Hand-Pinched Dumplings
Csipetke

**Makes 1 batch; serves 4 with goulash**

---

*2 cups all-purpose flour, plus more as needed*

*2 extra-large eggs, beaten*

*2 teaspoons vegetable oil, plus more for coating*

*¼ teaspoon kosher salt*

---

1. Mound the flour in the middle of a large, clean work surface. Make a well in the center of the flour and add the eggs, 2 teaspoons of the oil, and the salt. Using a fork, begin to incorporate small amounts flour from the inner edge of the well into the eggs.

2. Continue to incorporate flour, whisking with the fork, until the dough begins to come together. This will become messy, but don't worry. The dough will come together smoothly in no time. When you can no longer whisk, scrape the dough from the fork and return it to the mass.

3. Working with your hands and with the help of a bench scraper or metal spatula, start pushing larger amounts of the remaining flour over the (still eggy) dough and gently work it in. When the mass finely begins to resemble a rough dough, set it aside and clean the work surface. Scrape up the loose flour as well as any separate dried bits of flour and egg, and then sift it all through a coarse-mesh sieve back onto the work surface, discarding the dried bits. Continue to incorporate the sifted flour into the dough mass.

4. Knead the dough until it can't absorb any more flour without turning dry. Continue to knead the dough until very smooth and still barely moist, 5 to 7 minutes longer. Wrap tightly with plastic wrap and let rest for 30 minutes at room temperature.

5. Working in 2 batches if necessary, roll out the dough on a lightly floured work surface to a ⅛-inch thickness (any shape is fine). Cut into 2 or 3 easy-to-handle pieces and, working with your floured thumb and forefinger, pinch off roundish pieces of dough about ⅜ inch in diameter. They will appear irregular and look a little like thick miniature cornflakes. As you work, let each finished dumpling fall onto a lightly floured baking sheet or jelly-roll pan. Repeat to use all the dough. The uncooked dumplings can touch one another, but don't let them overlap too much or they might stick; use additional pans to hold them as needed. The uncooked dumplings can sit uncovered for a few hours, although the drier they are, the longer they take to cook.

6. In a large pot of salted boiling water, cook the dumplings just until tender but still firm to the bite and no longer floury tasting, 6 to 10 minutes depending on the thickness and dryness of the dumplings. Do not overcook. Drain and rinse under running water until cool.

7. Toss the dumplings in a large bowl with a few teaspoons of oil to coat and keep them separated. Keep at room temperature for up to a few hours or store, covered, in the refrigerator overnight.

# Beef Stew Flavored with Black Olives and Orange

Estouffade de Boeuf Provençal

**Serves 4**

The name of this recipe says it all. It's no wonder it's a favorite in Provence, the sunny south of France, where the earth, air, water, and skill of the French farmers and cooks conspire to come together in a simple stew flavored with the best of the Mediterranean. Try it with steamed or braised carrots and potatoes. The recipe relies on salt pork, which is cut from the belly or side of the hog, for flavor. Sold in supermarkets and at butcher shops, salt pork usually has some streaks of lean meat, similar to bacon.

**Butcher's Note:** We use beef chuck in five recipes in this book because, frankly speaking, it's the best choice for pot roasting, stewing, and braising—all basically the same technique, where meat is cooked in liquid over relatively low heat or in a moderate oven over a long period of time, usually an hour or more. (We also like brisket for some pot roasts, as for the recipe for Marinated Beef Pot Roast with Vinegar and Riesling on page 69. Read more about brisket there.) Other books may call for beef top or bottom round, but we advise you stay away from the round. Round looks great in the market—nicely colored and plump—but once it's cooked, it tends to be dry and relatively tasteless. When it's reheated, it's even less appealing.

On the other hand, chuck, cut from the neck, is the opposite of round in every way. It won't win any beauty contests in the market, but it's nicely marbled, marvelously flavorful and moist, and stands up to reheating. We suggest you buy first- or center-cut chuck, the most flavorful and moistest cuts of the chuck. Buy chuck boneless if you can, because it's

much easier to work with that way, but it's delicious on the bone, too.

**Wine Note:** To go with our Provençal beef stew, we tried a number of regional reds, and two stood out: Château Petit Sonnailler, from the *appellation* Coteaux d'Aix-en-Provence, and the Domaine de Pradeaux from the small and very special appellation of Bandol perched on the Mediterranean Sea.

Any number of other medium-rich wines from the Coteaux de Aix-en-Provence would be good choices, so let your merchant guide you. But take care when buying a young wine from Bandol; many are too bold for this stew. Look for alcohol levels below 13.5 percent (therefore more delicate) and, if you can find them, wines with a few years of aging (which mellows them still more). Our eight-year-old bottle of Domaine de Pradeaux—whose wines are not only lower in alcohol but often released at four or five years of age—is a very special companion to this dish and is worth seeking out. In warmer weather, a chilled bottle of the same winery's beautifully old-fashioned rosé tastes surprisingly delicious next to the stew's Provençal flavors.

From the States, there are a number of producers who have southern France on their minds when making wine. One favorite, made from the variety that is the basis of the reds of Bandol, is Jade Mountain Mourvèdre, made in Napa Valley from fruit grown in Contra Costa County, California.

======

*6 tablespoons extra-virgin olive oil, plus more for drizzling*

*4 ounces fatty, skinless salt pork, cut into pieces about 1½ inches long, ¼ inch wide, and ¼ inch thick*

*Kosher salt*

*3 pounds boneless beef chuck, cut into pieces about 3 inches long, 1½ inches wide, and 1½ inches thick*

*2 medium yellow onions, quartered and peeled, root end intact*

*12 large cloves garlic, 8 lightly crushed, 4 thinly sliced*

*2 large carrots, peeled and chopped*

*1½ cups dry rosé or white wine*

*½ cup water*

*2 large sprigs fresh thyme, plus 1 teaspoon finely chopped thyme leaves for garnish*

*Generous ⅛ teaspoon freshly grated nutmeg*

*2 whole cloves*

*Two 1-by-2-inch strips orange zest (see Note), the rest of the orange reserved*

*One 15-ounce can peeled whole tomatoes, drained and very coarsely chopped*

*1 cup small or medium mild black olives such as Niçoise or Nyons*

*2 tablespoons finely chopped fresh flat-leaf parsley*

======

1.  In a large, flameproof casserole or Dutch oven with a tight-fitting lid, heat 3 tablespoons of the olive oil over medium heat and cook the salt pork, uncovered, until pale gold and crispy. Using a slotted spoon, transfer to a small plate and set aside.

2.  Salt the beef pieces generously on all sides.

3.  Raise the heat under the pot to medium-high. Working in two batches, cook the beef until deeply browned all over, 10 to 12 minutes per batch, reducing the heat if it threatens to burn. Transfer the meat to a plate and set aside.

4. Pour off all but 4 tablespoons of the fat and return the pot to medium-high heat. Cook the onion quarters until deeply browned on 1 side. Turn the onions (try to keep them in 1 piece) and brown for 3 minutes more. Add the crushed garlic cloves and the carrots and cook, stirring occasionally, until the garlic just begins to color. Add the wine and simmer for 2 minutes, scraping the bottom of the pot to loosen any browned bits. Add the water, thyme sprigs, nutmeg, salt pork, and ½ teaspoon salt. Stick a clove firmly into each piece of orange zest and add them to the casserole.

5. Return the meat and any accumulated juices to the casserole and bring to a bare simmer. Reduce the heat to very low, cover, and cook, maintaining a bare simmer, until the meat is somewhat tender but not yet fork-tender, about 3 hours.

6. Using a slotted spoon, transfer the meat to a plate. Gently pour the liquid and vegetables through a colander set over a bowl. Pick out the onion quarters, transfer them to the plate with the meat, and cover the meat and onions with aluminum foil. Press lightly on the vegetables in the colander to extract most of the liquid. Discard the solids. Let the strained liquid rest for about 10 minutes. Skim off the fat and set aside.

7. Meanwhile, wipe out the pot and add the remaining 3 tablespoons olive oil. Place over medium-low heat, add the sliced garlic, and cook until pale gold at the edges. Stir in the tomatoes and cook, stirring occasionally, for 5 minutes.

8. Return the skimmed liquid and the meat and onions to the pot and stir gently. Taste the liquid: If you can't detect the flavor of orange, stir in the juice of the reserved orange, a little bit at a time, until the flavor is just noticeable. If you can already taste an orange flavor, leave out the juice.

9. Return the stew to a bare simmer, cover, and cook until the meat is very tender, 1 to 1½ hours longer. Remove from the heat and stir in the olives. If you have time, let the stew rest off the heat, uncovered, for 30 minutes. Reheat if necessary and divide among shallow serving bowls. Drizzle with a bit of olive oil and sprinkle with the chopped thyme and parsley. Serve immediately.

**Note:** To remove large strips of citrus zest, use a small, sharp knife or vegetable peeler to cut away the colorful portion of the peel, being careful to leave the bitter white pith underneath.

# Beef in the Style of Burgundy

### Boeuf à la Bourguignonne

**Serves 4**

Arguably the most legendary of braises to come out of France, this stew traditionally is made with relatively tough cuts of beef, such as chuck or shoulder. Both cuts are from the forequarter, with the shoulder cut from the bottom portion of the chuck, and both become wonderfully flavorful and tender with long, slow cooking. In the original stew, a calf's or pig's foot was used to provide a smoothness from naturally occurring gelatin. Here, we've added a little powdered gelatin to duplicate the texture. This pared-down version, prepared without the pearl onions and mushrooms used in some recipes, really emphasizes the flavors of the beef and wine. To emphasize this simplicity, we like to serve it with steamed or braised carrots and baby potatoes.

**Wine Note:** What else but a red Burgundy for this? But when buying red Burgundy, specific wine suggestions should take a backseat to a larger concern: More than any other wine, red Burgundy should be purchased from a reputable merchant who carries the wines of equally reputable importers, as Burgundy is expensive and fragile. So go with any wine your merchant thinks well of and is in your price range. A tip: Mellower, brick-colored, easygoing Burgundies are preferable here to the darker, tighter, and more forceful styles. That said, one of the favorites in our tasting was an offbeat wine worth mentioning, Bourgogne Passetoutgrains. Made from a large percentage of Pinot Noir and a smaller amount of Gamay grapes (rare for the region), Passetoutgrains is most often a lightweight, simple country wine, but the one that captured our fancy, Domaine Michel Lafarge Bourgogne Passetoutgrains, is a rich, spirited wine from a top Volnay producer and a great match for the braised beef. Beyond Europe, we loved the bright and earthy Te Kairanga Pinot Noir from Martinborough, New Zealand, a region that any lover of red Burgundy should get to know.

*5 ounces fatty, skinless salt pork,*
*cut into pieces about 1½ inches long,*
*¼ inch wide, and ¼ inch thick*

*2 tablespoons vegetable oil*

*Kosher salt*

*3 pounds boneless beef chuck, cut into pieces about*
*3 inches long, 1½ inches wide, and 1½ inches thick*

*4 large cloves garlic, lightly crushed*

*2 medium yellow onions, chopped*

*2 large carrots, peeled and chopped*

*2 tablespoons all-purpose flour*

*2 tablespoons marc de Bourgogne,*
*Cognac, or similar brandy*

*2 cups good-quality, medium-bodied*
*red Burgundy or Pinot Noir (see page 32*
*for notes on cooking with Pinot Noir)*

*Bouquet garni: 2 chopped green onions, 2 sprigs*
*fresh thyme, 2 sprigs fresh flat-leaf parsley,*
*1 bay leaf, and 5 black peppercorns*

*One ¼-ounce packet unflavored gelatin*

*2 tablespoons finely chopped fresh flat-leaf parsley*

1. Bring a small saucepan of water to a boil and blanch the salt pork for 2 minutes. Drain well. Transfer the salt pork to a large, flameproof casserole or Dutch oven with a tight-fitting lid. Add the oil and cook, uncovered, over medium heat until the salt pork is pale gold and crispy. Using a slotted spoon, transfer to a small plate and set aside.

2. Salt the beef generously on all sides.

3. Raise the heat under the pot to medium-high. Working in two batches, cook the beef until deeply browned all over, 10 to 12 minutes per batch, reducing the heat if it threatens to burn. Transfer the meat to a plate and set aside.

4. Pour off all but 4 tablespoons of the fat and return the pot to medium-high heat. Add the garlic, onions, and carrots and cook, stirring occasionally, until the onions are pale gold at the edges, 5 to 8 minutes. Sprinkle the flour over all and cook, stirring, for 1 minute more. Add the brandy and cook until it nearly evaporates. Add the wine and bring to a simmer over high heat. Reduce the heat and simmer for 5 minutes, scraping the bottom of the pot to loosen any browned bits.

5. Make the bouquet garni by tying the green onions, herb sprigs, bay leaf, and peppercorns in a square of cheesecloth. Add the meat and any accumulated juices

on the plate to the pot along with the bouquet garni and ¼ teaspoon salt. Bring to a gentle simmer and cook, uncovered, for 5 minutes more.

6. Ladle about ¼ cup of the hot wine from the pot into a small bowl. Sprinkle the gelatin over the wine, stir, and let dissolve. Stir the dissolved gelatin into the stew. Reduce the heat to very low, cover, and cook at a bare simmer until the meat is very tender, about 4 hours.

7. Let the stew rest off the heat for 30 minutes. Skim off some of the fat and use a slotted spoon to transfer the meat to a plate. Gently pour the liquid and vegetables through a colander set over a bowl, pushing hard to extract the flavorful liquid from the vegetables. Allow some of the mashed carrots to pass through to help thicken the cooking liquid, but don't push everything through; you want a slightly thickened, flavorful sauce that's fluid enough to thinly coat the beef. Discard the vegetables and bouquet garni.

8. Return the meat and sauce to the pot and reheat gently. Divide the meat and sauce among serving plates or shallow bowls. Garnish with the parsley and serve.

# Beef Stew with Cumin and Horseradish

Manzo con Comino e Rafano

**Serves 4**

The presence of horseradish and cumin in an Italian dish raises interesting points. Although it may seem surprising, horseradish is found in the cooking of many regions of Italy and is especially beloved in the Friuli-Venezia Giulia region in the northeastern corner of the country. Its abundant use there bespeaks Germanic influences: Hundreds of years prior to and up through the end of World War I, the region was part of or allied with the far-flung Austrian Empire. This explains the horseradish, but what about the cumin?

As Fred Plotkin points out in *La Terra Fortunata*, his survey of the food and culture of Friuli-Venezia Giulia, the region's character was in part shaped by its largest city, Trieste, which served as the sole port for the powerful but landlocked Austrian Empire. Not only did spices enter here from Africa and Asia, to be distributed throughout the empire and beyond, but Trieste also served as the exit point for many of the flavorings that were produced and enjoyed within the empire itself (in this, it surpassed even Venice). Cumin, it seems, tasted so good to the locals who trafficked in it that they found a place for it in their kitchens. This abundantly beef-filled stew has not a vegetable in sight; braised baby turnips or bitter greens would be welcome side dishes. Serve this rich, cold-weather dish over simply prepared polenta or, better still, stone-ground yellow grits, which, if you can find them, are much better than most imported Italian polenta in the United States.

**Wine Note:** If you stick to the recipe as written, the effect of the horseradish is fairly mellow, as the accompanying wine should be. One recommendation is the Tenuta Villanova Merlot, an easygoing partner that's lighter and less fruity than many more familiar American versions. If you think you might shower the dish with more horseradish at the table, as we do, then you'd benefit by pouring Refosco, the best indigenous red of the region, made from the grape of the same name. Its penetrating tang and great personality won't take nothin' from no horseradish.

Among the handful of these wines available in the United States, try the excellent Ronchi di Manzano Refosco. Another Friulian favorite with beef adds a goodly dose of Merlot and Cabernet Sauvignon to its Refosco fruit, creating an all-around richer companion to the dish: Rather than simply complementing the beef (Villanova Merlot) or standing up to the horseradish with its own sass (Ronchi di Manzano Refosco), the Bastianich Vespa Rosso we tasted wrapped its suave self around the entire dish in a kind of delectable bear hug.

From the eastern United States, the Chaddsford Winery Cabernet/Chambourcin, like the Bastianich wine, is made by blending the international (Cabernets Sauvignon and Franc) with the local (Chambourcin) to achieve a blend that has more of the piquancy and savor familiar to lovers of European wine.

---

*1 cup all-purpose flour*

*Kosher salt*

*2 ½ pounds boneless beef short ribs, cut into 1 ½-inch pieces (see Butcher's Note, page 54; if only bone-in ribs are available, buy 5 to 6 pounds)*

*5 tablespoons olive oil*

*1 large yellow onion, finely chopped*

*½ cup dry red wine*

*1 ¾ teaspoons ground cumin*

*2 cups Beef Stock (page 212) or canned low-sodium beef broth, or 1 cup stock or broth and 1 cup water*

*¾ cup (1 ½ sticks) unsalted butter*

*3 tablespoons lightly packed grated fresh horseradish (see Note, page 44), plus more for serving, if desired*

*3 tablespoons finely chopped fresh flat-leaf parsley*

---

1. In a large bowl, mix the flour with 2 tablespoons salt and set aside. Toss the meat in the flour mixture to coat and shake off the excess.

2. Heat a large stockpot over medium-high heat and add the olive oil. When hot, working in batches, cook the beef until crusty and deeply browned on two sides, about 6 minutes per side, reducing the heat if it threatens to burn. Transfer to a plate and set aside.

3. Reduce the heat to medium, add the onion, and cook, stirring occasionally, until soft and pale gold at the edges, 8 to 10 minutes. Add the wine and simmer until nearly evaporated, scraping the bottom of the pot to loosen any browned bits. Add ¾ teaspoon of the cumin, ¾ teaspoon salt, and the stock, along with the meat and any accumulated juices.

4. Bring to a simmer, reduce the heat to very low, cover tightly, and cook at a bare simmer until the meat is very tender, 4 to 6 hours.

5. When the meat is very tender, the sauce should have thickened somewhat, clinging just lightly to the beef pieces. Gently simmer the stew, uncovered, to thicken if necessary. Using a wooden spoon, lightly push on the beef to collapse the chunks partly, which allows them to absorb more of the sauce, but take care that the meat does not shred. Add salt to taste, if necessary, and let the stew rest off the heat for at least 15 minutes while you make the horseradish–brown butter.

6. In a light-colored skillet, so that you can watch the milk solids brown, melt the butter over medium heat. Reduce the heat to low and cook, swirling the butter regularly, until the milk solids just begin to turn to pale brown and the butter gives off a nutty aroma, 3 to 5 minutes. Watch the butter carefully and continue to swirl until the solids have deepened to the color of saffron, no more than 30 seconds more. Do not let burn. Immediately stir in

the horseradish, the remaining 1 teaspoon cumin, and a pinch of salt. Keep warm over low heat.

7. Gently reheat the stew, if necessary. Divide the stew among warmed serving bowls and spoon 2 to 3 tablespoons of the warm horseradish–brown butter sauce over each. Garnish with the parsley and serve immediately, passing any remaining horseradish-brown butter and more freshly grated horseradish, if desired, at the table.

**Make-Ahead Tip:** The stew can be prepared through step 4 up to 3 days ahead. Cover, reheat gently with a few tablespoons of stock or water, and continue as directed. The horseradish–brown butter sauce can be made up to 2 hours ahead and reheated gently.

# Spiced Portuguese-Style Pot Roast with Bacon, Onions, and White Wine

Alcatra

**Serves 4 to 6**

Don't be surprised by the number of onions in this beloved Portuguese dish. The meat needs to be completely surrounded by aromatic slivers of onions, so that when it's done, both beef and onions are rich, smoky, slightly spiced, and bathed in a thin but intensely flavorful sauce. A good way to savor the juices is to serve generous helpings of rice in shallow bowls, spoon the meat and onions over it, and then ladle on lots of sauce. See page 59 for information on beef chuck.

**Wine Note:** This dish is a great showcase for Portugal's wealth of unique and affordable wines. From fresh, juicy (and unbelievably low-priced) JP Tinto Terras do Sado to the intense Caves Aliança Aliança Particular Palmela to the more full-bodied richness of José Maria da Fonseca and Van Zeller "Domini" from the Duero, the country offers great choices for pairing with the oniony beef in this recipe. Although the acidity levels range from moderate to low, the easygoing fruit flavors—always a food-loving trait among reds—these wines have in common make them perfect with this dish. These fruit flavors vary in intensity from one to the next, but none are "tight" or "tough" wines, and all are free of excessive tannin and wood. Even those that flash a little new wood (like the Caves Aliança Palmela) are so very good-natured that you hardly notice its presence.

Wines with more tannin made waves here. In our tastings we found the spicy, brothy nature of the braised beef and onions exaggerated the tannins, leaving a raw, bitter taste that upset the harmony of the dish. Even the medium-weight, delectable, and pleasingly tannic Luis Pato Casta Baga felt out of place, so the even more powerful (often tannic) Portuguese "high expression" wines are also best left for another meal. From California, try the juicy Bonny Doon "Clos de Gilroy," a mellow, nearly tannin-free wine made from Grenache grapes that's very much in the spirit of these Portuguese reds.

---

*3 tablespoons unsalted butter*

*8 ounces smoked slab bacon, cut into pieces about 1 inch long, ¼ inch wide, and ¼ inch thick*

*Kosher salt*

*One 2-pound piece beef chuck uniformly shaped like a roast, cut crosswise into 4 equal steaks*

*6 medium yellow onions, thinly sliced*

*12 large cloves garlic, thinly sliced*

*20 allspice berries*

*10 black peppercorns*

*¼ teaspoon crushed red pepper flakes*

*1 bay leaf*

*3 cups dry white wine*

*1 cup water*

*2 tablespoons finely chopped fresh flat-leaf parsley*

*4 to 6 cups cooked white rice for serving*

1. In a 5- or 6-quart flameproof casserole or Dutch oven with a tight-fitting lid, melt 2 tablespoons of the butter over medium heat. Stir in the bacon and reduce the heat to medium-low. Cook, stirring occasionally, until the bacon is crispy but still tender, about 10 minutes. Using a slotted spoon, transfer to a plate, leaving the bacon fat in the pot. Set the bacon aside.

2. Generously salt the steaks.

3. Raise the heat under the pot to medium-high and cook the steaks until nicely but not heavily browned on both sides, 3 to 4 minutes per side. Work in batches if necessary. Transfer to another plate and set aside.

4. Stir the onions, garlic, and 1 teaspoon salt into the drippings in the pot and cook over medium-high heat, stirring regularly, until reduced in volume and slightly softened, 6 to 8 minutes. If the moisture from the onions has not deglazed the bottom of the pot, add ½ cup water and scrape to loosen any browned bits. Transfer the contents of the pot to a bowl and set aside; let the pot cool.

5. Preheat the oven to 350°F.

6. Rub the inside of the pot with the remaining 1 tablespoon butter. Distribute half of the onion mixture evenly across the bottom. Lay the meat in a single layer over the onions. Scatter the allspice berries, peppercorns, red pepper flakes, bay leaf, and half of the reserved bacon over the meat. Distribute the remaining onion mixture over the meat, completely covering it. Scatter the remaining bacon over the top and pour the wine, water, and any onion and beef juices on the plates into the pot. Add more water to just cover the solids, if necessary.

7. Bring to a simmer and let bubble gently for 5 minutes. Cover, transfer to the oven, and cook for 20 minutes. Reduce the oven temperature to 250°F and continue cooking until the meat is very tender, 3 to 3½ hours more. Adjust the oven temperature as needed to maintain a very gentle simmer.

8. Turn off the oven, uncover the pot, and let the stew rest in the oven for about 30 minutes to concentrate the flavors.

9. Divide the meat among wide, shallow bowls. Spoon over abundant amounts of onions and broth, garnish with the parsley, and serve with the rice.

# Beef Braised in Barbera Wine

Brasato al Barbera

Serves 4 to 6

There was a time when this historic dish from Piedmont, Italy, made use of the region's best wines, Barolo and Barbaresco. Today, because of their expense, only wine producers and a few restaurants continue the practice of cooking with these wines. Good-quality Barbera is readily available and makes a delicious braise.

This dish differs from most other Italian braises in that it uses one large piece of meat rather than smaller cubes. In Piedmont, both beef and veal rump and round roasts are called for in this dish. Instead, we use chuck roast for its beefier flavor and moister texture, although it doesn't slice as nicely as do the rump and round roasts. The sauce is made by puréeing the vegetables along with the braising liquid to create a delicious, thick, wine-flavored "gravy." Serve this with mashed potatoes or polenta and braised root vegetables such as carrots, turnips, or parsnips.

🔪

**Wine Note:** If you want to pull out the big guns—Barbaresco and Barolo—you would do your best to find a wine of some age, because harder, tannic wines are no fun with this dish. Two wines from top traditional producers stood out in our tests: An eight-year-old Produttori del Barbaresco Barbaresco "Pora" and a seven-year-old Aurelio Settimo Barolo "Rocche." Luciano Sandrone Barbera d'Alba, a more modern-style wine from a third top grower, was just as fine. The first two wines complemented the dish with the low-keyed, warm, and woodsy complexity that it seems only aged Nebbiolo-based wines can deliver. The Barbera, because of its tangy focus, provides a different sort of companion, one that creates a delicious contrast between the homely stew and the suavely spiced electricity of the wine itself. The Nebbiolo grape—the sole ingredient in the great Barolo and Barbaresco wines—has proven to be a frustrating variety to cultivate beyond Italy's Piedmont and Lombardy regions. One California winery, however, has had more than a little luck: Palmina in Santa Barbara County has issued a number of lovely Nebbiolo-based wines true to the spirit of Piedmont. Look to Palmina "Stolpman" Nebbiolo or their vibrant Barbera "Bien Nacido" for excellent partners for our Beef Braised in Barbera.

*Kosher salt*
*One 3-pound boneless beef chuck roast, tied*
*¼ cup extra-virgin olive oil*
*2 carrots, peeled and chopped*
*1 large yellow onion, chopped*
*1 stalk celery, chopped*
*3 large cloves garlic, crushed*
*1 tablespoon tomato paste*
*1 bottle (750 ml) good-quality Barbera wine*
*2½ teaspoons finely chopped fresh rosemary*
*½ teaspoon freshly grated nutmeg,*
*plus more for garnish*
*⅛ teaspoon ground cinnamon*
*1 bay leaf*
*Freshly ground black pepper*

1. Generously salt the beef on all sides.

2. In a medium, flameproof casserole or Dutch oven with a tight-fitting lid, heat the olive oil over medium heat. When hot, cook the roast until deeply browned on all sides, about 15 minutes, reducing the heat if it threatens to burn. Transfer to a plate and set aside.

3. Preheat the oven to 350°F.

4. Add the carrots, onion, celery, and garlic to the pot and cook over medium high heat, stirring occasionally, until the onions are pale gold at the edges, 8 to 10 minutes. Stir in the tomato paste and cook for 1 minute longer. Add the wine and bring to a boil over high heat, scraping the bottom of the pot to loosen any browned bits. Cook over medium-high heat until the wine has reduced by one-third, about 10 minutes.

5. Stir in 1½ teaspoons of the rosemary, the ½ teaspoon of nutmeg, the cinnamon, bay leaf, and ½ teaspoon salt. Return the meat and any accumulated juices to the pot, cover, and bring to a simmer.

6. Transfer to the oven and cook for 20 minutes. Reduce the heat to 250°F and continue cooking until the meat is very tender, about 3½ to 4 hours more, turning the roast over in the liquid every hour or so and adjusting the oven temperature as needed to maintain a bare simmer.

7. Remove from the oven and, if you have time, let rest for 30 minutes, covered, basting occasionally. Using a slotted spoon, transfer the roast to a plate, cover tightly with aluminum foil, and keep warm in a very low (200°F) oven.

8. Transfer the cooking liquid and vegetables to a blender and process until very smooth, about 1 minute, adding salt to taste. Reheat before serving if necessary.

9. Transfer the roast to a cutting board. Snip the strings and remove. Using a serrated knife, cut into slices about 1 inch thick (don't worry if the slices fall apart—keep them together as best you can). Transfer the slices to serving plates and smother with a generous amount of the sauce. Garnish with the remaining 1 teaspoon rosemary, grated nutmeg, and coarsely ground black pepper and serve immediately.

# Marinated Beef Pot Roast with Vinegar and Riesling

Sauerbraten

**Serves 4 to 6**

With this dish, you'll discover one of the granddaddies of regional wine cookery, rich with the flavors of the sixteenth century. Because we use beef brisket, our version is much moister than those made with traditional beef round. Ask for a "point," or second-cut, brisket (see Butcher's Note). This dish reheats well with the addition of stock, water, or a mixture of both, and because of the extended marinating in wine and vinegar, it lasts for up to two weeks in the refrigerator. Serve with spaetzle or egg noodles.

**Butcher's Note:** Many people are in the habit of asking for the leaner first cut of brisket, perhaps because that's what their mothers and grandmothers used, but since you probably only cook brisket every now and then, indulge in the fattier and therefore far more flavorful second cut. Beef brisket, cut from the breast, always needs long, slow cooking to tenderize it and bring out its flavor. In this recipe, we tell you to cut or tear the meat *with* the grain because, as the meat has been cooked for so long, it virtually falls apart into appetizing chunks. In other cases, if you are preparing a brisket dish that instructs you to slice it against the grain, let the meat cool a little first so that it firms up, and then use a very sharp knife to slice it.

**Wine Note:** Although the sauerbraten is made with dry Riesling (which we use to regulate the sweetness in the recipe), the wine in your glass should have a touch of sweetness to be compatible with the raisins and gingersnaps in this dish (remember the principle of "like with like"). Many good-quality, less dry German Rieslings offer a sweet-tart harmony, the result of a bracing, steely acidity balanced by a just-perceptible sweetness. Like everywhere else, Germany has its share of lousy wines, but in the good examples, this harmony comes from the mouthwatering taste and texture of the wine's various fruit flavors (from the cool of lime to the deeply peachy) shot through with a mineral savor sucked up from the soil, making these among the most interesting white wines in the world.

It's unlikely that any other dish better illustrates how well white wine can complement beef. In fact, there is no better wine for sauerbraten than a German Kabinett or Spätlese Riesling. More austere, less succulent whites screech alongside sauerbraten, and most reds get beaten up and dismantled between bites of the tangy beef and densely flavored sauce. One favorite for sauerbraten, from the Sarr River Valley, is the dryish, earthy, and concentrated Van Volxem Kanzemer Altenberg Riesling Spätlese, but any number of German Rieslings would be just as good. (See page 103 for more information on German wines.) Seek out a wine merchant with a real interest in German wine—not always an easy task, but well worth it. Beyond Germany, Austria, and Alsace in France, which together serve as the masters of Riesling, there are few really fine sources for this variety. Recently, Oregon has emerged as another. Look for the Holloran "La Pavillion" Riesling from the Willamette Valley, styled much like its German siblings.

*Kosher salt and freshly ground black pepper*

*2 ¾ pounds beef brisket,*
*preferably point, or second, cut*

*¼ cup bacon fat or olive oil*

*2 carrots, peeled and chopped*

*2 stalks celery, chopped*

*2 large cloves garlic, peeled and crushed*

*1 large yellow onion, chopped*

*2 cups good-quality dry Riesling wine*

*1 cup good-quality white wine vinegar*

*10 juniper berries*

*6 cloves*

*4 large sprigs fresh thyme*

*3 bay leaves*

*2 cups Veal Stock (page 213), Beef Stock (page 212), or canned low-sodium beef broth*

*2 cups water*

*5 tablespoons unsalted butter*

*¼ cup all-purpose flour*

*1 tablespoon sugar*

*½ cup golden raisins*

*⅔ cup crushed (but not powdered) gingersnaps*

1. Generously salt the brisket on both sides and season with pepper.

2. In a large skillet, heat the fat over medium-high heat and cook the meat until deeply browned on both sides, about 5 minutes per side, reducing the heat if it threatens to burn. Transfer to a deep baking dish or heatproof bowl just large enough to contain it and the marinade. Set aside.

3. Pour off all but 3 tablespoons of the fat and return the skillet to medium heat. Add the carrots, celery, garlic, and onion and cook, stirring occasionally, until softened, about 5 minutes. Add the wine, vinegar, juniper berries, cloves, thyme, and bay leaves, bring to a simmer, and cook for 3 minutes. Pour the hot marinade over the meat. If the meat is not entirely submerged, add some of the 2 cups stock or water to just cover. (Be sure to measure and subtract the amount from the 2 cups listed in the ingredient list.) Let cool slightly, cover tightly, and refrigerate for 4 days. Turn the meat once a day during this time, keeping the vegetables around and on top of the meat so it stays fully immersed.

4. Preheat the oven to 350°F.

5. Bring the meat and marinade to room temperature and transfer to a large, flameproof casserole or Dutch oven with a tight-fitting lid. Stir in the stock and water (less any amount used in the marinade) and 1 teaspoon salt. Cover and bring to a gentle simmer over medium heat. Uncover and skim off any foam. If you scoop out any vegetables or other seasonings while skimming, rinse and return them to the pot.

6. Cover, transfer to the oven, and cook for 20 minutes. Reduce the oven temperature to 250°F and continue cooking until tender but not quite falling apart, about 5 hours. Adjust the oven temperature as needed to maintain a bare simmer.

7. Transfer the pot to the stove top and transfer the meat to a plate. Leave the oven on. Cover the meat and set aside.

8. Simmer the cooking liquid over medium-high heat until the liquid is reduced to about 3 cups, 12 to 15 minutes.

9. Meanwhile, make a roux: In a skillet, melt the butter over medium-low heat and whisk in the flour and sugar until smooth. Reduce the heat to low and cook, whisking regularly and occasionally scraping down the sides of the skillet with a rubber spatula, until pale nut brown in color, about 5 minutes. Remove from the heat and set aside.

10. When the cooking liquid and vegetables have reduced, whisk in the roux until incorporated. Stir in the raisins and the meat, along with any accumulated juices. Baste the meat thoroughly with the thickened sauce, cover, return to the oven, and cook for 30 minutes longer. Transfer back to the stove top. At this point the sauce should be very thick and just slightly fluid. Cook to reduce it a little more or thin with stock or water, if necessary.

11. Transfer the meat to a cutting board and tent loosely with aluminum foil.

12. Stir the gingersnaps into the sauce over very low heat. Taste the sauce; it should be subtly sweet and sour and very flavorful. Add a few drops of vinegar or a pinch of salt, if necessary.

13. Cut or tear the meat along the grain into 3 or 4 chunks per serving and place on warmed serving plates. Ladle the sauce generously over the meat and serve.

-Chapter 4-
# VEAL

# Veal Scallopini with Prosciutto and Sage

Saltimbocca alla Romana

**Serves 4**

Originally a dish from the north of Italy, this now is a Roman favorite and one that our American customers will particularly appreciate because it comes together in a matter of minutes, bursting with flavor and interest. A little easy organization is needed to make sure these delicious *saltimbocca,* or "jump in your mouth," veal scallops cook perfectly. So, as always, read through the recipe once or twice before cooking. If the butcher pounds the veal for you, these will be on the table in less than half an hour. Our favorite accompaniment is baby spinach briefly sautéed in olive oil flavored with a crushed clove of garlic, a pinch of crushed red pepper flakes, and salt. Cook the greens before the veal and then reheat gently and sprinkle with fresh lemon juice just before serving.

**Butcher's Note:** Whether you or the butcher pounds the meat, the cutlets should be of uniform thickness so that they all cook at the same rate. We suggest aiming for a thickness midway between ⅛ and ¼ of an inch, admittedly an awkward instruction, but this seems to be the ideal for creating thin and delicate veal scallopini that do not dry out when cooked quickly. Don't be confused about labels: The veal may be called cutlets, scallops, or scallopini, all words for the same thin, boneless pieces of meat. For more on flattening meat, see page 136.

**Wine Note:** It turns out that Rome's hometown white wine, Frascati, is the perfect foil for the thinly pounded veal made pleasingly salty and savory with prosciutto and sage. Produced in the hills outside the city, Frascati has never been a fancy wine; but in the hands of the best producers, Frascati's flavors and aromas are heightened without sacrificing the citrusy refreshment that makes this wine so good with a number of the local specialties, *saltimbocca alla Romana* among them. One favorite is the Villa Simone Frascati Superiore. When looking for an American wine to accompany the saltimbocca, understand that crisp, light-bodied white wines like Frascati are not the strong suit of most New World producers, California included. However, California's very fine sparkling wines would make a great partner for the savory, prosciutto-topped scallopini. One favorite is Roderer Estate Brut from the Anderson Valley.

*Sixteen 1½-ounce veal cutlets,*
*(about 1½ pounds total), pounded into*
*similar shape about halfway between ⅛ and*
*¼ of an inch thick (see Butcher's Note)*

*16 fresh sage leaves*

*16 paper-thin slices prosciutto di Parma*
*or similar cured ham*

*Kosher salt and freshly ground black pepper*

*6 tablespoons extra-virgin olive oil, or as needed*

*All-purpose flour for dredging*

*⅔ cup dry white wine*

*⅔ cup Chicken Stock (page 215)*
*or canned low-sodium chicken broth*

1. Preheat the oven to 200°F. Put an ovenproof plate or platter in the oven to warm.

2. Lay the pounded veal cutlets side by side on a work surface and rub each with a sage leaf without tearing the leaf. Reserve the sage leaves.

3. Cut a slice of prosciutto to fit just within the dimensions of the cutlet and press it into the meat to help it adhere. Center a reserved sage leaf on top of the prosciutto. Working lengthwise, weave a toothpick in and out of the veal to secure the prosciutto and sage, keeping the veal as flat as possible. Repeat with the remaining veal, prosciutto, and sage (if any leaves have torn, replace them with fresh leaves). Lightly sprinkle both sides of all the cutlets with salt and pepper.

4. Divide the 6 tablespoons of olive oil between 2 large skillets and set each over high heat. While the oil heats, dredge half of the cutlets with flour, shaking off the excess.

5. When it begins to smoke, swirl the oil to coat the bottoms of the skillets and cook 4 cutlets, prosciutto side down, in each of the skillets for 1 minute. Turn and cook for 45 seconds to 1 minute longer. Transfer to the warmed plate and return to the oven. The cutlets will continue to cook gently in the oven.

6. Repeat with the remaining 8 cutlets, adding more oil to the skillets, if necessary.

7. When all the cutlets are in the oven, let the skillets cool for 30 seconds and then divide the wine between them. Simmer the wine over medium heat until reduced to 2 to 3 tablespoons, 35 to 45 seconds. Divide the stock between the skillets and cook until the liquid is reduced to ⅓ cup, 35 to 45 seconds longer, scraping the bottoms of the pans to loosen any browned bits. Combine the liquids in 1 skillet and add any accumulated juices from the veal. If necessary, continue to simmer a few seconds to concentrate the flavor. You only need enough sauce to lightly moisten the veal. Taste and season with salt, if needed.

8. Divide the veal scallops among 4 warmed serving plates, attractively overlapping them in a shingle pattern. Drizzle the sauce over each and serve immediately.

# Lobel's Veal-BLT Burgers

**Serves 4**

With a nod to both American tradition and beloved veal dishes from France, these unique burgers fuse storied French flavors and techniques with this country's classic trio of bacon, lettuce, and tomato.

🗝️

**Wine Note:** We pay homage to the American spirit of the burgers in a soft, simple, and lightly fruity Pinot Noir; try the Rex-Goliath Pinot Noir from California. We also explored the French influence, evidenced with the tarragon compound butter and tomatoes, by serving a light and vibrant Beaujolais. In our tests, all the wines we tried suited the burgers beautifully, but our favorite was the Georges Duboeuf "Jean Descombes" Morgon. Serve them cool in summer.

---

*4 high-quality hamburger buns or Kaiser rolls,*
*split and toasted*

*1 small head Bibb or Boston lettuce,*
*separated into leaves*

*16 Roasted Tomato halves (recipe follows)*

*8 slices bacon, cooked to taste*

*1½ to 1¾ pounds ground veal*

*4 tablespoons White Wine–Tarragon Butter,*
*frozen (recipe follows)*

*Kosher salt*

*4 tablespoons Homemade Mayonnaise,*
*or more to taste (recipe follows)*

---

1. Prepare a fire in a charcoal or wood grill or preheat a gas grill to medium-high. Lightly oil and preheat the grate.

2. Put the buns open-faced on 4 serving plates. On 1 half of each bun, lay 1 or 2 lettuce leaves, 4 tomato halves, and 2 strips of bacon. Set aside.

3. Gently shape the veal into 4 equal patties. Cut the frozen butter into 4 tablespoon-sized disks. Using your fingers, make a hole in the side of each patty and insert a disk of the butter so that it sits in the center of the patty and its flat side is parallel to the flat side of the patty. Gently pinch the hole closed, completely enclosing the butter within the patty so that it won't leak during cooking.

4. Generously salt the patties and grill for 3 to 4 minutes on each side for medium-rare. (Alternatively, cook the patties in a skillet with a little olive oil over medium-high heat.) Transfer the burgers to the bottom buns and top each with a tablespoon of the mayonnaise. Serve immediately, passing additional mayonnaise at the table, if desired.

## Roasted Tomatoes

**Makes about 20 tomato halves**

---

*One 28-ounce can peeled whole tomatoes,*
*drained, tomatoes cut in half lengthwise*

*Olive oil*

*Kosher salt*

---

1. Preheat the oven to 325°F. Line a baking sheet with aluminum foil and grease the foil with olive oil.

2. Put the tomatoes cut side up on the prepared baking sheet. Drizzle olive oil over each tomato half and sprinkle lightly with salt.

3. Roast the tomatoes for 45 minutes to 1 hour (smaller tomatoes may take less time), or until they have shrunk but are still moist. Cool, cover, and refrigerate until needed, up to 3 days ahead of time.

## White Wine–Tarragon Butter

**Makes about ½ cup**

*1 cup dry white wine*

*2 tablespoons minced shallots*

*Freshly ground black pepper*

*2 tablespoons finely chopped fresh tarragon*

*Kosher salt*

*½ cup (1 stick) unsalted butter, slightly softened
and cut into pieces*

1. In a small saucepan, combine the wine, shallots, and a few grindings of pepper and bring to a boil over medium-high heat. Reduce to medium and simmer until the wine is reduced to 1 or 2 tablespoons, 8 to 10 minutes.

2. Remove the pan from the heat and add the tarragon and a generous pinch of salt. Let cool for 5 to 10 minutes, then, while the wine mixture is still warm, combine it with the butter in a small bowl and mash to mix it thoroughly.

3. Lay a double thickness of 16-inch-long pieces of plastic wrap on a work surface. Using a rubber spatula, scrape the butter from the pan onto the plastic in a mass. Roll it tightly in the plastic, twisting the ends and pressing on the butter to form a sausage shape about 1½ inches thick. (If the butter is too soft to roll easily, chill it slightly first.) Freeze or refrigerate as needed for a recipe, up to 3 days.

## Homemade Mayonnaise

**Makes about 1½ cups**

*2 large egg yolks, at room temperature*

*Kosher salt*

*½ cup extra-virgin olive oil*

*½ cup vegetable oil*

*¾ teaspoon fresh lemon juice*

1. In a very clean, dry mixing bowl, whisk together the egg yolks and salt.

2. Whisking continuously, begin adding the olive oil, a drop at a time, until the mixture thickens considerably (it may be easier to add the initial drops of oil from the oil bottle's screw cap or a measuring spoon). Once the emulsion forms, add the remaining olive oil in small amounts, still whisking continuously to incorporate fully.

3. Continue adding the vegetable oil in the same fashion. You should now have a thick, creamy mayonnaise.

4. Whisk in the lemon juice. Add more salt and lemon juice to taste. Use right away, or cover and refrigerate for up to 5 days.

# Classic Breaded Veal Chops with Parmigiano-Reggiano and Balsamico

Cotoletta all'Emilana

**Serves 2**

A luxurious northern Italian version of Wiener schnitzel, these golden-crusted veal chops, developed in Emilia-Romagna in Italy, are one of the most satisfying ways to enjoy veal. Our recipe incorporates two of the three most famous products from Italy's Emilia-Romagna region: hard, salty Parmigiano-Reggiano cheese and traditional balsamic vinegar. (The third, of course, is prosciutto di Parma.)

Some variations of this dish finish the chops with a warmed topping of Parmigiano and prosciutto di Parma, others leave the garnishes raw, and still others don't include balsamic vinegar at all. We think this is one of the best occasions for the syrupy, aged, sweet-yet-pungent vinegar. If you don't want to splurge on balsamic vinegar aged for twenty-five, fifty, or even a hundred years, substitute our Mock Balsamico.

**Butcher's Note:** Moist and tender veal rib chops, cut from the rack, when cooked quickly in a hot skillet, as they are here, are simply out of this world. Frenched veal chops, like lamb chops, have had the meat scraped from the tail end of the rib bone to leave at least 1½ inches of bone exposed, although chefs (and anyone who wants to make a statement) usually cut all the meat from the slender, curving tail bone, leaving only the eye (the succulent round piece of meat at the end of the chop). While we agree this is a gorgeous presentation, if you are making this for your family, you may opt to leave the meat on the bone so that everyone can enjoy it.

**Wine Note:** If you can find it, here's a great invitation to try another of Emilia-Romagna's glorious products: Lambrusco wine. You may remember the cheap, sweet, soda-capped Lambrusco sold in the 1970s, but of course that's not what we're suggesting here. Traditional Lambrusco, while neither fancy nor complicated, is nonetheless excellent and distinctive. The difference between '70s-esque versions and the good stuff is mostly a matter of a producer choosing among various subvarieties of the Lambrusco grape and whether to sweeten or not. Worthy Lambrusco contains better grapes and (usually) no perceptible sweetness, and it is closed with a cork or sometimes a Champagne-style cork and cage. The cheap stuff is usually closed with a screw cap.

The best Lambrusco is red, dry, light to medium in body, slightly fizzy, pleasingly tart, and altogether invigorating. Served cool and on its own or as a companion to a platter of prosciutto di Parma and other *salumi*, it's also delicious alongside the creamy pastas and fried specialties of the region. You could serve a slightly fuller-bodied red or white wine with these crusted veal chops, but there may not be a better accompaniment than a good Lambrusco. Among favorites with the veal chop is the Ca'De'Medici "Piazza San Prospero" Lambrusco Rubino Scuro. As an alternative from these shores, look for a medium-bodied Oregon Pinot Noir to accompany the crispy, luscious veal chops. One favorite: Domaine Drouhin Pinot Noir from the Willamette Valley.

*2 tablespoons unsalted butter*

*1 small yellow onion, finely chopped*

*4 fresh sage leaves, finely chopped,*
*plus 2 small sprigs for garnish*

*¾ cup dry white wine*

*2 large eggs*

*1½ ounces Parmigiano-Reggiano cheese,*
*very finely grated, plus shavings for serving*

*Kosher salt*

*Two 10- to 14-ounce veal rib chops,*
*any bits of chine bone removed, the bones frenched*
*and the meat trimmed of excess fat (see Butcher's*
*Note), pounded evenly to ½-inch thickness*
*(see Butcher's Note, page 136)*

*Freshly ground pepper*

*1 cup dried bread crumbs, preferably homemade*
*(see Note, page 42)*

*6 tablespoons unsalted butter, clarified (see Note)*

*Traditional, very old, artisan-made*
*balsamic vinegar or Mock Balsamico*
*(recipe follows) for drizzling*

1.  In a small skillet, melt the butter over medium heat. Add the onion and sage leaves, reduce the heat to medium-low, and cook, stirring occasionally, until the onion is soft and pale gold at the edges, about 10 minutes. Add the wine and cook slowly until reduced by half, 4 to 5 minutes (the mixture should be slushy). Cool for 5 minutes in the freezer.

2.  In a baking dish just large enough to hold the veal chops in a single layer, beat together the eggs and one-third of the grated cheese.

3.  Generously salt the veal chops on both sides. Press the salt into the meat. Repeat with a few generous grindings of pepper.

4.  Mix the cooled onion mixture into the egg mixture. Dip the chops in the egg-onion mixture and turn several times to coat. Arrange the chops in the dish and spoon the mixture over them. Let stand at room temperature for 1 hour.

5.  In a wide, shallow bowl or plate, mix the bread crumbs and the remaining grated cheese.

6.  Put a wire rack on a baking sheet and, one at a time, lift the chops from the marinade, scraping off the excess. Push the onions to the side of the dish and dip the chops in the egg sauce again, avoiding the onions as much as possible. Thickly coat each side of the chops with the bread-crumb mixture, firmly pushing the crumbs into the meat. Lay the chops on the wire rack and refrigerate for 15 minutes.

7.  In a large skillet, heat the clarified butter over medium-high heat. When the butter is hot, swirl it to evenly coat the bottom of the skillet. Reduce the heat to medium-low and cook the chops until deep golden brown on both sides, about 3 minutes per side for medium-rare. If you're unsure as to the degree of doneness, you can make a small cut and peek inside a chop. Though there will be a trace of raw meat next to the bone, 6 minutes of total cooking should give you perfectly cooked veal throughout the rest of the chop.

8. Transfer the chops to warmed serving plates, garnish with the sage sprigs. Drizzle a very small amount of balsamic vinegar next to the chops and serve. Pass the shaved Parmigiano-Reggiano cheese and additional balsamic at the table.

**Note:** Clarifying butter removes the milk solids that cause butter to brown and burn when cooked. To clarify butter, melt in a small saucepan over medium-low heat and then let it stand without stirring for about 20 minutes; the water will evaporate and the milk solids will collect at the bottom. Remove from the heat and skim any foam off the top of the butter. Carefully pour the clear butter through a fine-mesh sieve into a glass measuring cup, leaving the solids in the pan. Discard the solids. For our Breaded Veal Chops, you'll need to begin with about ½ cup (1 stick) of butter to yield the 6 tablespoons needed for the dish.

## Mock Balsamico

**Makes 2 tablespoons**

*½ cup balsamic vinegar*

*1 tablespoon brown sugar*

1. In a small skillet or saucepan, bring the vinegar and brown sugar to a boil over medium-high heat. Reduce the heat to medium and simmer until reduced to a generous 2 tablespoons.

2. Transfer to a small glass bowl and let cool. When cooled, the Mock Balsamico will be the consistency of very thin syrup. Thin with a few drops of balsamic vinegar, if necessary.

# Pan-Fried Veal Medallions with Chestnuts and Pearl Onions

Médaillons de Veau à la Aixoise

**Serves 2**

While this recipe is based on an authentic recipe from Savoy, France, we have omitted two items usually found in the local dish: chunks of braised carrot and celery root. These vegetables would make a perfect accompaniment, steamed and tossed with butter or braised in butter, stock, and fresh thyme.

While the remaining ingredients are also traditional, the techniques used and the final results are more like something you might find in a fancy regional restaurant. The richness depends a great deal on the veal stock; canned beef broth is an acceptable substitute but not nearly as good.

**Wine Note:** It's not always easy to locate wines from the Savoy, but a handful do make it to the United States. The smooth and roundly crisp Rousette de Savoie is very good with the veal and chestnuts and offers more weight and body than most other Alpine whites from this region. Look for the Pierre Boniface Rousette de Savoie. The most dramatic wine choice—and perhaps the best—comes not from the Savoy at all but from the flatlands a hundred miles to the northeast. There is great mutual flattery, it turns out, between this dish and aged white Burgundy, one of the wine world's true treats. And if you're feeling flush, this dish does right by the big names—Meursault, Puligny-Montrachet, Chassagne-Montrachet—and their best wines, ideally with at least six or eight years of age. The mild veal, woodsy chestnuts, and browned pearl onions offer a rich and engaging background for the complexity of these wines. "Merely" a village wine, Marc Colin's Puligny-Montrachet "Le Trezin," at nine years old, was especially good, but lots of white Burgundies would be equally fine; let a good merchant be your guide. Any number of California's finest Chardonnays would suit the veal medallions, too. One favorite: Talbott Chardonnay "Diamond T Estate" from Monterey County.

---

### Chestnuts and pearl onions

*2 tablespoons unsalted butter*

*24 fresh pearl onions, peeled (see Note),*
*or thawed frozen pearl onions*

*12 whole fresh chestnuts, peeled (facing page)*

*2 tablespoons green Chartreuse liqueur*

*1 teaspoon finely chopped fresh thyme*

*Kosher salt*

### Sauce

*2 tablespoons unsalted butter*

*3 tablespoons finely chopped shallots*

*2 tablespoons green Chartreuse liqueur*

*½ cup dry white wine*

*2 cups Veal Stock (page 213)*

*2 large sprigs fresh thyme*

*1 small bay leaf*

*¼ teaspoon kosher salt*

*Kosher salt*

*Two 6-ounce veal medallions cut from the loin,*
*each about 1½ inches thick*

*Freshly ground pepper*

*2 tablespoons vegetable oil*

*1 tablespoon unsalted butter*

*3 tablespoons heavy cream*

*½ teaspoon finely chopped fresh thyme*

---

1. For the chestnuts and pearl onions, in a skillet, melt the butter over medium heat and cook the onions and chestnuts, stirring constantly, until the onions are flecked with golden brown, about 10 minutes. Stir gently to avoid breaking up the nuts.

2. Add the Chartreuse and continue to cook for another 2 minutes, stirring constantly to help glaze the vegetables with the liqueur. Stir in the thyme and a generous sprinkling of salt. Remove from the heat and set aside.

3. To make the sauce, in a saucepan, melt the butter over medium-low heat and cook the shallots, stirring occasionally, until softened but without color, about 5 minutes. Add the Chartreuse and carefully ignite with a kitchen match. When the flames die down, raise the heat to medium and add the wine. Simmer for 3 minutes, then add the stock, thyme, bay leaf, and salt. Return to a simmer and cook until reduced to ⅔ cup, about 10 minutes. If not concentrated and flavorful, reduce a little further and add more salt if needed. Remove from the heat and set aside.

4. Generously salt the veal on both sides and season with a few grindings of pepper. In a skillet, heat the vegetable oil in over medium-high heat. When very hot, swirl the oil to coat the bottom of the skillet. Add the veal, reduce the heat to medium, and cook until nicely browned on the first side, about 3 to 4 minutes. Turn the veal and add the butter. Continue to cook, basting regularly with the butter and oil, until cooked to the desired doneness, about 4 minutes more for medium-rare. Transfer the veal to a plate, tent loosely with aluminum foil, and keep warm in a very low (200°F) oven.

5. Meanwhile, reheat the chestnut-onion mixture, moistened with a little stock, water, or butter if it appears dry. Reheat the sauce, discarding the thyme sprig and bay leaf. Add the cream and accumulated juices from the plate holding the veal to the sauce and bring to a simmer. Simmer gently for 1 to 2 minutes to thicken slightly. Add salt to taste.

6. Divide the chestnuts and pearl onions between 2 warmed serving plates, placing them in a cluster just off center. Lean the veal medallions attractively against the vegetables and surround with the sauce. Garnish with the finely chopped thyme and serve.

**Note:** To more easily peel fresh pearl onions, trim the root end of each bulb and blanch the onions in boiling water for 1 to 2 minutes. Cool under running water. Using your fingers, slip the onions from their outer skins or peel with the help of a paring knife.

## FRESH CHESTNUTS

Precooked and peeled packaged whole chestnuts, labeled fresh or fresh frozen, are convenient, readily available, and work well in most dishes. Out of season, you really don't have much choice, but if you can find fresh whole chestnuts in the shell, mostly available in the fall and winter, the extra effort of peeling them is worth it.

To peel fresh, raw chestnuts, you have to blanch them first. Working with one nut at a time, firmly hold the chestnut in a kitchen towel and, using a sharp paring knife, make an X incision on the flat face, cutting through only the shell and the skin beneath. Simmer the nuts in a saucepan of lightly salted boiling water for 5 minutes. Remove from the heat and use a slotted spoon to lift the chestnuts from the water one at a time. Carefully peel them, using the knife to help pry off the shells. (This is the best method for Pan-Fried Veal Medallions with Chestnuts and Pearl Onions.)

Alternatively, you can roast or deep-fry chestnuts for a richer taste. This is especially good for eating them out of hand. To roast, cut an X into the chestnuts as described above, spread on a baking sheet, and bake in a preheated 400°F oven until the shells curl at the X, about 15 or 20 minutes. Peel when cool enough to handle. To deep-fry, heat 1 quart of peanut oil in a deep saucepan and heat the oil to about 325°F on a deep-frying thermometer. Fry in batches of 5 chestnuts at a time for about 3 minutes. Transfer to paper towels to drain. Peel when cool enough to handle.

# Catalan-Style Veal Stew with Prunes and Potatoes

Carn Estofada amb Prunes i Patates

**Serves 4**

Using unsweetened chocolate as an ingredient in savory European dishes dates back to the sixteenth century, when Spanish explorers first carried it back to Europe from Mexico. Today, the Catalan people of northeastern Spain continue to use chocolate in a number of preparations where its ability to thicken, flavor, and generally fill in the gaps is valued in stew making. Not immediately recognizable in the finished dish, the chocolate helps it become, like any good stew, truly greater than the sum of its parts, mingling here with the sweetness of prunes and succulent chunks of veal.

**Butcher's Note:** Meat from the breast and shoulder makes for the most flavorful veal stews. Breast meat, because of its higher fat and collagen content, cooks to a more tender, rich, and meltingly soft result, which for many is the hallmark of a great stew. On the other hand, cubed breast meat tends to fall apart, so that the finished dish has fewer prominent chunks of meat than stews made with other cuts. Additionally, veal breast has alternating layers of fat and lean, much like pork belly, and you may find yourself having to separate the soft, flavorful meat from the remaining pieces of fat as you eat. None of this poses a problem for us, though, because the taste and texture of a stew made with veal breast is rich, silky, and simply without peer.

For a chunkier stew and less fat to contend with, choose shoulder meat. It is nearly as good as breast meat, and the cubes retain their shape and gently collapse in your mouth. As it cooks, the veal shoulder has less fat, so there's less skimming in the end. Each cut is delicious and distinct in its own way. If you purchase boneless veal breast or shoulder, you will need 2½ pounds of meat and 1½ pounds of bones; ask your butcher to save the bones for you.

**Wine Note:** Because veal itself is fairly neutral, when thinking about wines to drink alongside this dish, we looked to the ingredients that surround it. Here, the ripe sweetness of prunes together with tomatoes, cinnamon and a bit of chocolate steered our choices. As we've stated elsewhere, when there's sweetness in a dish—even a just a little—it usually tastes better with a white wine that has a touch of sweetness itself or a red that has a rich core of fruit flavors (see pages 23 to 24). In either case, what you don't want are wines that are bone-dry, austere, or, for reds, tannic. Two whites and one red stood out in our veal stew tasting: Torres "Viña Esmeralda," a lightly sweet, tangy, and aromatic Muscat-Gewürztraminer blend from the most important winery in the region; R. López de Heredia "Viña Tondonia" Reserva, a well-aged white Rioja that—surprise—was dry, yet still deliciously mellow with the stew; and Castell del Remei "Gotim Bru," a warm and deeply fruit-filled blend of mostly Tempranillo with Merlot and Cabernet Sauvignon, from the Catalan *denominación* of Costers del Segre, west of Barcelona. From outside Spain, choose a moderately rich but easygoing red wine like the Steltzner Claret, a Cabernet-Merlot blend from California's Napa Valley or, for a white, an off-dry wine like the Robert Mondavi Chenin Blanc.

*6 tablespoons extra-virgin olive oil*

*4 to 4½ pounds bone-in veal breast or shoulder, meat cut into 1-inch cubes, bones reserved (see Butcher's Note)*

*1 yellow onion, finely chopped*

*4 large cloves garlic, finely chopped*

*3 tablespoons Spanish brandy, Armagnac, or other similar brandy*

*1½ cups dry white wine*

*One 16-ounce can peeled whole tomatoes, drained and finely chopped*

*Two 2-by-1-inch strips orange zest (see Note, page 62 )*

*3 sprigs fresh thyme*

*1 large bay leaf*

*Kosher salt*

*1½ pounds thin-skinned, waxy potatoes, such as Yukon Gold, peeled and cut into ½-inch dice*

*¾ ounce bittersweet or semisweet chocolate, finely grated*

*⅛ teaspoon ground cinnamon*

*⅛ teaspoon cayenne pepper*

*¾ pound prunes, soaked in hot water for 30 minutes and drained (see Note)*

*2 tablespoons finely chopped fresh flat-leaf parsley*

1. Preheat the oven to 350°F.

2. In a flameproof casserole or Dutch oven with a tight-fitting lid, warm 3 tablespoons of the olive oil over medium-high heat. Working in two batches, cook the veal and veal bones until golden brown on at least two sides, about 5 minutes per side, reducing the heat if they threaten to burn. Transfer to a large plate and set aside.

3. Let the casserole cool slightly and return it to medium heat. Add the onion and garlic and cook, stirring occasionally, until pale gold at the edges, about 10 minutes. Add the brandy and wine and simmer until the liquid has reduced by half, about 10 minutes longer, scraping the bottom of the pot to loosen any browned bits.

4. Stir in the tomatoes, orange zest, thyme, bay leaf, and 1 tablespoon salt, then add the meat, bones, and any juices accumulated on the plate. Add just enough water to cover the meat (cover the meat only; it's okay if the large bones stick up). Bring to a bare simmer, cover, and transfer to the oven.

5. After 20 minutes, reduce the heat to 250°F and continue to cook until the meat is somewhat tender but not yet falling apart, about 2 hours more. Adjust the oven temperature as needed to maintain a bare simmer.

6. Remove the pot from the oven and let rest, uncovered, for at least 15 minutes. Skim off most of the fat collected on the surface. Pick off any meat remaining on the bones and add it to the pot. Discard the bones, thyme sprigs, and bay leaf.

7. Meanwhile, in a large skillet, heat the remaining 3 tablespoons of olive oil over medium-high heat until just smoking. Add the potatoes and, using a spatula, toss them until coated with the oil. Reduce the heat to medium and fry the potatoes, tossing them constantly, until they're golden and crispy on at least two sides and tender within, about 20 minutes, reducing the heat if they threaten to burn. As they finish cooking, sprinkle them with salt to taste. Set the potatoes aside in their skillet.

8. Return the casserole to the stove top over medium heat and return the stew to a simmer. Stir in the chocolate,

cinnamon, cayenne, and drained prunes. Simmer, uncovered, stirring occasionally, until the liquid has thickened slightly so that it is midway between a broth and a sauce, about 30 minutes. If necessary, add salt to taste. If the pieces of veal seem a bit dry and firm, break them up somewhat with the back of a wooden spoon to help them absorb the sauce.

9. To serve, reheat the potatoes to recrisp them, if necessary, and ladle the stew into large, shallow serving bowls. Top each serving with a handful of potatoes and a sprinkling of the parsley. Serve immediately, passing any remaining potatoes at the table.

**Note:** Pitted prunes also work well here, so if you like, you can remove the pits. We think the stew looks best with plump, whole fruits with pits. If serving prunes with pits, just be sure to let your guests know.

**Make-Ahead Tip:** If you skip the cooking of the potatoes in step 7, you can prepare the stew up to 2 days ahead. Cover and refrigerate. Reheat the stew gently, covered, thinning with a bit of water or stock if it seems too thick. Then, while it's reheating, prepare the potatoes as directed in step 7. When the stew is hot and the potatoes are cooked through and crisp, simply serve as directed in step 9.

# Rioja-Style Braised Veal with Thyme

Morcillo de Ternera Estofado con Tomillo

**Serves 4**

This appealingly simple yet deeply flavored dish uses an unusual technique in which the meat from the veal shank is cut from the bone before it's cooked. It is then browned and braised in a wine-flavored vegetable purée that's enriched with the bone marrow and flavored with thyme. Though a shadow of itself after four hours of cooking, a traditionally styled Rioja wine marks the finished dish with its special aroma and flavor, and so it should be considered a unique (though optional) ingredient. This isn't a soupy braised dish but one with a very thick, satiny gravy that clings to the tender veal. Serve it with steamed baby potatoes and a salad.

**Butcher's Note:** When you ask for veal shanks, ask for the hind shank. It's firmer and less bony than the foreshank and does not fall apart as easily when cooked. Veal shanks are worth trying to find, although you may have to special order them from your butcher.

**Wine Note:** Red Rioja comes in a range of styles, many in lockstep with the demands of the international marketplace. So a wine drinker may be forgiven for not knowing of one of the most distinctive and food-friendly wines in this or any other region: the traditionally made red wine of Rioja, today produced by just a handful of bodegas that continue to make wines like no other. Few wines in the world, except some red Burgundies, combine this relative lightness of body with a great complex of aromas and flavors. And more rarely still does this kind of delicate wine get a chance to refine further by aging, sometimes twenty or thirty years or more. A great example of this style also happened to be our favorite among eight wines tasted alongside this straightforward and satisfying braised veal: Bodegas Riojanas "Monte Real" Reserva. For a New World companion to the dish, try a full-flavored but refined Pinot Noir like the Marimar Torres Estate "Don Miguel Vineyard" Pinot Noir from the Russian River Valley in Sonoma, California.

*4 pounds veal shanks, cut by the butcher as for*
*osso buco (see Butcher's Note, page 89)*

*¼ cup Spanish-Style Lard Paste (page 217)*
*or extra-virgin olive oil*

*Kosher salt*

*All-purpose flour for dredging*

*3 yellow onions, chopped*

*2 carrots, peeled and chopped*

*8 large cloves garlic, thinly sliced*

*1½ cups red Rioja wine or other dry red wine*

*1½ cups dry white wine*

*2 cups Beef Stock (page 212)*
*or canned low-sodium beef broth*

*1 cup water*

*¾ cup drained and chopped canned tomatoes*

*1½ teaspoons finely chopped fresh thyme,*
*plus 1½ teaspoons whole leaves for garnish*

1. Cut the meat from each shank into 4 large, roughly equal-sized chunks, about 2 inches each, and reserve the bones.

2. In a heavy stockpot, warm the lard paste over medium-high heat. Generously salt the veal pieces and veal bones. Coat with the flour and knock off any excess. Working in two batches, cook the meat and the bones, turning the pieces until deeply browned on at least two sides, 10 to 12 minutes per batch. Reduce the heat if the meat threatens to burn. Transfer the meat and bones to a plate and set aside.

3. Add the onions, carrots, and garlic to the pot and cook, stirring occasionally, until somewhat reduced in volume, 5 or 6 minutes. Reduce the heat to medium and cook, stirring occasionally, until the vegetables just begin to brown, about 15 minutes longer. Adjust the heat as necessary to prevent burning and use a spatula to scrape up any floury bits that form on the bottom of the pot.

4. Add both wines and simmer until reduced by half, scraping the bottom of the pot to loosen any browned bits, 12 to 15 minutes. At this point, the mixture should resemble onion slush.

5. Stir in the stock, water, tomatoes, and 1 teaspoon salt. Add the bones. Return the mixture to a simmer and cook for about 5 minutes. Lift the bones from the pot and, using a small knife, scrape the marrow from them onto a plate.

6. Working in two batches, transfer the liquid to a blender and add half of the marrow and half of the chopped thyme to each batch. Purée until smooth, holding the blender top with a kitchen towel to prevent splattering or burns. Return the purée to the pot.

7. Return the bones, meat, and any accumulated juices to the pot. Cover partially, leaving a ½-inch-wide crack, and cook at a bare simmer over medium-low heat, stirring occasionally, until the meat is tender, 3 to 4 hours. The resulting sauce should be very thick and abundant, and it should easily cling to the meat while remaining fluid. If after a few hours of cooking the liquid seems to be getting too thick, put the lid tightly on the pot or add small amounts of stock or water, or do both. If the sauce seems thin once the meat is tender, then simmer gently, uncovered, until thickened as described.

8. Discard the bones and divide the meat and sauce among warmed serving plates. Serve immediately, garnished with the thyme leaves.

# Traditional Milanese-Style Braised Veal Shanks

Osso Buco alla Milanese

**Serves 4**

In its older, more traditional form, dating probably from the early nineteenth century, *osso buco alla Milanese* seems to have been simply sections of veal shank braised with onion and white wine. At some point it became common to energize the dish with the last-minute addition of a *gremolata,* a lovely mixture of garlic, parsley, lemon zest, and sometimes anchovies.

Most contemporary recipes for osso buco tend to include lots of other things, such as carrots and celery and a variety of herbs. Sometimes a sizable dose of white wine is part of the plan, along with tomatoes or tomato sauce—never mind that the dish most likely predates the arrival of tomatoes in Italy. We decided to develop a recipe that reflected the earlier, simpler dish, though we're not total purists, as we do add veal stock and a touch of tomato paste. Once you've made this stripped-down osso buco—especially when served alongside its classic partner, a saffron-scented *risotto alla Milanese*—you may never go back to the ingredient-heavy version again.

**Butcher's Note:** These veal shanks are prepared as for osso buco. This means the shanks are cut into pieces 1½ to 2½ inches thick and then tied with butcher's twine to hold the meat in place during cooking. Ask your butcher to tie them, or to do it yourself, tie the twine around the circumference of the piece, securing it with a tight knot. The twine should encircle the shank piece so that a little of the round bone is visible.

**Wine Note:** There are some very good Italian red, white, and sparkling wines produced in Lombardy, but none that we tried alongside our osso buco excited us. So we looked to the neighboring Veneto and Piedmont regions, where we found our favorite, a high-quality, fairly traditionally styled Valpolicella from the Veneto. Our winner displayed a skill that many wines lack: The ability to accommodate nearly everything on the plate at once, including the mellow veal shank, its oniony sauce, and in our tasting, a pile of saffron-flavored risotto alla Milanese. Some wines just suited the veal, which is surprisingly delicate. Others were great with the rice but not the veal or the sauce. Only the Valpolicella sang with all three. Valpolicella means different things to different people, so if all it brings to mind for you is the watery, sharp, pale red drink served in red sauce joints, you only know part of the story. In and around the town of Valpolicella, they continue to crank this '60s- and '70s-style wine out (and it's still great with red sauce and pizza), but more recently the wines have been made respectable by a number of producers whose commitment to quality has fleshed out and improved them without giving away their tangy, lighter-bodied, cherry red, food-friendly souls. But because Valpolicella is a wine zone in transition (due to its checkered reputation) and is also, by its nature, confusing, as there are currently a number of very different styles of wine that sport the name Valpolicella on their labels. What you want is a Valpolicella Classico or Classico Superiore from a producer who makes so-called traditional-style Valpolicella at the highest level. It should be light- to medium-bodied, briskly cherry-flavored, and made with little or no fancy new oak aging. Nor do you want to see the words "Rispasso" or "Appassimento" on the label—this is a delicious sort of supercharged Valpolicella that fared less well in our osso buco tasting. Your wine merchant can help you make sense of all this. A favorite at our tasting was Agricola ca' la Bionda Valpolicella Classico. When looking beyond Valpolicella for an osso buco mate, the best partners will be medium-bodied, attractively tangy, and smooth. One Italianate favorite: Columbia Winery's "Alder Ridge" Barbera from Washington State's Yakima Valley.

---

*Kosher salt*

*Four 8- to 10-ounce veal shanks,*
*cut by the butcher as for osso buco about 1½ inches*
*thick, tied (see Butcher's Note)*

*All-purpose flour for dredging*

*6 tablespoons olive oil*

*3 tablespoons unsalted butter*

*1 yellow onion, finely chopped*

*1 teaspoon tomato paste*

*½ cup dry white wine*

*2 cups Veal Stock (page 213)*
*or canned low-sodium beef broth, or 1 cup canned*
*low-sodium beef broth and 1 cup water*

*1 loosely packed tablespoon finely chopped*
*fresh flat-leaf parsley*

*¾ teaspoon finely minced garlic*

*2 teaspoons finely grated lemon zest*

---

1. Preheat the oven to 350°F.

2. Generously salt the veal shanks on all sides. Coat them with flour and knock off any excess.

3. Heat a large flameproof casserole or Dutch oven over medium-high heat and add the olive oil. When hot, cook the shanks until deeply browned, 8 to 10 minutes on the first side and 6 to 8 minutes on the second, reducing the heat if they threaten to burn. Stand the shanks on their edges and, holding them with tongs, brown these surfaces, working your way around the circumference

of each shank (lean them against the sides of the pot, if necessary). This will take another 5 to 7 minutes. Transfer to a plate and set aside. Discard the fat in the pot and wipe out any blackened bits.

4. Return the pot to medium heat, melt the butter, and reduce the heat to medium-low. Add the onion and cook, stirring occasionally, until pale gold and soft, 15 to 17 minutes. Stir in the tomato paste and cook for 1 minute. Stir in the wine and simmer until almost evaporated. Stir in the stock and ½ teaspoon salt, scraping the bottom of the pot to loosen any browned bits. Add the veal shanks and any accumulated juices and bring just to a simmer.

5. Cover tightly, transfer to the oven, and cook for 20 minutes. Reduce the oven temperature to 250°F and continue cooking until the meat is very tender, 2 to 3 hours longer. Adjust the oven temperature as needed to maintain a bare simmer. Carefully turn the shanks over once or twice during braising.

6. The sauce, while somewhat thickened and very flavorful, should still be brothy. If necessary, gently simmer for a few minutes more to concentrate the flavor, but don't concentrate it too much. The sauce should provide good moisture to the meat. Season the sauce to taste with salt, if necessary.

7. Transfer the shanks to warmed serving plates and remove the strings.

8. Stir the parsley, garlic, and lemon zest into the sauce. Spoon generous amounts over the shanks and serve immediately.

# Catalan-Style Braised Veal Ribs with Green Olives

*Platillo de Vedella amb Olives*

**Serves 4**

This is our adaptation of a fabulous traditional dish we first encountered in Colman Andrews' essential *Catalan Cuisine.* Among other modifications, our version calls for veal ribs (see Butcher's Note), whose bones add flavor and texture to the intensely delicious, garlic-scented green olive and tomato sauce that coats the finished ribs.

**Butcher's Note:** There are two kinds of veal ribs that work for this dish. One choice is veal spare ribs, which are cut from those ribs that extend from the luxurious rib roast. These lean and elegant ribs have the classic rack of ribs shape familiar to lovers of beef or pork spare ribs, and they are best eaten with your fingers. To ready veal spare ribs for this dish, first have your butcher cut a rack of nine or ten ribs in half crosswise through the bones, so that you have two half-racks with 3- to 5-inch rib lengths. Next, slice between the bones of each half-rack to make the 3- to 5-inch riblets for use in the recipe. The only problem with veal spare ribs is actually finding them, due largely to the way that most veal is cut and sold. They're especially good, so it's worth asking your butcher, or contact us at Lobels.com.

There's a second choice, which, although different in texture, is just as delicious: ribs cut from the breast of veal. These are meatier than spare ribs and are best eaten with a knife and fork. To ready breast of veal for this dish, ask your butcher for a 4- to 4½-pound section of meaty, bone-in veal breast. Next, have them cut it crosswise, through the bones, into three or four pieces so that each piece now has rib lengths of approximately 3 inches. Next, slice between the bones of each piece to make the 3-inch "riblets" for use in the recipe.

Even if you can't find veal ribs, by all means try the dish with boneless veal breast cut into thick strips roughly the size of the ribs called for in the recipe: about ¾ inch thick and 3 inches long.

**Wine Note:** As with so many dishes, it's the sauce that points the way to the wine. Veal is fairly neutral, but the combination of tomato, abundant garlic, and green olive is anything but. In keeping with our regional theme, two northeastern Spanish wines stood out in our tasting. The favorite was the Scala Dei "Negre" from the Priorat region in Catalonia, a wine that (despite a family resemblance) is a bit different from the densely powerful and dramatic wines that put this region on the world's wine map. As impressive and delicious as Priorat's top wines are, most have a feature that makes them less than friendly around complex foods: high alcohol levels. This "baby" Priorat, however, is relatively mild mannered compared to its siblings and has impeccable table manners—our bottle of Scala Dei's "Negre" had a mouthwatering acidity and a taste and texture not unlike a peppery Côtes du Rhône from France, just right alongside the salty tang of the green olives in the dish. Our next favorite wine belongs to a class of wines that almost always shine alongside green olives: rosés. Our fruit-filled Artazuri rosé from Navarra in north-central Spain has, like many rosés, a refreshing but slightly bitter quality (kind of like watermelon rind) that seemed designed to match the slightly bitter green olive flavor. For a pair of California choices in the same spirit, you could choose a wine from this duo of great values from Cline Cellars in Sonoma: A red Cline California Syrah or pink Cline Oakley rosé.

### Marinade

⅓ cup extra-virgin olive oil

20 large sprigs fresh thyme

15 large garlic cloves, halved lengthwise
and thinly sliced

4 to 4 ½ pounds veal spareribs (9 to 10 ribs)
or bone-in veal breast, cut into riblets
(see Butcher's Note)

### Tomato base

¼ cup extra-virgin olive oil

2 yellow onions, finely chopped

1 large stalk celery, finely chopped

1 carrot, peeled and finely chopped

½ red bell pepper, seeded and finely chopped

One 15-ounce can peeled whole tomatoes,
drained and chopped

¼ teaspoon kosher salt

Kosher salt

All-purpose flour for dredging

¼ cup extra-virgin olive oil, plus more if needed

1 ½ cups dry white wine

2 cups Beef Stock (page 212)
or canned low-sodium beef broth

1 cup water

2 bay leaves

1 teaspoon sweet paprika

¼ teaspoon cayenne pepper

Freshly ground black pepper

2 to 4 tablespoons Catalan Picada (recipe follows)

1 ¼ cups pitted, coarsely chopped green olives,
rinsed or soaked if salty

1. To make the marinade, in a large mixing bowl, stir together the olive oil, thyme, and garlic. Thoroughly rub the ribs with the marinade and then put the ribs in the bowl. Cover and refrigerate for at least 6 hours or up to overnight.

2. Remove the ribs from the refrigerator and let come to room temperature. Meanwhile, make the tomato base: In a large skillet, heat the olive oil over medium-high heat. Add the onions, reduce the heat to medium-low, and cook for 5 minutes, stirring occasionally. Add the celery, carrot, and bell pepper.

3. Discard the thyme sprigs (leaving any loose leaves behind) and collect the garlic slices from the veal. Add the garlic to the skillet and cook gently until the vegetables are golden at the edges, about 20 minutes, stirring occasionally. Stir in the tomatoes and salt and continue cooking until reduced to a paste, about 25 minutes more. Remove from the heat and set aside.

4. Meanwhile, brown the veal for the braise: Remove the ribs from the marinade and salt generously on all sides. Coat half of the ribs on both sides with flour and knock off any excess. Heat the olive oil in a large, flameproof casserole or Dutch oven with a tight-fitting lid over medium-high heat. Cook the floured ribs until a rich, golden brown on all the meaty sides, including the edges, 3 to 4 minutes per side. Transfer to a plate. Coat the remaining ribs with flour and cook in the same way. Add more oil if needed. Transfer to the plate with the first batch of ribs.

5. Preheat the oven to 350°F.

6. Pour off most of oil in the pot and scrape up and discard any blackened bits of flour. Add the wine and bring to a boil, scraping the bottom of the pot to loosen any browned bits. Reduce the heat to medium and simmer until reduced by one-third, about 5 minutes. Stir in the tomato base. Add the stock, water, bay leaves, paprika, cayenne, and a few generous grindings of black pepper.

7. Add the veal ribs to the pot, placing them on their edges if necessary to make room enough for all. Add any accumulated juices from the plate. Bring to a simmer, cover the pot, and transfer to the oven. After 20 minutes, reduce the heat to 250°F and cook at a bare simmer until the meat is very tender but not quite falling off the bone, about 3 hours. Adjust the oven temperature as needed to maintain a bare simmer. Remove from the oven and let the stew rest for at least 15 minutes.

8. Using a slotted spoon, transfer the ribs to a plate, cover with aluminum foil, and keep warm in a very low (200°F) oven.

9. Skim off most of the fat. Stir 2 tablespoons of the picada and the olives into the pot. Add more picada to taste. (The picada should add a warm, savory flavor to the stew, but it shouldn't dominate the other flavors in the dish.) Simmer for 10 minutes to let the picada slightly thicken the stew and to give the flavors time to develop. The sauce should cling to the veal but still be slightly fluid. Divide the ribs among serving bowls, top each with a generous ladleful of sauce, and serve.

## Catalan Picada

**Makes 4 to 5 tablespoons**

*3 tablespoons extra-virgin olive oil*

*1 piece good-quality country-style white bread
about ¾ inch thick and 3 inches square,
crust removed*

*6 blanched roasted almonds*

*6 blanched roasted hazelnuts*

*1 large garlic clove, thinly sliced*

*2 tablespoons finely chopped fresh flat-leaf parsley*

*1 tablespoon cold water*

1. In a small skillet, heat 2 tablespoons of the olive oil over medium heat. Add the bread and toast until golden brown, 2 to 3 minutes per side.

2. In the bowl of a food processor fitted with the metal blade, pulse the almonds, hazelnuts, garlic, and toasted bread, scraping the sides and bottom of the bowl between pulses, until very finely chopped, about 2 minutes.

3. Add the remaining 1 tablespoon olive oil, the parsley, and the water and process for another 20 seconds, or until the mixture resembles a coarse paste. Add a few more drops of olive oil, if needed.

4. Transfer the paste to a mortar and work the mixture with the pestle until the solid pieces of nuts and bread are no longer visible or nearly so. Cover and refrigerate for up to 24 hours. The picada is best made shortly before using.

# Braised Veal Breast Stuffed with Wild Mushrooms

*La Poitrine de Veau Farcie*

**Serves 4 to 6**

Here, we turn to one of our favorite cuts, boneless veal breast. In this recipe, we stuff it with wild mushrooms and ham, roll it and tie it with kitchen string, and braise it in a small amount of white wine until tender. Serve this dish with egg noodles or spaetzle and the mixture of peas and carrots that are typical in its native Alsace.

**Wine Note:** Here's a dish that shows off the refinement and food-friendliness of dry Alsatian Riesling, in two different styles: the first steely and youthful, the second dense and aged. Our favorite was a Charles Schleret Riesling, an expressive wine with beautiful detail and a crisp mineral quality. In spite of its youth (two years old), it had an earthy depth of flavor that encouraged sip after sip with the veal—itself earthy with wild mushrooms. Our other favorite was the *grand cru* Albert Mann "Schlossberg," a densely flavored and delicious wine with altogether more weight. This wine's impact had mellowed with six years of aging, which is what made it, in a way, different from the Schleret Riesling, an equally great partner to the veal breast. From beyond Alsace, look for a firm, richly flavored dry Riesling like Pikes Riesling Reserve from the Clare Valley in South Australia.

*6 tablespoons unsalted butter*

*1 cup finely chopped shallots*

*1 pound mixed wild mushrooms such as chanterelle, black trumpet, or porcini, coarsely sliced or chopped, or 2 to 3 ounces dried reconstituted wild mushrooms*

*½ cup plus 3 tablespoons chopped fresh herbs such as chives, tarragon, parsley, and chervil, in equal parts*

*¾ cup crème fraîche*

*Kosher salt*

*One 3-pound boneless veal breast, cut to measure about 12 by 8 inches*

*Freshly ground black pepper*

*¼ pound very thinly sliced baked or boiled ham*

*¼ cup vegetable oil*

*1 cup dry white wine such as Riesling*

*¼ cup water*

*1 large sprig fresh thyme*

*1 bay leaf*

1. In a large skillet, melt the butter over medium-low heat and cook the shallots for about 5 minutes until translucent, stirring occasionally. Raise the heat to medium-high, add the mushrooms, stir to coat, and cook, stirring often, until reduced in volume, about 5 minutes (if using dried mushrooms, reduce the heat to medium and cook for about 3 minutes). Reduce the heat to low and stir in the ½ cup herbs and ½ cup of the crème fraîche. Add salt to taste, stir, and remove from the heat to cool.

2. Put the veal on a work surface with the short side facing you. Sprinkle lightly with salt and pepper and lay the ham in overlapping slices over the veal to cover it. Top with half of the mushroom mixture, spreading it about 1 inch from the edges.

3. Carefully roll the veal away from you to enclose the mushrooms. Push any filling that falls out back into the roll. Turn one end toward you and tie the roast with kitchen string snugly (but not too tightly) in about ¾-inch increments widthwise and then once lengthwise. Sprinkle again with salt and pepper.

4. Heat a large, heavy flameproof casserole or Dutch oven with a tight-fitting lid over medium-high heat and, when hot, add the oil. Brown the veal roast on all sides for about 20 minutes, reducing the heat if it threatens to burn.

5. Add the wine and water and simmer gently for 3 minutes, scraping the bottom of the pot to loosen any browned bits. Add the thyme and bay leaf and cover the pot. Reduce the heat to very low and cook at a bare simmer until tender, 4 to 5 hours, basting and turning the meat occasionally.

6. Transfer the veal to a cutting board. Stir the remaining ¼ cup crème fraîche and mushroom mixture into the cooking liquid and heat until warmed through.

7. Snip the strings and remove. Using a very sharp or serrated knife, cut the veal into ½- to ¾-inch-thick slices. Divide among warmed serving plates and top with the mushroom sauce. Garnish with the remaining 3 tablespoons herbs and serve.

-Chapter 5-
# PORK

# Portuguese-Style Marinated Pork and Caramelized Onion Sandwiches

Bifanas de Porco

**Serves 4**

These delicious, habit-forming sandwiches are worth the overnight wait the marinating requires, but if you must, shorten the marinating time. This robust pork and onion sandwich is a variation of a recipe in Ana Patuleia Ortins's book *Portuguese Homestyle Cooking*; we've also seen versions made with beef and others with tomatoes. Don't be surprised by the margarine; it has its uses, and the Portuguese understand them all. Butter on this sandwich can taste a little too rich, sweet, and dairyish; margarine is traditional. Here, it can contribute another layer of flavor and some extra moisture that mingles beautifully with the hot pepper paste.

In Portugal, the peppers that go into the red pepper paste are traditionally salted and packed in large containers, where their flavors concentrate. After about a week, they are transferred to jars and stored beneath a blanket of olive oil. For ease, we've adapted the recipe for fresh peppers. Use any red-colored medium-hot pepper with sweet, flavorful flesh. In the United States, those commonly available include red jalapeños, red cherry peppers, or tapering Dutch peppers (our favorite). Remember to wear gloves when handling the chilies and avoid touching your eyes. The recipe yields more pepper paste than you'll need for the sandwiches; try the leftovers with eggs, burgers, or fish.

**Butcher's Note:** We urge shoppers to look for good marbling and pinkish gray finely textured meat with just a little creamy outer fat when they buy pork. Luckily, much of the pork produced today is of good quality, but if your butcher, supermarket, or gourmet shop carries heirloom or specialty pork, try it. Take our word for it: You will have a hard time going back to more run-of-the-mill pork!

The flavor of heirloom pork is so amazingly satisfying, you will immediately understand why in days gone by the pork raised right there on the farm was so cherished and why the pigs were so carefully tended and well fed. We sell meat from pure- and crossbred Tamworths, Gloucestershire Old Spots, and Large Black hogs, raised for us in Vermont in a stress-free environment. They are fed a diet free of subtherapeutic antibiotics and growth hormones. The result? Flavor so deep and rich it echoes the good pork from that bygone era. The meat is gloriously juicy and tender, and will make these sandwiches (or any recipe in this chapter) burst with flavor. For more on our heirloom pork, visit Lobels.com.

**Wine Note:** Vinho Verde is hardly a complex wine, but what it lacks in complexity it more than makes up for it in its water-like drinkability and impressive flexibility with food. Our favorite wine with these spicy pork *Bifanas* was the Casa de Vila Verde Vinho Verde, a slightly richer but still brisk and delicious Vinho Verde grown in a single vineyard and stamped with a vintage date, unusual for these wines. At 11 percent alcohol rather than the usual 9 percent, it is bigger than most of its peers and better able to complement more fully flavored dishes. But any of the lighter-weight, crackling-crisp Vinhos Verde are equally fine (there are other Vinhos Verde made with fancier, single varietals and higher price tags that, while good, are not as food friendly as the more basic stuff). What you want are the lively, light-bodied and fully dry versions that are shot with a bit of effervescence and rarely exceed ten dollars. More importantly, you want

to buy and drink these wines as young as possible, that is, at no more than a year and a half of age. After that, they lose considerable freshness and by age two they're on their way to becoming flat tasting, dull, and . . . a waste of money. But because so many Vinhos Verde don't list a vintage date on the label, how's a shopper to tell how old these wines are? Here's a secret passed on to us by food and wine sleuth David Rosengarten: On the back of the bottle you'll find the Portuguese governmental seal of guarantee (*selo de garantia*). On the seal is a serial number followed by a slash and a date. The date is what's important here because it tells you the year in which the wine was bottled. Since the bottling always occurs after the New Year, if you subtract one year from that date, you get the vintage date! So 2005 on the seal means you have a wine from the autumn 2004 vintage in your hands, and if you're looking at this bottle in the summer of 2006, the wine is therefore approaching two years old and you should pass it up; in this example, you want only a Vinho Verde from the 2005 vintage (the seal will read 2006)—the most recent available. Beyond Vinho Verde, a number of the light, crisp and often overlooked wines made throughout the Northeast would be just the thing with these spicy pork sandwiches: Clinton Seyval Blanc from New York's Hudson Valley is one of the best. Or have a beer.

---

*1 pound boneless pork loin, cut into 8 slices*
*about ½ inch thick*

### Marinade

*4 large cloves garlic*

*½ teaspoon kosher salt*

*¼ cup dry white wine*

*2 tablespoons Portuguese-Style*
*Hot Red Pepper Paste (page 216)*

*2 teaspoons sweet paprika*

### Caramelized onions

*¼ cup olive oil*

*3 yellow, white, or sweet onions,*
*halved and thinly sliced*

*2 teaspoons kosher salt*

*1 teaspoon sweet paprika*

*About 1 ½ cups olive oil*

*Kosher salt*

*4 Portuguese-style or hard rolls, split*

*Margarine*

---

1. Working in batches, put the pork slices in a heavy plastic bag, lay the bag on a work surface, and gently pound the pork with a meat mallet or the back of a small, heavy skillet to an even thickness of ¼ inch.

2. To make the marinade, on a cutting board, crush the garlic with the flat side of a knife and chop. Sprinkle with the salt and work into a paste by repeatedly mashing it with the flat side of the knife. Transfer the garlic paste to a large, shallow bowl.

3. Add the wine, hot pepper paste, and paprika and mix well. Put the meat in the bowl and turn to coat with the marinade. You may want to rub the mixture into the meat with your fingers. Cover the bowl tightly and refrigerate for at least 6 hours or up to overnight.

4. To make the caramelized onions, in a large skillet, heat the oil over medium heat. Add the onions and salt, and cook, stirring occasionally, until somewhat reduced in volume but without color, about 15 minutes.

5. Reduce the heat to medium-low and continue to cook, stirring often, until the onions are pale brown, sweet, and soft, about 1 hour. Reduce the heat if the onions

threaten to burn. Stir in the paprika to mix thoroughly and set aside.

6. When you're ready to make the sandwiches, let the pork come to room temperature and preheat the oven to 200°F. Gently reheat the onions, if necessary, and season to taste with salt.

7. Remove the pork slices from the marinade and lightly salt both sides (do not scrape off the marinade). In a large skillet, pour in the olive oil to a depth of ¼ inch and heat over medium-high heat. When it begins to smoke, carefully slide a few slices of pork into the oil. Fry, turning once, until just barely cooked through, 45 seconds to 1 minute per side. Do not overcook. Using a slotted spoon, transfer to a shallow baking dish and keep warm in the oven. Repeat to fry all of the pork.

8. Meanwhile, warm the split rolls in the oven. Spread each side with a thin layer of margarine.

9. Put 2 pork slices on the bottom half of a roll and top with caramelized onions and the top of the roll. Serve right away, with extra margarine and pepper paste to spread on the sandwiches, if desired.

**Make-Ahead Tip:** The caramelized onions can be made up to 1 day ahead. Reheat gently before serving.

# Pork Cutlets with Apples, Onions, and Marjoram

Scweinsmedallions mit Marjoran

**Serves 2**

This dish displays the excellent cooking traits of good-quality German Riesling wine, which is not surprising considering the preparation originated in Germany's Rhineland. While it's relatively simple and quick to put together, it nevertheless boasts vibrant and complex flavor, due in part to the gentle sweetness, balance, and perfume of these wines. The key to success is to have the all the ingredients and equipment at hand when you are ready to fry. Not only is this safer, but because the cutlets cook quickly, it allows you to focus on getting them in and out of the pan without overcooking. To double the recipe, use two skillets.

🔧

**Wine Note:** German Riesling! For those who aren't familiar with it, here's a chance to learn about the most refined and nimble food wine there is. You could do little better than to try two favorites from our wine and pork cutlet session. Both matches work so well because of the principle of "like goes with like": In this case, a slight sweetness in the wines finds a partner in the apples of the dish. From the Rheingau, the Joseph Leitz Rüdesheimer Klosterlay Kabinett is a sweet-tart style of Riesling that sumptuously complements the pork in a creamy and expressive style. But it's the slightly dryer *halbtrocken* style of Riesling that really makes the match take off. From the Rheinpfalz: Lingenfelder's Freisenheimer Musikantenbuckel Kabinett Halbtrocken. Try pronouncing this if you like, but a notepad works when asking your merchant for the wine. As is true for most German wines, the first word in this name is the producer; the second is the town, as "from Freisenheim"; third is the vineyard in which the grapes grew; fourth is the level of ripeness the grapes achieved, which is important in lands as far north as this part of Germany; and the fifth indicates that the wine is half-dry as opposed to dry, or *trocken*. Although a great number of German wines in the United States have no indication of dryness at all—which means they generally display a rounder sweet-tart feel in the mouth than the others, regardless of quality or price—they are often described as off-dry. Riesling wines from other parts that display the qualities of the best German versions are rare. One of the best places to look is New Zealand, where wines like the Felton Road Rieslings from Central Otago—one dry and one off-dry—would work handsomely next to our apple-sweetened pork cutlets.

---

*¾ cup off-dry Riesling wine*

*¼ cup golden raisins*

*About 1¼ cups vegetable oil*

*1 large yellow onion, thinly sliced*

*2 sweet apples such as Gala or Fuji, peeled, cored, halved, and cut into thin half-moon slices*

*¾ cup Pork Stock (page 212), Chicken Stock (page 215), or canned low-sodium chicken broth*

*3 teaspoons finely chopped fresh marjoram*

*Kosher salt*

*1 pound boneless pork loin, cut into 6 slices (cutlets), each about ⅜ inch thick, at room temperature*

*Freshly ground black pepper*

*All-purpose flour for dredging*

*2 tablespoons whole-grain or smooth German-style mustard such as Inglehoffer's*

---

1. In a small saucepan, bring the wine and raisins to a simmer over medium-high heat. Reduce the heat so that the wine simmers gently and cook until reduced by half, about 4 minutes. Set aside.

2. In a large skillet, heat ¼ cup of the oil over medium heat and cook the onion slices, stirring occasionally, until softened and pale gold at the edges, 8 to 10 minutes. Stir in the apples and cook for 5 minutes more. Add the wine-raisin mixture, the stock, 2 teaspoons of the marjoram, and ¾ teaspoon salt and bring to a simmer.

3. Reduce the heat to medium low and simmer gently until the liquid has reduced by two-thirds but the mixture is still slightly liquid, 5 to 7 minutes. Set aside.

4. Preheat the oven to 200°F. Sprinkle the pork slices on both sides generously with salt and lightly with pepper. Put about 1 cup of flour on a large plate.

5. In a large skillet, pour enough oil to reach a depth of about ¼ inch and heat over medium heat. While the oil heats, spread both sides of each pork slice with mustard and then dredge with the flour. Shake off the excess flour and when the oil begins to smoke carefully slide 2 to 3 pork slices into the skillet. Reduce the heat slightly and fry for 1½ to 2 minutes per side. The pork slices will be barely pink in the center. Transfer to a paper towel–lined plate and keep warm in the oven. Repeat to fry the remaining pork slices, letting the oil get hot again between batches.

6. Gently rewarm the reserved onion-apple mixture over low heat. Divide the mixture between 2 serving plates and top each with 3 pork cutlets. Garnish with the remaining 1 teaspoon marjoram and serve immediately.

# Pork Chops with White Wine and Mustard Sauce

*Côte de Porc Vigneronne*

**Serves 2**

Mâconnais, in the southern part of France's Burgundy region, is home to the world-famous white wine–based mustard of Dijon, which shapes much of the region's cooking. These chops are a tasty example of what the French can do with just a few choice ingredients.

**Wine Note:** Here is a dish that shows the value of the easygoing, crisp refreshment of the region's most common wine, Mâcon-Villages. Though quality levels vary, with some being a little dull and others quite dramatic, a well-made, basic Mâcon-Villages is nevertheless the prototype for a certain style of Chardonnay-based wine that is delicious, refreshing, affordable, and very flexible at the table. One favorite in our tasting was the simple but rewarding Domaine des Verchères Mâcon-Villages. A fancier wine was also good with the pork and represents the best of the new breed of Mâcon wine: Mâcon-Milly-Lamartine "Clos du Four" from the Héritiers du Comte Lafon. In spite of the oceans of Chardonnay made all over the globe, very little of it resembles the wine of the Mâconnais, home to two other well-known *appellations*, Pouilly-Fuissé and St. Véran. And so, it is a style that seems to be increasingly distinctive, especially because the talented wine makers in so-called New World wine regions seem less able or willing to make Chardonnays of such modest beauty. That said, there are a few wineries beyond France issuing more restrained and elegant Chardonnay, particularly as suitable vineyard sites are discovered and as consumer appreciation grows for wines

with delicacy rather than sheer impact. One favorite: Chateau Ste. Michelle "Canoe Ridge" Chardonnay from Washington State's Columbia Valley.

---

*3 ounces fatty, skinless salt pork, cut into ⅜-inch dice*

*1 tablespoon vegetable oil*

*Two ¾-pound bone-in pork loin chops, each about 1 inch thick*

*Kosher salt and freshly ground black pepper*

*All-purpose flour for dredging*

*3 tablespoons finely chopped shallots*

*½ cup dry white wine*

*1 tablespoon tomato paste*

*½ cup Chicken Stock (page 215) or canned low-sodium chicken broth*

*2 tablespoons Dijon mustard*

*1½ tablespoons finely chopped fresh chives*

---

1. In a large skillet, cook the salt pork in the oil over medium-low heat, stirring occasionally, for about 5 minutes, or until the salt pork is pale gold and crisp. Using a slotted spoon, transfer the salt pork to a plate and set aside.

2. Generously season the pork chops on both sides with salt and pepper. Coat with flour and shake off the excess.

3. In the same skillet, cook the pork chops over medium-high heat for 4 to 6 minutes on each side for medium (do not overcook). Transfer the chops to a plate, tent loosely with aluminum foil, and keep warm in a very low (200°F) oven.

4. Let the skillet cool slightly and pour off all but 2 tablespoons of the fat. Reduce the heat to medium-low, add the shallots, and cook, stirring occasionally, until softened, about 4 minutes. Raise the heat to medium-high and add the wine, scraping the bottom of the skillet to loosen any browned bits. Simmer rapidly until reduced by one-third, about 2 minutes.

5. Transfer 3 or 4 tablespoons of the hot wine mixture to a small bowl and whisk in the tomato paste until dissolved. Add the dissolved tomato paste and the stock to the skillet and simmer for about 2 minutes, or until thickened slightly. Reduce the heat to very low and whisk in the mustard and half of the chives.

6. Return the pork chops and any accumulated juices on the plate to the skillet, turning the chops to coat with the sauce.

7. To serve, transfer the chops to warmed serving plates and top with the sauce. Garnish with the bits of crispy salt pork and the remaining chives.

# Pork Chops with Tomato and Roasted Red Pepper Stew

*Chuletas de Cerdo con Tomate y Pimientos del Piquillo Asados*

**Serves 4**

Because these chops are just ½ inch thick, they need to be nicely browned in very hot oil in a short period of time. This dish greatly benefits from the use of high-quality heirloom meat like our Kurobuta pork (see Butcher's Note, page 100). But even with any pork, use either loin or rib chops. Loin chops are slightly more expensive than rib chops and include the T-bone; rib chops are cut from the rack, or rib. Both are great, although as a rule we prefer rib chops because we find them just a little more flavorful. In any case, take care not to overcook them. So that you don't crowd the pan, you many need to work in batches or use several skillets. Serve these with crispy-edged fried potato slices.

This dish from the Rioja region of Spain relies on one of the most delicious products from that country: roasted *pimientos del Piquillo*. These 2- to 3-inch-long peppers boast a rich, wood-roasted flavor and an appealing prickle of chili heat. Available in the United States in jars and tins, they are now quite common in fancy food markets. If you can't find them, you can substitute a similar quantity of good-quality roasted red bell peppers, but add a pinch of cayenne pepper to the tomato sauce to reproduce the mild heat of the Piquillos.

**Wine Note:** Piquillo peppers are the soul of this dish, which like some far hotter members of the pepper family, can cause trouble for some wines. This is an especially important time to choose wines that display the virtues of food friendliness, discussed at length in chapter one. Those that don't will simply fail to please with this dish. In the Rioja, this means wines from either the quality-minded traditional producers who build their wines on a tart and delicate framework or those more modern producers who keep the new oak and alcohol levels in check. One favorite among reds is the old-school Bodegas Riojanas "Viña Albina" Reserva. For a New World choice, a good bet is to pour a brisk, fairly simple Pinot Noir like the Pipers Brook Vineyard "9th Island" Pinot Noir from Tasmania, Australia.

---

5 tablespoons Spanish-Style Lard Paste
(page 217; variations) (optional)

Eight 6- to 7-ounce bone-in pork loin or rib chops,
each about ½ inch thick

6 tablespoons extra-virgin olive oil

1 yellow onion, chopped

6 large cloves garlic, thinly sliced

One 28-ounce can peeled whole tomatoes

1 teaspoon finely chopped fresh thyme,
plus 1 teaspoon whole leaves for garnish

1 teaspoon sweet paprika

¼ teaspoon sugar

Kosher salt

16 ounces jarred roasted Piquillo peppers
(pimientos del Piquillo asados),
drained and quartered lengthwise

¾ cup dry white wine

---

1. If using the lard paste, rub a thin layer onto both sides of each pork chop. Cover and set aside at room temperature. Otherwise, let the chops come to room temperature until needed.

2. In a skillet, heat 3 tablespoons of the olive oil over medium-high heat. Add the onion and garlic, reduce the heat to medium, and cook, stirring occasionally, until pale gold at the edges, 8 to 10 minutes.

3. Add the tomatoes and half of their juices, the chopped thyme, the paprika, the sugar, and 1½ teaspoons salt. Coarsely crush the tomatoes with a wooden spoon. Bring to a gentle simmer and cook, stirring occasionally, until the sauce thickens and most of the liquid has evaporated, about 30 minutes.

4. Stir in the Piquillo peppers to warm through. Remove the stew from the heat and set aside.

5. Generously salt the chops. (If already rubbed with lard paste, use less salt.)

6. In one large or two smaller skillets, heat the remaining 3 tablespoons olive oil over medium-high heat (if using two skillets, you'll need a little more oil). When the oil begins to smoke, cook the chops, working in batches if necessary, until golden brown on the first side, about 3 minutes. Turn and cook on the other side until just barely pink in the center, about 1½ minutes more. Arrange the chops in a low-sided earthenware casserole or baking dish, slightly overlapping.

7. Preheat the oven to 325°F. Gently reheat the stew.

8. Pour off the fat in the skillet and place the skillet over medium heat. Add the wine, scraping the bottom of the skillet to loosen any browned bits. (If using two skillets, add the wine to one skillet and scrape to loosen any browned bits. Pour this liquid into the second skillet and repeat.) Cook the wine until reduced to about 3 tablespoons. Stir the wine reduction into the stew.

9. Distribute the stew between and over the chops to cover and transfer to the oven. Bake for 15 minutes.

10. Garnish with the thyme leaves and serve from the casserole, topping each portion of chops with the red pepper stew and then spooning some of the pork juices at the bottom of the casserole over each.

**Make-Ahead Tip:** You can prepare the dish through step 4 up to 1 day ahead. Cover and refrigerate the tomato–red pepper stew until ready to proceed.

# Medallions of Pork with Prunes in the Style of the Loire Valley

Noisettes de Porc aux Pruneaux

**Serves 4**

Pork served with prunes is a classic combination, and this recipe from France's Loire River Valley makes good use of the marriage of fruit and meat. The only trick is to let the skillet get very hot so that the very lean pork medallions brown nicely before the meat cooks through or dries out. Browning them to a light golden color on both sides intensifies the flavor of the pork, and the cooked bits left in the pan nicely flavor the sauce.

**Butcher's Note:** Purchase 2¼ to 2½ pounds pork tenderloin and cut the medallions from the thickest part. Reserve the remainder for another use; it freezes very nicely for up to three months.

**Wine Note:** Vouvray, made from Chenin Blanc grapes grown in the relative cool of France's Loire Valley, is another wine world original. These are wines that handily accompany not just French food, but any cuisine, because of their moderate alcohol levels and a keen, refreshing acidity (contrasted in many versions by a barely perceptible soft sweetness).

There is a sec, or fully dry, style of Vouvray and a demi-sec, or half dry (no sweeter tasting than most American Chardonnay, for example). Falling between these two, there is an unofficial style called *sec-tendre*. It's a phrase not (yet) found on the label, so ask your wine merchant. All three are among the most flexible food wines that exist.

Beyond these styles, most producers make a fully sweet "Moelleux" (among the world's longest-lived and most complex wines) and a sparkling wine or two. Like many German wine regions, the northerly latitude of Vouvray is both the region's bane and its blessing. It's not easy for grapes to ripen fully here, but those that do produce wines unlike any other. These vibrantly textured wines carry all kinds of flavors that dance and shift. One moment there are pearlike flavors, next an undertow of something mineral, followed by an unexpected whiff of honey. None of these wines gets near a new oak barrel. There's a wide range of quality available, but you can enjoy many of the best without spending a fortune: Look for a demi-sec or sec-tendre style from Didier and Catherine Champalou or the slightly more costly, standard-bearing wines of Philippe Foreau (a.k.a. Domaine de Clos Naudin), both of whose wines stood out in our tastings. From California, try Chapellet Chenin Blanc from the Napa Valley, a simple but delicious classic.

*8 ounces pitted prunes*

*Kosher salt*

*1¾ pounds pork tenderloin, cut into 8 medallions about 1½ inches thick (see Butcher's Note)*

*3 tablespoons vegetable oil*

*2 tablespoons unsalted butter*

*½ cup finely chopped shallots*

*1 cup off-dry white wine, such as Vouvray Demi-Sec*

*½ cup Chicken Stock (page 215) or canned low-sodium chicken broth*

*2 teaspoons fresh thyme leaves*

*⅛ teaspoon ground cinnamon*

*Freshly ground black pepper*

*1½ tablespoons red currant preserves*

*2 tablespoons crème fraîche*

1. Soak the prunes in very hot tap water for 30 minutes, or until somewhat softened. Drain and set aside.

2. Generously salt the pork medallions on both sides.

3. In a large, heavy skillet, heat the oil over high heat until it smokes. Add the pork and cook until the first side is golden brown, about 4 minutes. Reduce the heat if the medallions threaten to burn. Turn and cook the second side for no more than 3 to 4 minutes (they should still be slightly raw in the center). Transfer to a plate, cover tightly with aluminum foil, and keep warm in a very low (200°F) oven.

4. Pour off all but 1 tablespoon of the oil and let the skillet cool slightly. Return to medium-low heat and melt the butter. Add the shallots and cook, stirring occasionally, until softened, about 3 minutes. Add the wine and the prunes, scraping the bottom of the skillet to loosen any browned bits. Raise the heat slightly and simmer for 3 minutes.

5. Add the stock, thyme, cinnamon, and a few grindings of pepper. Using a spatula, gently push on the prunes to release their flavor and thickening power, but don't crush them completely. Return to a brisk simmer and cook until the liquid is reduced by half, 8 to 10 minutes.

6. Stir in the preserves. Add the pork and any juices that have accumulated on the plate and return to a low simmer. Simmer gently until the pork is warmed through and cooked to medium (140°F to 145°F on an instant-read thermometer), basting the medallions regularly.

7. Divide the medallions among warmed serving plates. The sauce should be thick but pourable; if necessary, reduce it for a minute or so more to thicken it and concentrate its flavor. Whisk the crème fraîche into the sauce and add salt to taste. Pour the sauce over the medallions and serve immediately.

# Roast Loin of Pork with Rosemary, Sage, and Garlic

*Arista*

**Serves 6**

In our version of this Tuscan classic, we perform an easy bit of butchering that results in a moister roast that's simple to carve (see Butcher's Note). You can follow this recipe using a boneless loin pork roast placed on a roasting rack, although the results aren't quite the same. The beauty of this dish is that it is good both hot and, later in the week, sliced even thinner and served cool. We like it with white beans and a sautéed leafy green vegetable such as kale, Swiss chard, or spinach, all drizzled with extra-virgin olive oil.

**Butcher's Note:** For this recipe, you begin with a bone-in center-cut pork roast, separate the rack of bones from it, and then, once seasoned, tie the two pieces together curved side up. (You can ask your butcher to remove the ribs for you.) Strapping the ribs on backward provides a protective "rack" to elevate the meat above the roasting pan and minimize moisture loss during cooking. The bone also adds to the drippings for the pan sauce. At the end of cooking, the ribs are simply untied and removed, and the tender meat is easily sliced to ideal thinness. The bones are great to gnaw on. What might appear to be an elaborate boning and tying process is really very simple. For a treat, order high-quality heirloom pork from us (see Butcher's Note, page 100); its flavor and tenderness make a big difference in this dish.

**Wine Note:** Though boldly flavored on the outside with herbs and garlic, this pork loin roast still presents, in the end, a very delicate mouthful of pork. Although most of the Sangiovese-based Tuscan wine favorites would work quite well with this classic dish, some are better than others. It is not the particular flavors of these wines that matter; it's their relative weights and textures. Among the many subregions of Chianti itself, we found that the regular, *normale* bottlings harmonize best. These are medium- to medium–full-bodied wines with warmly tart black cherry flavors; their tannins offer support and no more. Wines like this should go down without a catch; bigger wines will breathe too much of their alcoholic fire into the delicate pork. From Chianti country, the modest scale and easy drinkability of Badia a Coltibuono's Chianti "Cetamura" is just right. For entertaining, the richer refinement of the Castello di Ama Chianti Classico heightens the experience without hogging the stage. Thinking American? From the North Fork of Long Island, the medium weight and polish of the Schneider Vineyards Cabernet Franc would make a great pair with the richly herbed Tuscan-style pork.

*One 4-pound center-cut bone-in pork loin roast
with a generous layer of fat left on*

*⅓ cup extra-virgin olive oil, plus more for
garnish (optional)*

*6 large cloves garlic, finely chopped*

*3 tablespoons finely chopped fresh sage*

*3 tablespoons finely chopped fresh rosemary*

*1 teaspoon coarsely ground black pepper*

*Kosher salt*

*¾ cup dry white wine*

*2½ cups Pork Stock (page 212)
or equal parts canned beef broth and water*

1. Using a sharp knife, separate the rib bones from the loin or ask the butcher to prepare the roast for you (see Butcher's Note). Score the fat on top of the loin in a crosshatch pattern, cutting ¼ inch deep (don't cut into the flesh).

2. In a small bowl, stir together the olive oil, garlic, sage, rosemary, and black pepper. Rub all but about 1 tablespoon of the herb mixture into the slits in the pork roast and over the entire surface of the loin. Rub the remaining mixture into the ribs. Let the loin and ribs stand at room temperature for at least 1 hour and up to 3 hours. (Alternatively, you can apply the marinade a day before and store the pork, tightly wrapped in plastic wrap, in the refrigerator overnight. Bring to room temperature before proceeding.)

3. Preheat the oven to 450°F.

4. Very generously salt the loin and ribs on all sides. Tie the loin and ribs together with butcher's twine or kitchen string, with the rounded side up (see Butcher's Note), and put in a roasting pan just large enough to hold the meat, bone side down. Roast for 20 minutes. Reduce the oven temperature to 300°F and roast until an instant-read thermometer registers 140°F to 145°F when inserted in the center of the roast, 1¼ to 1½ hours.

5. Put the roasting pan on the stove top and transfer the roast to a cutting board. Let rest, tented loosely with aluminum foil, for 15 minutes.

6. Meanwhile, skim the fat from the drippings in the roasting pan, if you like. Add the wine and bring to a simmer over medium-high heat. Simmer until reduced by two-thirds, 4 to 5 minutes.

7. Add the stock and continue simmering until reduced by almost half (to 1½ cups), 12 to 15 minutes. The pan sauce should be flavorful but still quite liquid, midway between a broth and a sauce in consistency. Cook to reduce further and add salt to taste, if necessary. (For an additional flavor boost, stir a few whole leaves of sage, a small sprig of rosemary, and a crushed clove of garlic into the sauce and let them infuse it while you slice the roast. Remove before serving.)

8. Snip the strings on the roast and separate the loin from the ribs. Slice the loin into slices slightly less than ¼ inch thick and divide them among serving plates, 4 to 5 slices per plate, laying them attractively over or up against any accompanying vegetables, if using.

9. Slice and plate the ribs or reserve them for another use.

10. Reheat the sauce, if necessary, and spoon it over and around the meat. Serve immediately, drizzled with extra-virgin olive oil, if you like.

# Pork with Cockles in Sweet Red Pepper Sauce

*Porco à Alentejana*

**Serves 4**

The delicious combination of pork and clams has long been a favorite in many parts of Portugal and Spain. There's a time-honored religious aspect to dishes of this kind because eating pork and shellfish combinations was seen as an irrefutable emblem of one's Christianity. During a time when Christians, Jews, and Muslims shared the Iberian Peninsula in large numbers, this held a certain significance. In any event, it's a delectable dish that in our version is prepared somewhat differently than usual. Typically, the sweet red pepper paste—the most unique ingredient in the dish—serves as an overnight marinade for the pork, and then the pork and pepper paste are cooked until the meat is tender. We found that cooking the pepper paste for so long robs the dish of one of its greatest assets, the rich flavor and sweetness of red peppers, so, in our version, we simply stir it in toward the end of cooking.

**Wine Note:** With Portuguese food on the lighter side, it's long been an automatic response to pull the cork on a bottle of the affordable, food-friendly, and crackling-crisp Vinho Verde. And very good with this dish it is. But we threw a ringer from across the border in Galicia, Spain, into our tasting, and we loved it even more with the pork and clams: Albariño. Made wholly from the grape by the same name (which is a sometime component of Vinho Verde itself), Albariño manages a trick rare in a dry white wine: It is full of rich fruit flavor and briskly refreshing at the same time. One favorite was the Fillaboa Albariño. Perhaps surprisingly, there is very good Albariño being grown at the southernmost end of the Napa Valley. Ask your merchant for Havens Albariño.

*½ cup extra-virgin olive oil,
plus more for drizzling*

*2 pounds boneless pork blade or shoulder,
cut into ¾-inch cubes, at room temperature*

*Kosher salt*

*1 large yellow onion, finely chopped*

*5 large cloves garlic, 4 minced, 1 cut in half*

*1½ cups dry white wine*

*2 teaspoons tomato paste*

*1½ cups water*

*3 large bay leaves*

*3 sprigs fresh thyme*

*1 teaspoon sweet paprika*

*12 slices of baguette about ½ inch thick,
cut on the diagonal*

*5 to 6 cups loosely packed, stemmed, and
chopped mustard greens or other tender,
slightly bitter greens*

*¾ cup Portuguese-Style
Sweet Red Pepper Paste (page 216)*

*Freshly ground black pepper*

*2 pounds New Zealand cockles
or 24 small littleneck clams, well scrubbed*

*3 tablespoons finely chopped fresh cilantro*

1. In a large Dutch oven or casserole with a tight-fitting lid, heat ¼ cup of the olive oil over medium-high heat until very hot. Working in batches, cook the pork until golden brown on at least two sides, about 10 minutes per batch, reducing the heat if it threatens to burn. Transfer to a bowl. Toss the pork generously with salt and set aside.

2. Let the Dutch oven cool slightly and place over medium heat. Add half of the onion and half of the minced garlic. Cook, stirring occasionally, until pale gold at the edges, about 8 minutes. Add the wine, scraping the bottom of the pot to loosen any browned bits. Simmer gently until reduced by about one-third, about 5 minutes. In a bowl, combine the tomato paste and water, stir to dissolve, and add to the pot. Stir in the bay leaves, thyme, paprika, ½ teaspoon salt, and the pork and any accumulated juices. Bring just to a simmer, cover the pot, and cook until the pork is tender, about 1½ hours, adjusting the heat as needed to maintain a gentle simmer.

3. Rub the bread slices with the garlic halves and drizzle with a bit of olive oil. Toast or broil the bread until crisp but still tender inside and set aside.

4. Add the mustard greens to the pork stew a handful at a time, stirring until each handful wilts. Stir in the sweet pepper paste and a few generous grindings of black pepper. Cover and keep warm over low heat.

5. In a medium saucepan with a tight-fitting lid, heat the remaining ¼ cup olive oil over medium heat. Cook the remaining onion and minced garlic, uncovered, until pale gold at the edges, about 8 to 10 minutes. Add the cockles, raise the heat to high, cover, and steam, shaking the pot occasionally, until they open, 3 to 4 minutes. (If you're using littleneck clams, they'll take a little longer). Discard any that don't open.

6. Transfer the entire contents of the saucepan to the pork stew, stirring gently to combine without knocking the cockles from their shells. Cook gently for 1 minute, adding salt if necessary. Divide the stew and broth among 4 warmed shallow soup bowls, distributing the cockles attractively around the bowl. Drizzle each serving with additional olive oil and sprinkle with the cilantro. Garnish with the garlic toasts and serve immediately.

**Make-Ahead Tip:** The dish can be prepared through step 2 up to 1 day ahead. Cover and refrigerate. Reheat gently and proceed as directed.

# Pork with Celery and Lemon-Egg Sauce

*Hirino me Selino Avgolemono*

**Serves 4**

This Greek classic is a homey and satisfying stew that features celery in four forms: celery stalk, celery leaves, celery root, and celery seeds. These flavors are bound together with the pork by a smooth, lemony egg sauce that pulls the dish together at the end of the cooking. Serve this over orzo or other pasta, with a green salad alongside.

**Butcher's Note:** Cut from the shoulder blade, these chops are fattier than other pork chops, and when they are split, they're sometimes sold as country-style ribs. Country-style ribs are generally readily available in many supermarkets and specialty shops with a butcher's counter. They're sold both bone-in and boneless and work well either way. (If you buy bone-in chops, get 3 to 3½ pounds and have the butcher cut them into 1½-inch pieces for you, reserving the bones.) In fact, since you'll probably want another 3 pounds of bone-in ribs to make our quick pork stock (see page 212), any reserved bones can count toward that total. In the end, this cut is nothing more exotic than meat that is cut from the pork shoulder. Any pork labeled "country-style ribs," "blade pork chops," "shoulder pork chops," "end-cut pork chops," or "shoulder pork" will work well here. All are essentially the same meat.

**Wine Note:** There's a lot happening in the world of Greek wine. Top-quality, fascinating red and white wines are being made from a wealth of unusual indigenous grape varieties, some with long histories and many of which, it turns out, are especially good with food. Surprisingly, our favorite among the flight of Greek whites we tried with the dish was a completely unfancy and widely available longtime favorite, Boutari Santorini. The wine had a gentle, softly crisp quality that was not particularly aromatic. Nor was it fruity. Set in a medium-bodied frame, the wine was without any truly memorable features but without faults either. It was as if the wine maker had asked of it, "First, do no harm" (which it didn't) and then said, "You will be a good companion to whatever is served" (and it was). A good non-Greek choice would be a soft and citrusy Semillon from Australia. One favorite: Brokenwood Semillon from the Hunter Valley in New South Wales.

*Kosher salt*

*2 ½ pounds boneless blade (country-style)
pork chops, cut into 1 ½-inch pieces*

*¼ cup extra-virgin olive oil*

*1 yellow onion, finely chopped*

*1 large leek, white and pale green parts only, split,
well rinsed, and thinly sliced crosswise*

*⅔ cup dry white wine*

*3 ½ cups Pork Stock (page 212),
Chicken Stock (page 215), canned low-sodium
chicken broth, or water*

*¼ teaspoon celery seed, plus more for garnish*

*10 stalks celery, leaves reserved and
chopped for garnish*

*1 pound celery root, peeled and
cut into ½-inch dice (about 2 ½ cups)*

*3 large egg yolks, plus 1 large whole egg*

*1 tablespoon cornstarch
dissolved in 3 tablespoons water*

*5 to 6 tablespoons fresh lemon juice*

1. In a bowl, generously salt the pork, tossing to coat.

2. In a heavy stockpot, heat the olive oil over medium-high heat. Working in batches, cook the pork until deeply browned on at least two sides, about 10 minutes per batch, reducing the heat if it threatens to burn. Transfer to a plate and set aside.

3. Reduce the heat to medium-low, add the onion and leek, and cook, stirring occasionally, until very soft but without color, about 15 minutes. Add the wine and let it evaporate, scraping the bottom of the pot to loosen any browned bits. Add the stock, celery seed, 1 teaspoon salt, and the pork along with any accumulated juices and bring just to a simmer. Cover and cook until tender, about 2 hours, adjusting the heat as needed to maintain a bare simmer.

4. Meanwhile, bring a large pot of very generously salted water to a boil. Using a vegetable peeler, peel the celery stalks to remove most of the tough strings and cut into 3-inch lengths.

5. Add the celery root to the boiling water and simmer for 5 minutes. Add the celery stalk pieces and continue simmering until the vegetables are softened but still a bit firm, about 5 minutes more. Drain and set aside.

6. When the pork is tender, stir the celery and celery root into the pot, cover, and cook gently for 15 minutes longer.

7. Meanwhile, in a mixing bowl, whisk together the egg yolks, whole egg, cornstarch mixture, and 5 tablespoons of lemon juice. Set aside until ready to finish the dish.

8. Whisk a few ladlefuls of hot cooking liquid, a little at a time, into the reserved egg mixture. Return this to the pot in a thin stream, stirring thoroughly to distribute. Cook very gently, uncovered, to thicken the sauce for 5 minutes, stirring occasionally. Do not let it boil. If necessary, add more lemon juice and salt to taste. At this point, the sauce should have the thickness of very heavy cream that just coats the back of a spoon. The consistency of the sauce is important. If it isn't thick enough, cook gently for a few more minutes. If it still isn't thick enough, whisk another egg with a little of the hot sauce and stir it into the pot. If it's too thick, thin it with a little water.

9. Divide the pork and sauce among the plates. Garnish with celery seed and the celery leaves and serve immediately.

# French Basque-Style Pork with Red Bell Peppers and Cinnamon

Le Ragoût de Porc Basquaise

**Serves 4**

Think of this as a kind of Basque chile con carne. French Basque dishes of this sort, from the far western part of France near the Spanish border, are often seasoned with (in addition to bell peppers) the full-flavored, lightly spicy, local pepper called *piment d'Espelette,* which may be sold as a paste or dried and ground to a powder. To approximate its taste, we combined sweet paprika with cayenne. Be sure to use recently bought fresh paprika and cayenne. If you find piment d'Espelette, substitute about 2 teaspoons of the dried powder for the paprika and cayenne. Serve this with a big green salad and thick slices of lightly toasted country-style bread rubbed with a clove of garlic and drizzled with good olive oil.

**Wine Note:** We had hoped to enjoy the French Basque country's most famous red, Madiran, the ancient and vigorous wine made from the local Tannat grape (now sometimes "helped" with of a bit of Merlot), with this aromatic stew of pork and beans. But most available vintages are, sad to say, just too powerful and dry in their early years to complement the dish. We found that what is needed is an aged wine of mellow warmth. If you have access to Madiran wine at least eight years old, by all means serve it; the famous Château de Montus Madiran improves for upward of fifteen years (and its Prestige bottling even more). Because of the difficulty of finding the hoped-for Madirans, we threw in some ringers from other parts of southwest France and therefore discovered our favorite, the Mas Jullien Coteaux du Languedoc. Although this wine is much plusher, it benefits from a little aging, too, to help the wine navigate the light spiciness of the beans, often a problem for dry, tannic wines. It's not uncommon for retailers to carry bottles of Mas Jullien with five or more years of age (as ours was), so look for them. For a more affordable and widely available choice, try one of southwest France's greatest values (and a fabulous cooking wine, too): Corbières. One favorite is Domaine de Fonsainte Corbières. For an American choice, try the Sean Thackrey "Pleiades," a deeply fascinating (and ever-changing) blend of all sorts of southern French varieties.

¼ cup extra-virgin olive oil

Kosher salt

3 to 3 ½ pounds bone-in blade (country-style) pork chops, cut into pieces (see page 116) about 3 inches long and 1 inch wide

1 ½ tablespoons powdered sugar

2 yellow onions, finely chopped

2 stalks celery, finely chopped

5 large cloves garlic, thinly sliced

2 cups full-bodied dry red wine

One 15-ounce can peeled whole tomatoes, drained and chopped

1 tablespoon sweet paprika

Scant ½ teaspoon ground cinnamon

⅛ teaspoon cayenne pepper

2 red bell peppers, seeded and cut into ½-inch dice

One 15-ounce can red kidney beans, drained

2 tablespoons finely chopped fresh flat-leaf parsley

1. In a heavy stockpot, heat the olive oil over medium-high heat. Working in two batches, generously salt the pork and sprinkle each batch with the powdered sugar. Cook until deeply browned on both sides, about 10 minutes, reducing the heat if it threatens to burn. Transfer to a plate and set aside.

2. Reduce the heat to medium and add the onions, celery, and garlic. Cook, stirring occasionally, until the onion is translucent, about 5 minutes.

3. Raise the heat to medium-high and add the wine. Bring to a boil, reduce the heat to medium, and simmer for 3 minutes, scraping the bottom of the pot to loosen any browned bits. Stir in the tomatoes, paprika, cinnamon, cayenne, and 1 teaspoon salt. Add the pork and any accumulated juices and bring just to a simmer. Cover and cook until tender, about 2 hours. Adjust the heat as needed to maintain a bare simmer.

4. Stir in the bell peppers and simmer gently, uncovered, for 15 minutes. Stir in the beans and simmer, uncovered, for 15 minutes longer. If you have time, let the stew rest for 30 minutes before serving. Reheat gently and serve, garnished with the parsley.

# Braised Pork Shank with Wine-Pickled Turnips

Stinco di Maiale con Brovada

**Serves 4**

Although there is no wine in this braise, the accompanying wine-pickled turnips are flavored with lots of it, and their sweet-and-sour dimensions provide a great contrast to the long-cooked pork shanks and mildly spiced braising liquid. The only difficult part in producing this dish is finding pork shanks, which in the United States are more commonly turned into smoked ham hocks (these would be excellent with the pickled turnips, too). You can substitute other cuts of pork (see Butcher's Note), but if you find shanks, they yield particularly rich-flavored results and, along with the turnips, a glimpse of a unique cuisine from Friuli-Venezia Giulia, a little-known corner of Italy. Serve these with grilled or pan-fried rectangles of polenta.

The turnip pickle, an old specialty of Friuli, is typically made with grape skins left over from the wine-making process and whole turnips, which require months of pickling before they are grated. Our quick version is made with turnips cut into matchsticks, and it has more of a sweet-sour character than some traditional turnip pickles. We find it's very easy to like.

**Butcher's Note:** We are the first to admit that it's hard to find pork shanks, but you can special order them from us at Lobels.com or from another high-end purveyor. Chances are you may have to order more shanks than necessary for this recipe, but they freeze well—and once you taste the braise, you might well want some shanks on hand for another go at it. If you buy them with a layer of skin or fat, they will be even tastier. The fat will render as the shanks braise and then be discarded, but enough of the flavor will remain.

Alternatively, there are a few other cuts that work well in this dish. For example, 3 pounds of bone-in pork picnic shoulder, cut near the shank, works well. Ask the butcher to cut it so that you get four smaller, shanklike pieces with lots of skin. (In fact, ask for extra skin, if possible, and include it in the braise. That way, you'll have enough braised skin to crisp under the broiler for a few minutes and serve with the meat.)

About 1¾ pounds of boneless pork shoulder also works well, although there won't be any skin. If you prefer a single

tied roast, follow the recipe and, when the meat is done, cut it into four pieces for serving. Or, cut the boneless shoulder into 1-inch cubes and brown them on at least two sides in olive oil (omit the large amount of vegetable oil required for the shanks and shoulder roast). When ready to serve, ladle the meat, vegetables, and reduced sauce over the pickled turnips. Finally, if you choose boneless pork shoulder, replace the water here with Pork Stock (page 212) or Chicken Stock (page 215) or broth for more intense flavor.

🔩

**Wine Note:** The Wine-Pickled Turnips were the ingredient we thought about when it came to selecting the wine for this dish. Though mellowed somewhat by their cooking with the pork broth, they are a tangy presence on the plate, and so the wine needed to be tangy itself, that is to say, filled with a vibrant acidity. Our top choice was the local red Refosco (from the grape by the same name) that is ready-made for strongly flavored dishes or dishes—like this one—that have one strongly flavored ingredient on the plate. In addition to its tangy profile, Refosco has a mouthwatering, red-fruited quality not unlike the wine-pickled turnips themselves. Our favorite was Ronchi di Manzoni Refosco. Almost as good (and far easier to find than Refosco) was Marco Felluga Merlot, a wine emblematic of the uniquely refined style of Merlot wines made in Friuli. If you haven't discovered them, you should. For a non-Italian choice, try a Malbec from Argentina. One favorite: Valentin Bianchi "Famigli Bianchi" Malbec from the Mendoza region.

---

*Kosher salt*

*Two 2- to 2 ½-pound pork shanks,
surrounded by a layer of fat or skin, if possible
(see Butcher's Note)*

*6 tablespoons vegetable oil*

*7 tablespoons Italian-Style Lard Paste (page 217)
or extra-virgin olive oil*

*1 yellow onion, chopped*

*1 carrot, peeled and chopped*

*1 stalk celery, chopped*

*6 large cloves garlic, 2 left whole, 4 minced*

*½ teaspoon ground coriander seed*

*¼ teaspoon freshly grated nutmeg*

*¼ teaspoon ground cinnamon*

*¼ teaspoon freshly ground black pepper*

*3 whole cloves*

*3 ½ cups water, plus more for the baking dish*

*Olive oil for drizzling*

*6 cups Wine-Pickled Turnips (page 123), drained,
½ cup of pickling liquid reserved*

---

1. Generously salt the shanks on all sides.

2. In an 8- to 10-quart flameproof casserole or Dutch oven with a tight-fitting lid, heat the vegetable oil over medium-high heat. When hot, cook the shanks until deeply golden brown all around their circumference, 6 to 8 minutes per side, or about 30 minutes total, reducing the heat if they threaten to burn. Transfer to a plate and set aside. Discard the oil in the pot and wipe out any blackened bits.

3. Preheat the oven to 350°F.

4. Return the pot to the stove top and heat 3 tablespoons of lard paste over medium-low heat. Add the onion, carrot, celery, and whole garlic cloves and cook, stirring occasionally, until the onion and garlic are pale gold at the edges, 8 to 10 minutes. Stir in the coriander, nutmeg, cinnamon, pepper, cloves, ½ teaspoon salt (omit the salt if using lard paste), and the water. Bring to a simmer, scraping the bottom of the pot to loosen any browned bits.

5. Return the shanks and any accumulated juices to the pot. Bring to a simmer, cover, transfer to the oven, and cook for 20 minutes. Reduce the oven temperature to 250°F and continue cooking, turning and basting the shanks once or twice, until the shanks are very tender and nearly falling off the bone, about 4 hours.

6. Transfer the shanks to a cutting board and let them stand just until cool enough to handle, no more than 5 minutes. Reserve the braising liquid.

7. With the end of one shank pointing toward you, carefully pull the meat away from the bone in 2 intact and equal-sized pieces, splitting it lengthwise and keeping the surface skin or fat as intact as possible. Discard the bones and reserve any other loose skin or fat. Repeat with second shank.

8. Place each rounded shank half (4 in all), rounded side up, on a small, lightly oiled baking dish. Lay any reserved pieces of skin or fat over the exposed flesh, if possible. Drizzle the meat with olive oil and add a few tablespoons of water to the dish. Cover tightly with aluminum foil and keep warm in the oven.

9. Skim some or all of the fat from the braising liquid and strain the liquid through a fine-mesh strainer into a bowl, pushing repeatedly on the vegetables until all of their liquid has been extracted. Return the liquid to the pot and cook over medium-high heat until reduced to 1½ cups, 10 to 12 minutes. The liquid should be very fluid but flavorful. Cook to reduce a little more, if necessary, and season with salt to taste. Remove from the heat, transfer to a small saucepan, and set aside.

10. Wipe out the pot and place over medium-low heat. Heat the remaining 4 tablespoons lard paste and add the minced garlic. Cook, stirring occasionally, until pale gold at the edges, 2 to 3 minutes.

11. Stir the Wine-Pickled Turnips and the reserved pickling liquid into the pot and mix thoroughly with the garlic. Raise the heat to medium and stir in ⅓ cup of the reduced braising liquid. Cook, stirring occasionally, until the braising liquid and pickling juices are completely reabsorbed by the turnips, 10 to 20 minutes. Add salt, if necessary. Set aside and keep warm.

12. When ready to serve, remove the reserved shank meat from the oven and preheat the broiler. When the broiler is hot, uncover the meat and brush it lightly with 1 or 2 tablespoons of the braising liquid.

13. Broil the meat until the fat or skin on top is crisp, basting with more braising liquid if necessary to prevent the meat from drying out if it's short on fat or skin, 2 to 4 minutes.

14. To serve, gently reheat the wine-pickled turnips and the remaining reduced braising liquid. Divide the turnips among warmed serving plates, placing them in a neat mound in the center. Top each mound with a piece of meat, surround each serving with the braising liquid, and serve.

**Make-Ahead Tip:** The dish can be prepared through step 7 up to 2 days ahead. After removing the meat from the shanks, immerse them in the braising liquid and refrigerate, with plastic wrap pressed against the shanks and also tightly covering the pot. Refrigerate the skin or fat, covered with plastic wrap, separately.

# Wine-Pickled Turnips

Brovada

**Makes 6 to 7 cups**

---

*2 ½ pounds seedless black or red grapes*

*2 tablespoons sugar*

*2 tablespoons kosher salt*

*One bottle (750 ml) dry red wine*

*2 cups good-quality red wine vinegar*

*3 pounds turnips, peeled and cut into very thin matchsticks, 2 to 3 inches long*

---

1. In the bowl of a food processor, process the grapes until chopped into small but still distinct pieces suspended in their liquid. (Do not purée.) Set aside.

2. In a large mixing bowl, dissolve the sugar and salt in 1 cup of the wine. Stir in the remaining wine and the vinegar. Add the turnips and the chopped grapes and mix thoroughly.

3. Cover and refrigerate for at least 2 days. This keeps well for at least 3 months. (Excess liquid is usually drained before use in recipes.)

-Chapter 6-

# LAMB

# Roman-Style Lamb Chops with Artichokes

Braciolini di Agnello con Carciofi

**Serves 2**

The Romans' love for artichokes is reflected in the low-key genius of their preparations. For example, artichokes are stuffed and baked with olive oil, garlic, mint, and bread crumbs for *carciofi alla Romana*; they're spread open like a flower, deep-fried, and sprinkled with salt for *carciofi alla Giudia.* In this dish, small wedges of artichoke are braised in water, wine, herbs, and aromatic vegetables, and the resulting artichoke stew is poured over tender little rib lamb chops that have been seared in a separate pan. Because artichokes are able to yield a tasty braising liquid in a relatively short time—a feat rare among vegetables—when this liquid is slightly reduced, it's all the sauce that's needed. Once the artichokes are cleaned, the whole process takes about thirty minutes. You can substitute 2 tablespoons of olive oil for the ham fat, but we hope that you don't; it adds an ineffable "Italianness" that helps make the dish special.

**Butcher's Note:** For the ham fat, ask at the butcher's or a good deli for a few pieces of rind from a cured ham. They have to do this before slicing the hams anyway, so they will probably happily oblige. These pieces have a layer of delicious fat still attached to them, which is easily detachable from the rind with a knife. Another source is the butt ends of the hams, which are often sold cheaply when the deli can no longer slice from them. Remove the fat for use in this recipe and finely chop the rest of the ham for use in salads and pastas, or toss a chunk into a simmering soup or stew for a big flavor boost.

**Wine Note:** Artichokes raise a red flag for many wine drinkers because an acid unique to them, cynarin, stimulates the sweetness receptors in the mouth. The result is that everything tastes sweeter. We have made some observations, though, that alleviate worries about the "artichoke problem" with wine. First, this phenomenon has more impact on some mouths than others. Second, the effect is quite temporary (it lasts seconds, not minutes). Third, certain kinds of dishes seem to mitigate the impression of sweetness (we think this dish is one of them). And fourth, wines with the food-friendly qualities of balance, good acidity, and reasonable alcohol levels can happily bring those virtues to a pairing with artichokes.

Balanced, untannic red wines that have definite but not forceful characteristics work well with this dish. There's little red wine imported from around Rome and the larger region of Lazio that surrounds it, so we turned instead to neighboring regions to find wines that pleased us with the dish. For red, the medium weight and smoky fruit flavors of young, vibrant high-quality Chianti work beautifully. The wine enhances both the lamb and the artichokes, and it in turn is enhanced by each. What you want is young Chianti, from an excellent producer (save the fancier Riserva bottlings and super-Tuscans for a simple roast). Not always cheap but rarely expensive, they are widely available. One standout in our tasting was the Selvapiana Chianti Rufina. For white, look to a wine that some lamb lovers prefer over any red: Sauvignon Blanc. There's very little Sauvignon Blanc grown in central Italy, so we looked north to Friuli for our favorite, the Venica Sauvignon Blanc. Neither light nor heavy, good examples have a delectable savor that repeatedly presses its electric fruit into your taste buds. When combined with its unique taste—a citric herbaceousness—Sauvignon Blanc acts like a lively seasoning for the mildly gamy flavor of lamb. These qualities also leave it undaunted in the face of an artichoke. The artichoke, however, is improved by the encounter,

proof positive that artichokes and wine don't have to be enemies. For a red wine from outside Italy, try a light and zippy Pinot Noir like the Saint Clair "Vicar's Choice" Pinot Noir from Marlborough, New Zealand. For a white, look for the great food-friendly Kiwi: Sauvignon Blanc. One favorite hails from the Voss winery across the straits in neighboring Martinborough.

---

*4 tablespoons extra-virgin olive oil,
plus more for drizzling*

*1 ounce fat from a dry cured ham such as
prosciutto di Parma, very finely chopped
(see Butcher's Note)*

*1 yellow onion, finely chopped*

*1 large clove garlic, peeled and minced*

*⅔ cup dry white wine*

*1 cup water*

*1 tablespoon tomato paste*

*2 teaspoons finely chopped fresh marjoram*

*Finely grated zest of ½ lemon*

*Kosher salt and freshly ground black pepper*

*8 baby artichokes or 3 large artichokes,
cleaned (see facing page) and cut into wedges
¾ inch thick at their widest point*

*One 8-rib rack of lamb (1¼ to 1½ pounds),
trimmed of excess fat and cut evenly
into 8 thin chops*

---

1. In a large nonstick skillet, heat 1 tablespoon of the olive oil and the ham fat over medium-low and cook until the fat renders and the bits of meat turn golden, 3 to 5 minutes.

2. Raise the heat to medium, add the onion and garlic, and cook, stirring occasionally, until the onion begins to brown around the edges, about 10 minutes. Stir in the wine and cook at a simmer until reduced by half, about 10 minutes.

3. In a small bowl, whisk together the water and tomato paste. Add to the skillet with 1 teaspoon of the marjoram, the lemon zest, 1 teaspoon salt, and a few grindings of pepper and bring to a simmer.

4. Stir in the artichokes, return to a simmer, cover, and cook, stirring occasionally, until just tender when pierced with the tip of a knife, 15 to 20 minutes. When tender, a small amount of liquid should still surround the artichokes. Add a little more water, if necessary, and/or reduce slightly to concentrate the flavors. Taste and adjust the seasonings.

5. Remove the skillet from the heat and cover to keep warm while you finish the dish.

6. Salt the chops evenly on all sides. In another large skillet or two smaller ones (you need enough room to cook the chops in a single layer), heat the remaining 3 tablespoons olive oil over medium high-heat until it shimmers and slides easily in the pan. Cook the chops until nicely golden brown on both sides, about 3 minutes per side for medium-rare.

7. Divide the chops attractively between 2 plates and pour the artichoke mixture over and around the chops. Drizzle with more olive oil, sprinkle with the remaining 1 teaspoon marjoram, and serve.

**Make-Ahead Tip:** The artichokes can be cooked up to 3 hours in advance and kept at room temperature.

## HOW TO CLEAN ARTICHOKES

Both small and large artichokes are cleaned in much the same way, with the tough parts of the leaves, any thorny tips, and the hairy choke removed. Baby artichokes, which can be the size of a walnut and don't have fuzzy chokes, are completely edible.

To trim a large artichoke, pull off the tough outer leaves to expose the pale green leaves beneath. Trim off any tough or browned stem and, using a vegetable peeler or paring knife, remove the dark green layer of the peel surrounding the stem and the underside of the artichoke bottom. Peel any traces of dark green that remain, mostly where the leaves previously met the bottom. Using kitchen shears or a serrated knife, slice off the tops of the leaves to remove the thorny tips. Submerge the trimmed artichokes in a bowl of acidulated water, which is simply plain water mixed with the juice of 1 or 2 lemons to prevent browning. (Once they are trimmed, the artichokes can be held in the water for up to 2 days. Drain and pat dry before using.)

To trim a small artichoke, slice off the tops of the leaves, about ½ to ¾ inch from the tips. Submerge in acidulated water.

To finish cleaning the trimmed artichokes, quarter them and cut or scrape out the hairy choke, any purple spiky leaves, and any remaining dark green bits. As you work with artichokes, it's a good idea to dip them occasionally in the acidulated water to prevent browning. Use the artichoke as instructed in the recipe.

# Rioja-Style Grilled Lamb Chops

### Chuletillas de Cordero Asadas

**Serves 4**

This terrific informal dish, in which good lamb chops cut from the rib, or rack, and marinated in red wine are grilled over a hot fire, is from the wine country in Rioja, Spain. A wood fire will produce the most amazing results, but charcoal or gas will suffice. It's common practice in many of the world's wine regions to add vine cuttings to the fire for the special savor they impart to grilled meat, so seek them out if they're available where you live. The chops can also be cooked in a grill pan on the stove top or in a heavy skillet; use a couple of skillets or work in batches so they cook without crowding.

**Wine Note:** In the Rioja, as in many other Old World wine regions, the friction between tradition, technology, and the demands of the international marketplace result in the creation of wines in a wide range of styles, some more modern and some proudly traditional (see page 87 for more information). Happily, these lamb chops are not too finicky about their partners, and so both bolder, more modern-style wines as well as those with the delicate and mature tastes of traditional red Rioja are at home here. One favorite among "new-school" wines is Herencia Remondo "La Montesa" Crianza from Bodegas Palacios Remondo; for an old-school favorite, try R. López de Heredia Viña Bosconia Reserva. From beyond Rioja, look for the distinctive wines of Uruguay. The country's long-established wine industry has made a specialty of wines made from the Tannat grape, first planted by Basque settlers in the nineteenth century. Here, the variety yields briskly flavored, medium- to-full-bodied wines that are especially good with food—the sort of wine we could use more of. One favorite: Bodegas Carrau Tannat de Reserva.

---

*1⅓ cups dry red wine*

*6 tablespoons olive oil*

*6 large garlic cloves, minced*

*2 teaspoons finely chopped fresh thyme*

*Two 8-rib racks of lamb (1¼ to 1½ pounds each), trimmed and cut evenly into 16 chops*

*Kosher salt*

*15 to 20 dried vine cuttings, cut to fit inside your grill (optional)*

---

1. In a small saucepan, bring the wine to a simmer over medium-high heat. Reduce the heat and simmer gently until reduced to 1 cup, 3 to 4 minutes. Whisk in the olive oil, garlic, and thyme and set aside to cool to room temperature.

2. Put the lamb chops in an even layer in a nonreactive baking dish and pour the marinade over them. Turn to coat, cover, and let stand at room temperature for 2 hours, turning the chops once or twice.

3. Prepare a fire in a charcoal or wood grill or preheat a gas grill to medium-high. Lightly oil and preheat the grate.

4. Lift the chops from the marinade, blot dry with paper towels, and salt generously on both sides.

5. Spread the coals out evenly and lay the vine cuttings on top, if using. Grill the lamb chops to the desired doneness, 2½ to 3 minutes per side for medium-rare. Transfer the chops to a platter and serve.

# Pan-Fried Lamb Chops with Garlic Cream and Wild Mushrooms

Côtelettes d'Agneau Bordelais

**Serves 2**

This dish from Bordeaux incorporates four of the region's favorite ingredients: lamb, garlic, wild mushrooms, and wine. This is traditionally made with a rack of lamb, which would make it perhaps more elegant but certainly no more tasty than the loin chops we suggest here. The two-chop serving size makes this a light main course. If you are hungrier, up the number of chops to six, for three per diner; there is enough sauce in the recipe as is. (Or use six to eight rib lamb chops—just be sure to reduce the cooking time somewhat, as they are thinner.) Although we call for the more easily obtainable dried mushrooms here, if you can get fresh porcini (cèpes), we urge you to try them. You will want to add a little more butter when sautéing fresh mushrooms.

**Wine Note:** The dish is as good with white Bordeaux as it is with red. For white, look for the wines of Graves and Pessac-Leognan, local favorites known around the world. For a crisper white Bordeaux, try Château Graville-Lacoste and, for a richer wine, the widely available Château La Louvière. For the reds, stay with medium-bodied, Merlot-inflected wines such as the simple but lovely wine from Château Lacroix de Bellevue in the *appellation* Lalande-de-Pomerol that stood out at our tasting. Any number of similar wines from the Fronsac, Canon-Fronsac as well as medium-weight Pomerol and St. Emilion wines, would be equally fine. Let your merchant be your guide. From beyond Bordeaux, pour a Washington State Merlot. We especially like the Canoe Ridge Winery Merlot from the Columbia Valley.

*¾ ounce dried porcini mushrooms (cèpes),*
*or ⅓ pound fresh porcini, sliced*

*3 tablespoons unsalted butter*

*1½ tablespoons finely chopped shallot*

*⅓ cup dry white wine*

*1 sprig fresh thyme*

*Kosher salt*

*8 ounces (generous ⅔ cup) crème fraîche*

*12 large cloves garlic of about the same size,*
*peeled but left whole*

*Four 4-ounce loin lamb chops,*
*each cut about 1 inch thick*

*2 tablespoons vegetable oil*

*1 tablespoon finely chopped fresh flat-leaf parsley*

1. Rinse the dried mushrooms in two changes of water, draining each time. Place the mushrooms in a small bowl with just enough warm water to cover and let soak until softened, about 30 minutes. Lift the mushrooms from the bowl and squeeze gently to remove some of the moisture. Strain the soaking liquid through a fine-mesh sieve. Reserve ¼ cup of the soaking liquid and set the mushrooms aside.

2. In a small saucepan, melt 1½ tablespoons of the butter over medium-low heat and cook the shallot until softened, about 4 minutes.

3. Add the wine, thyme, and a generous ¼ teaspoon salt. Raise the heat to medium; simmer until the liquid is reduced to 2 tablespoons. Stir in the crème fraîche and all but 1 clove of the garlic. Return to a bare simmer and cook, stirring occasionally, until the garlic is completely tender, 30 to 40 minutes.

4. Transfer the garlic mixture to a blender and purée until very smooth, about 1 minute. Return the garlic cream to the saucepan. It should be thick enough to coat the back of a wooden spoon but still pour easily. If still a little thin, simmer briefly to thicken. Set aside, covered to keep warm.

5. In a small skillet, melt the remaining 1½ tablespoons butter over medium-high heat. Crush the remaining clove of garlic and add it to the skillet. Add the mushrooms and sauté, stirring constantly, until golden at the edges, 3 to 4 minutes. Reduce the heat if they threaten to burn. Stir in the reserved soaking liquid and salt lightly. Let the liquid nearly evaporate. Transfer to a small bowl, cover, and keep warm.

6. Salt the chops generously on both sides. Wipe out the skillet and heat over medium-high heat. Add the oil and when hot, cook the chops until nicely browned on both sides, 3 to 3½ minutes per side for medium-rare.

7. Put 2 chops in the center of each of 2 plates. Reheat the garlic cream if necessary and spoon it around the chops. Scatter the mushrooms over and around the chops. Sprinkle with the parsley and serve.

**Make-Ahead Tip:** You can make the garlic cream up to 8 hours ahead. Cover and refrigerate until ready to use.

# Marinated Greek-Style Lamb Kabobs

Arni Souvlaki

**Serves 4**

This straightforward recipe for kabobs is easy, simple, and appealing to everyone who likes grilled lamb—and who doesn't? What earns it the Greek designation is the simple oregano-kissed marinade

and the lemony sauce. When you prepare kabobs, cut the food to the same size, or as close as possible, so that every piece makes contact with the hot grill. If you have to choose, cut the vegetables a little smaller than the lamb to ensure that the meat hits the grill—otherwise it might steam instead of grilling. Serve over white rice or orzo, with a salad alongside.

**Wine Note:** Among Americans, Greek wine has mostly been experienced in one way: accompanied by a view of the azure Mediterranean beneath the warmth of the Greek sun. Given those circumstances, even the dullest local wines can taste like nectar. This helped to support a recent tradition of mediocre wine making in a country with thousands of years of experience. It's no surprise that many of these wines, although at times pleasant enough, are unrewarding to drink Stateside. And so Greek wine has been without too many boosters here—until now.

The changes in recent years, while not yet widespread, have taken deepest root in some of Greece's most important wine zones, where distinctive soils and indigenous grape varieties form the raw material of a small revolution. To glimpse what's going on, look for the bottle of red that flattered our lamb kabobs: Gaia Estate's "Nótios," a suave and succulent, red-fruited wine made from the Agiorgitiko (St. George) grape from the Nemea wine zone in the eastern Peloponnese. A brief six-week stay in new French oak barrels refines and softens the wine without sacrificing its juicy appeal and food friendliness. From outside of Greece, try alongside a not-too-tannic Cabernet like the Laurel Glen "Counterpoint" Cabernet Sauvignon from Sonoma.

### Marinade

*4 large cloves garlic, finely chopped*

*2 teaspoons dried oregano, preferably Greek*

*2 bay leaves, broken into pieces*

*3 tablespoons dry white wine*

*2 tablespoons extra-virgin olive oil,
plus more as needed*

*1½ tablespoons good-quality white wine vinegar*

*Kosher salt*

*2 to 2¼ pounds boneless leg of lamb,
trimmed and cut into 20 cubes about 1¼ inch
square (about 1½ pounds after trimming)*

### Lemon sauce

*1 cup Chicken Stock (page 215)
or canned low-sodium chicken broth*

*⅓ cup extra-virgin olive oil*

*2 tablespoons fresh lemon juice*

*⅛ teaspoon kosher salt*

*Six 8- to 10-inch metal or wooden skewers,
wooden skewers soaked in cool water
for 30 minutes*

*½ large red onion, cut into wedges, each about
⅔ inch wide at the widest point*

*1 slender zucchini, cut into 16 rounds,
each about ⅜ inch thick*

*1 red bell pepper, cored, seeded and cut into
sixteen 1¼-inch squares*

*Olive oil for basting*

*Kosher salt*

1. To make the marinade, in a large, shallow bowl, mix together the garlic, oregano, bay leaves, wine, olive oil, and vinegar and season to taste with salt. Stir to dissolve the salt. Add the lamb cubes and toss until well coated. Cover and let stand at room temperature for

2 hours, or refrigerate for up to 6 hours. Toss the meat once or twice during marinating.

2. To make the sauce, in a small saucepan, stir together the chicken stock, olive oil, lemon juice, and salt and bring to a boil over high heat. Reduce the heat to medium and simmer briskly until reduced by half, 6 to 8 minutes. Set aside.

3. Remove the lamb from the marinade and pat dry with paper towels. If the meat has been refrigerated, let it come to room temperature. Assemble 6 skewers, 4 that alternate lamb and vegetables and 1 or 2 more to hold the remaining vegetables: For the first, thread the meat on the skewers beginning with a cube of lamb followed by 2 nested layers of onion, another cube of lamb, 2 rounds of zucchini, another cube of lamb, 2 squares of red pepper, another cube of lamb, and 2 more nested layers of onion. Finish with a cube of lamb. Repeat with 3 more skewers. Alternate the remaining vegetable pieces on the remaining skewers and brush lightly with olive oil. Set the assembled skewers aside.

4. Prepare a fire in a charcoal or wood grill or preheat a gas grill to medium-high. Lightly oil and preheat the grate.

5. Salt the lamb kabobs lightly and the vegetable kabobs more generously. Grill to the desired doneness, turning the kabobs to expose all four sides to the heat, 12 to 14 minutes for medium-rare. Remove the all-vegetable kabobs sooner if they threaten to burn.

6. Meanwhile, reheat the lemon sauce over medium-low heat, whisking to smooth.

7. To serve, transfer the lamb kabobs to warmed serving plates. Transfer the all-vegetable kabobs to a bowl. Spoon the lemon sauce over the top of each kabob. Serve immediately, passing the vegetables at the table.

# Rack of Lamb with Eggplant Compote

Carré de Agneau à l'Aubergine

**Serves 2**

This simple, stylish recipe originated in the Languedoc region in southwest France and calls for an eight-rib rack of lamb. Cooking the rack whole and cutting it into chops afterward results in moister, more evenly pink meat. The compote is very much like a French version of baba ganoujh, the beloved Middle Eastern purée made with eggplant, lemon juice, tahini, olive oil, and garlic. This one uses no tahini but lots of garlic and vegetables instead. The compote is best made fresh, but you may prepare it a few hours ahead.

———

**Butcher's Note:** When you buy a rack of lamb, purchase one with eight or nine ribs. Racks are available with ten ribs, but the last rib is from the shoulder and is not as tender as the others. Look at the back of the rack; the bones should have visible streaks of red running through them, which indicates the youth of the animal. Any fat should be creamy white and the meat should be pink with light flecks of graining (fat).

When a recipe calls for the rack of lamb to be frenched, some or all of the meat and fat covering the rib bones is stripped away, leaving the "eye" of the meat with the naked bones extending from it (in fancy restaurants, this is where the paper frills are used). While a frenched rack of lamb is considered the most elegant way to present this cut, it's not a universal favorite; for many, the crispy bits nestled along the rib bones are as good as the eye itself. Whether you decide for elegance or a little more meat on the bones, make sure the butcher removes the chine bone for easy cutting between the chops. See page 186 for tips on properly browning entire racks of ribs.

**Wine Note:** The Languedoc, the vast and often rugged region that stretches from Provence to within thirty miles of the Spanish border, is, as far as wines are concerned, an area about which it is difficult to generalize, save this: Nearly all of the *appellations* contained within it will reward the adventurous wine lover. Corbières, Minervois, Fitou, St. Chinian, Faugères, Coteaux du Languedoc, Costières du Nîmes, and others are each chock-full of rewarding wines. In our tasting we focused on red wines, and it turned out, nearly all were good with the lamb and eggplant. Our favorite was the Château Saint Martin de la Garrigue "Bronzinelle," Coteaux du Languedoc, which walked a nice line between richness and refinement. To make your own selection, just take our little Languedoc shopping list (above) to a good wine merchant, and let them lead you through France's exotic "back door." Beyond France, look to Australia, whose vinters have made a specialty by blending Syrah with Cabernet Sauvignon, bottling wines that often have a suggestion of southern France within them. One favorite: Penfolds "Bin 389" Cabernet/Shiraz.

---

*¾ cup extra-virgin olive oil*

*10 large cloves garlic, 6 minced, 4 lightly crushed*

*2 tablespoons chopped fresh thyme*

*Freshly ground black pepper*

*One 8-rib rack of lamb (1¼ to 1½ pounds), trimmed of excess fat*

*2 large eggplants*

*Kosher salt*

*2 yellow onions, peeled and chopped*

*½ red bell pepper, seeded and cut into ⅜-inch dice*

*½ green bell pepper, seeded and cut into ⅜-inch dice*

*1 carrot, peeled and cut into ⅜-inch rounds*

*⅔ cup dry white wine*

*⅓ cup homemade Lamb Stock (page 214), Veal Stock (page 213), Chicken Stock (page 215), or canned low-sodium chicken broth*

---

1. Preheat the oven to 375°F.

2. In a small bowl, stir together ¼ cup of the olive oil, half of the minced garlic, 1 tablespoon of the thyme, and a few generous grindings of pepper.

3. Using a very sharp knife, score the fat covering the rib side of the lamb in a crosshatch pattern at about ½-inch intervals. Try not to cut into the flesh. Rub the oil-garlic mixture all over the lamb and into the slits. Let stand for 2 hours at room temperature, turning occasionally, or for up to 8 hours in the refrigerator.

4. Slice the eggplants in half lengthwise. Rub the cut surfaces with ¼ cup of the olive oil and sprinkle generously with salt. Place, cut side up, on a baking sheet lined with aluminum foil. Roast until tender and golden, 30 to 40 minutes. Remove from the oven and, when cool enough to handle, scrape the flesh from the skins with a large spoon. Discard the skins and briefly drain the flesh in a strainer to remove any excess water. Set aside.

5. Raise the oven temperature to 425°F.

6. Meanwhile, in a large skillet, heat the remaining ¼ cup olive oil over medium-high heat until almost smoking. Add the half of the onions, the bell peppers, and the remaining minced garlic. Cook, stirring constantly, until the edges of the vegetables begin to color, 3 to 5 minutes. Reduce the heat to medium-low and stir in the remaining 1 tablespoon thyme and 1 teaspoon salt. Cook, stirring occasionally, until the peppers are very tender but still brightly colored, 10 to 12 minutes

longer. Thoroughly stir in the reserved eggplant to the pan and cook for 2 to 3 minutes longer. Add salt to taste and set the skillet aside.

7. Using your fingers, scrape the bits of garlic from the rack of lamb and salt the lamb generously on all sides.

8. Strain the oil from the marinade into a large ovenproof skillet and heat over medium-high heat until almost smoking. Cook the lamb until nicely browned on all sides, reducing the heat if it threatens to burn, about 8 minutes. Transfer to a plate and set aside.

9. Add the remaining onions, the crushed garlic, and the carrot. Remove the skillet from the heat and toss well.

10. Push the vegetables into the center of the skillet to make a thick layer. Rest the rack of lamb, fat side up, on top. Gently pour the wine, stock, and any accumulated juices from the plate holding the lamb into the skillet and season with a pinch of salt. Roast the lamb to the desired doneness, 10 to 14 minutes for medium-rare, or when an instant-read thermometer registers 125°F to 130°F.

11. Transfer the lamb to a cutting board to rest for 5 minutes. Taste the liquid in the skillet; it should be thin but flavorful. If not, reduce it over medium heat for 1 or 2 minutes to concentrate the flavors, adding salt to taste if necessary.

12. Gently reheat the eggplant mixture and put about 1 cup in the center of each of 2 serving plates. Cut the lamb between the ribs into thin chops and prop them attractively against the eggplant. Stir in any lamb juices on the cutting board into the wine-vegetable sauce and divide the sauce between the plates. Serve immediately.

# Stuffed Lamb Rolls from Abruzzo

Braciole di Agnello all'Atessana

**Serves 4**

Even those who claim they don't especially like lamb will no doubt love these little bundles first created in Abruzzo, Italy. They are filled with a flavorful stuffing and smothered in a white wine and tomato sauce for a hearty, satisfying dish.

**Butcher's Note:** When we flatten boned meat cutlets or chicken breasts, we put them between two pieces of wax paper, plastic wrap, or in a plastic bag on a work surface. (We prefer a butcher's block, of course, but you may not have one in your home kitchen! A countertop is fine.) Use the bottom of a heavy frying pan, the flat side of a meat mallet or cleaver, or a rolling pin to flatten the meat. Begin with very light taps and increase the pressure just slightly as the meat thins out. Never pound too forcefully or you will break down the connective tissues and the meat will lose some of its texture. Gently pound the meat to form a shape that resembles a rectangle, or as close as you can. If there are holes in the rectangles, patch them with pounded scraps that are a little larger than the tear. Pound these into place.

**Wine Note:** Tomato sauces often cause trouble for fairly full-bodied red wines that are short on good levels of acidity, and so when it turns out that the soft and warmly flavored Montepulciano d'Abruzzo reds take so well to it, you wonder why. But beneath the generous and dark-fruited surface of these wines, there's a firmness, a kind of "silent" acidity that gives them the backbone to handle pesky tomato sauces and much more. A favorite in our tasting comes from one of the

region's best producers of Montepulciano d'Abruzzo, Cataldi Madonna, but any number of these widely available wines would be excellent. For a Montepulciano with an unusual provenance, look for Bonny Doon Vineyards' Il Circo: Montepulciano "Il Domatore di Leoni"—Italian grapes in a Santa Cruz, California, cloak.

---

*2 tablespoons olive oil*

*4 ounces thinly sliced pancetta or bacon,
cut into 1-inch pieces*

*4 large cloves garlic, minced*

*3 hard-cooked eggs, finely chopped*

*3 ounces Pecorino Romano cheese, finely grated*

*8 tablespoons finely chopped fresh flat-leaf parsley*

*6 tablespoons fresh bread crumbs, preferably
homemade (see page 42)*

*Kosher salt and freshly ground black pepper*

*3 pounds boneless leg of lamb,
trimmed of excess fat*

*1 yellow onion, chopped*

*2 tablespoons tomato paste*

*¾ cup dry white wine*

*1 cup Lamb Stock (page 214) or water*

*One 28-ounce can peeled whole tomatoes,
drained and chopped*

*Generous pinch of crushed red pepper flakes*

---

1. In a sauté pan, heat the olive oil and cook the pancetta over medium-low heat until crisp, tuning once. Lift the pancetta from the pan and drain. Leave the fat in the pan. Chop the pancetta very finely and set aside.

2. In a bowl, combine half the garlic, the eggs, cheese, 6 tablespoons of the parsley, the bread crumbs, ½ teaspoon salt, abundant pepper, and the pancetta. Stir the stuffing well.

3. Cut the lamb into 8 equal meaty pieces (avoid areas with lots of tough connective tissue and reserve this abundant scrap for lamb stock). Cover each piece with plastic wrap and, using a meat mallet or the bottom of a small, heavy skillet, pound the lamb into rectangles about ¼ inch thick (see Butcher's Note). Lay a piece of lamb, with a short side facing you, on a work surface and spread 3 heaping tablespoons of stuffing on the lamb, distributing it evenly up to ½ inch from the three nearest edges and 1 inch from the far edge. Lightly pat the filling into place. Carefully roll the lamb away from you into a roll. Repeat with the remaining lamb and stuffing. Tie the rolls by wrapping butcher's twine around them 2 or 3 times and set aside.

4. Salt the lamb rolls. Heat the reserved skillet over medium-high heat and, working in batches, brown the rolls on all sides, about 10 minutes per batch. Add a little more oil to the pan if needed. Transfer to a plate and set aside. If the stuffing leaks slightly and begins to burn, scrape the skillet and remove the browned bits.

5. Reduce the heat to medium-low and cook the onion, stirring occasionally, until pale gold at the edges, about 8 minutes. Add the remaining garlic and cook for 1 minute. Add the tomato paste and cook for 1 minute more, stirring. Add the wine and simmer for 3 minutes, scraping the bottom of the skillet to loosen any browned bits. Add the stock, tomatoes, red pepper flakes, and ½ teaspoon salt and bring to a simmer.

6. Add the lamb rolls and any accumulated juices to the skillet and reduce the heat to low. Cover and cook at a bare simmer until tender, turning the rolls and basting them every so often, about 1½ hours.

7. Remove the lamb rolls and set aside. Raise the heat to high and cook the sauce at a rapid simmer until concentrated but still pourable, about 5 minutes.

8. Meanwhile, snip and remove the twine from the rolls. Divide the lamb among serving plates and smother with the sauce. Sprinkle with the remaining 2 tablespoons parsley and serve.

**Make-Ahead Tip:** The lamb rolls can be assembled up to 8 hours in advance and refrigerated until ready to cook.

# White Bean and Lamb Casserole with Garlic

La Pistache de Agneau de Saint Gaudens

**Serves 4 to 6**

Although the French word *pistache* commonly refers to the pistachio nut, the word is also slang for drunkenness; by extension, in southwestern France, it refers to dishes in which the meat is prepared with a good dose of wine. It also refers to dishes that are eaten with a good bottle or two of wine. In the town of Saint Gaudens, in Gascony, the *pistache* resembles a quick and easy lamb cassoulet. Serve this with a bitter green salad of frisée, arugula, or watercress topped with Roquefort cheese and toasted walnuts.

**Butcher's Note:** We recommend lamb shoulder for braises and stews. It has more graining (which is what we call marbling in lamb and refers to the amount of thin streaks of fat running through the meat) and therefore is more moist and flavorful than leg meat. Lamb shoulder is easy to find in supermarkets, usually sold in the form of chops.

Any lamb chop labeled "bone-in lamb shoulder chop," "blade chop," "flat-bone chop," or "round-bone chop" works for recipes that call for shoulder meat. Round-bone chops are easier to cut into chunks than blade chops. If you buy blade chops, ask the butcher to separate the meat from the bones; it's tricky. If the recipe says that a little bone should be left on the meat, these chops work well, too. The bone just adds to the flavor, and so if you really can't find meat with bone, make the dish anyhow.

**Wine Note:** Côtes de Gascogne is a broad *appellation* whose name appears on many of the direct and simple white wines of the region. It can be made from a handful of local varieties whose most important function is their role in the production of the richly flavorful brandies of Armagnac. The wines made from these grapes are nothing like the rich and flavorful brandy, but the best of them are fresh and easygoing and serve as great all-purpose whites. They're also inexpensive. One favorite made from the local Ugni Blanc grape is Alain Lalanne Côtes de Gascogne. It ain't fancy, but it goes nicely with the casserole. This dish comes alive with reds, and our favorite lamb casserole mates came from outside of Gascony—not too far outside—from the appellation of Corbières. Though hardly refined wines, what makes these delicious, affordable, and so great at the table (and in a stew pot) is that many deliver a succulent fruit flavor and generous texture unencumbered by tannins. The favorite in our red wine and lamb casserole tasting, which showed this character in spades, was the Domaine Faillenc Sainte Marie Corbières. Whatever your choice, stick with juicy, full-flavored reds, free from excess tannin and aging in new oak barrels; they taste out of place here. Something from California? Try one of the state's longest-running values: Marietta Cellars "Old Vine Red," a proprietary blend from a Sonoma-based producer that, as much as any wine made in America, is exemplary of the kind of affordable, delicious, distinctive, food-friendly, and fuss-free wine that we could use more of.

*1 pound dried white beans such as cannellini,*
*picked over and rinsed*

*7½ cups water*

*2 cloves*

*3 yellow onions, 1 peeled and halved with*
*root end intact, 2 finely chopped*

*20 large cloves garlic, 5 left whole, 15 minced*
*(about 7 tablespoons)*

*1 small carrot, peeled and halved*

*1 stalk celery, halved*

*1 large sprig fresh thyme, plus 1 tablespoon*
*finely chopped fresh thyme*

*1 bay leaf*

*3 ounces fatty salt pork, with skin attached,*
*cut into 3 equal pieces*

*Kosher salt*

*8 tablespoons extra-virgin olive oil*

*1½ pounds boneless lamb shoulder,*
*cut into 1-inch cubes*

*1 cup dry white wine*

*One 15-ounce can peeled whole tomatoes,*
*drained and chopped*

*2 tablespoons finely chopped fresh flat-leaf parsley*

*Freshly ground black pepper*

*⅔ cup plain dried bread crumbs, preferably*
*homemade (see Note, page 42)*

1. In a large pot, combine the beans with enough cold water to cover by about 1 inch. Bring to a boil, remove from the heat, and let stand for 15 minutes, stirring occasionally. Drain and return to the pot.

2. Add the 7½ cups water to the pot. Stick 1 clove into each onion half and add to the pot. Add the whole garlic cloves, the carrot, celery, thyme sprig, bay leaf, and salt pork. Bring just to a boil over high heat. Reduce the heat and cook at a bare simmer, stirring occasionally, or until the beans are just tender but still whole, about 1 hour. (The time varies depending on the type and age of the beans.) Taste to make sure they are properly salted.

3. When the beans are nearly done, stir in 1 to 2 tablespoons of salt, making sure it is well mixed (if you add the salt earlier, the beans will toughen). When tender, remove from the heat and let the beans rest for at least 15 minutes.

4. Drain the beans in a colander set over a large bowl and reserve both the beans and the cooking liquid. Pick out the salt pork, bay leaf, thyme sprig, and most of the vegetable pieces and discard.

5. Wipe out the pot and heat 4 tablespoons of the olive oil over medium-high heat. Working in two batches, cook the lamb until deeply browned on at least two sides, about 4 minutes per side, reducing the heat if it threatens to burn. Sprinkle each side with salt as you cook. As each batch finishes browning, transfer to a plate.

6. Reduce the heat to medium-low and stir in the chopped onions and minced garlic. Cook gently, until the onion is pale gold at the edges, about 10 minutes. Add the wine and simmer for 3 minutes, scraping the bottom of the pot to loosen any browned bits. Add the tomatoes, chopped thyme, parsley, 3 cups of the reserved bean cooking liquid, and a few generous grindings of pepper. (If you have less than 3 cups of bean liquid, add water or chicken broth as needed.) Bring just to a simmer.

7. Meanwhile, preheat the oven to 350°F and position the oven rack in the middle. Grease an 8-by-12-inch earthenware or glass baking dish with 1 tablespoon of the remaining olive oil.

8. Spread half of the beans in the baking dish and distribute the lamb on top of the beans. Top with the remaining beans and set aside.

9. When the bean liquid comes to a simmer, pour it evenly over the lamb and beans. Sprinkle the bread crumbs over the entire surface and drizzle with the remaining 3 tablespoons olive oil.

10. Bake for 30 minutes. Reduce the oven temperature to 325°F and continue baking until the lamb is tender and the thickened liquid has evaporated about three-fourths of the way to the bottom of the baking dish, about 1½ hours longer. Adjust the oven temperature as needed to maintain a bare simmer. In spite of the level of evaporation in the baking dish, it will often appear that the liquid is still bubbling at the surface of the beans, so if you're unsure just how much liquid remains, peek down into the baking dish toward the end of cooking.

11. Preheat the broiler and slip the casserole briefly under it to brown and crisp. Let rest for 15 minutes, then serve, spooning the liquid at the bottom of the baking dish around each portion.

# Apulian-Style Lamb and Artichoke Casserole

### Fricassea di Agnello e Carciofi al Forno

**Serves 4**

To get an idea of what this dish is like, imagine an artichoke and lamb lasagna without the pasta, a dish for which we can thank the creative cooks of Apulia, in Italy's heel. Both the lamb and artichoke mixtures can be made, combined, and assembled in the baking dish up to 4 hours ahead and reserved at room temperature, or made ahead and refrigerated overnight. Bring to room temperature before cooking. The cheese-and-egg mixture must be made shortly before cooking. A salad is all you need to complete the meal.

**Butcher's Note:** If your butcher has trimmed boneless leg of lamb, you will need 1½ pounds. If you are trimming your own, begin with 2 to 2½ pounds of boneless leg of lamb. When trimmed of fat and silver skin, it will yield the 1½ pounds necessary for this dish.

**Wine Note:** The wines of the DOC Salice Salentino, as well as a welter of other related Apulian wines, seem tailor-made for lamb's earthiness. Produced mostly from two of the most common local grape varieties, Negroamaro (for its power, class, tannin, and acidity) and Malvasia Nera (for its aroma and its salubrious effect on Negroamaro), these wines are some of the most satisfying and affordable table wines in the world. And in spite of the hot climate from which they come, they're surprisingly fine companions for food, especially those with rich, roasted flavors as well as dishes with a slight sweetness. For instance, they are as delectable with American-style barbecue as with dishes such as this casserole.

Many of the most interesting products of Salice Salentino fuse modern and traditional tastes. They use modern grape growing and vinification techniques to help preserve the fresh fruit flavors as well as retain sufficient acidity in the wines, which in turn helps keep these wines refreshing and food friendly. At the same time, many of the best retain a certain rusticity and express themselves in a range of flavors and textures that suggest an aged wine, as well as the mellow harmony that older wines sometimes display. In fact, you'll find that many of the current vintages in our wine shops are often four or five years old, a reflection of the Apulian practice of holding wines before their release onto the market. What results is a sun-baked and sweetly earthy wine whose licorice-trimmed fruit flavors give immense pleasure with little pretense or cost. One favorite: Cosimo Tuarino Salice Salentino Reserva. A great American choice would be not-too-powerful Zinfandel. One favorite: Peachy Canyon "Westside" Zinfandel from Paso Robles, California.

---

*Two 1-inch-thick slices country-style bread,*
*crusts removed*

*¼ to ½ cup milk*

*1 pound very fresh lightly salted mozzarella cheese,*
*cut into ½-inch dice*

*1½ ounces Pecorino Romano or similar cheese,*
*finely grated*

*2 large eggs, beaten*

*Freshly ground black pepper*

*½ cup extra-virgin olive oil*

*1½ pounds trimmed boneless leg of lamb,*
*cut into 1-inch cubes (see Butcher's Note)*

*Kosher salt*

*8 large cloves garlic, chopped*

*1¼ cups dry white wine*

*1 yellow onion, chopped*

*12 green onions, white and pale green parts only,*
*trimmed and cut into ¾-inch pieces*

*6 large artichokes, cleaned (see page 129)*
*and cut lengthwise into eighths*

*½ cup water*

*6 tablespoons finely chopped fresh flat-leaf parsley*

---

1. In a mixing bowl, moisten the bread thoroughly with ¼ cup of milk and, using your hands, crumble the bread into pieces about ¼ inch thick (don't mash it into a paste). Add more milk if necessary to moisten and then drain any excess. Add the mozzarella, half of the Pecorino, the eggs, and a few generous grindings of pepper. Thoroughly combine the mixture and set aside.

2. In a large skillet, heat ¼ cup of the olive oil over medium-high heat. In a bowl, toss half of the lamb cubes with ½ teaspoon salt.

3. Working in two batches, cook the lamb until lightly browned on at least two sides, about 3 minutes per side. (As the first batch is cooking, toss the remaining lamb with salt.) When each batch finishes browning, transfer to a plate.

4. Reduce the heat to medium-low and return the lamb and any accumulated juices to the skillet. Add the garlic and a few generous grindings of pepper and cook for about 1 minute, stirring constantly to flavor the lamb. Add the wine, bring to a simmer, and cook gently for 3 minutes, scraping the bottom of the skillet to loosen any browned bits. Reduce the heat to low and cover the skillet, leaving the lid slightly ajar. Cook at the barest possible simmer for 30 minutes, stirring once or twice. The liquid should not completely evaporate during this time. Uncover the skillet and, if necessary, continue cooking to reduce the liquid to ¼ cup. Set aside.

5. Meanwhile, in another skillet, heat the remaining ¼ cup olive oil over medium heat and cook the yellow onion and green onions, stirring occasionally, until pale gold at the edges, 8 to 10 minutes.

6. Stir in the artichokes, ¾ teaspoon salt, and a few more grindings of pepper. Add the water, bring to a simmer, cover, reduce the heat to medium-low, and simmer gently for 20 minutes. Set aside.

7. Preheat the oven to 300°F.

8. In a large bowl, thoroughly combine the lamb-garlic mixture, the artichoke-onion mixture, any remaining liquid in the skillets, and the parsley. Transfer to an 8-by-10-inch earthenware or glass baking dish and spread evenly.

9. Stir the mozzarella-bread mixture and spread evenly over the lamb and artichokes. Sprinkle with the remaining Pecorino. Cover tightly and bake for 45 minutes.

10. Remove from the oven and preheat the broiler (let the dish rest during this time). When the broiler is hot, uncover the baking dish and broil until golden brown in spots, 3 to 6 minutes. Serve.

# Baked Lamb with Spanish Peppers

### Cordero en Chilindrón

**Serves 4**

This dish is originally from the region that noted Spanish cookbook author Penelope Casas calls "the region of the peppers," which includes much of northeastern interior Spain: Rioja, Aragon, Navarra, and the Basque country. Variations of this dish have become popular in other Spanish regions, as well. When you try it, you will understand its universal appeal. Serve with green beans, blanched until crisp-tender and sautéed in good olive oil and flavored with a crushed clove of garlic.

**Wine Note:** As with the Pork Chops with Tomato and Roasted Red Pepper Stew (page 107), the mildly piquant flavor of Piquillo peppers poses problems for fuller-bodied and more intense wines. Once again, it was a well-proportioned red Rioja that let the dish express its flavors and proved to be the most genial of those tasted. Our favorites won out over some of the most famous wines in this and other *denominaciónes* in northern Spain, including the intense and stylish wines of Ribera del Duero, Toro, Cigales, the emerging Bierzo, and Priorat. For simple, good-natured refreshment, try CUNE 2001 Rioja Clarete. For a more complex partner, try La Rioja Alta's 1998 Viña Alberdi Reserva, with its flavors of faded fruits and flowers framed by the savor of newer American oak barrels. For lovers of an oaky influence in their wines, here's a selection that offers these flavors in spades yet still remains incredibly flexible with a range of foods. From beyond Spain, pour an easygoing Pinot Noir in a lighter style. One favorite from California: the Saintsbury "Garnet" Pinot Noir.

*2 generous pinches of saffron threads (½ gram)*

*¼ cup warm water*

*6 tablespoons extra-virgin olive oil,*
*plus more as needed*

*One 1-inch-thick slice country-style bread,*
*crust removed*

*3 pounds 1-inch-thick bone-in lamb blade chops,*
*cut by the butcher into pieces about 2 inches*
*square (see Butcher's Note, page 138)*

*Kosher salt*

*1 yellow onion, finely chopped*

*¾ cup dry white wine*

*10 ounces jarred roasted Piquillo peppers*
*(pimientos del Piquillo asados), drained*

*3 large cloves garlic, sliced*

*1 teaspoon sweet paprika*

*2 cups water*

*2 tablespoons finely chopped fresh flat-leaf parsley*

*2 bay leaves*

1. In a small skillet over medium heat, toast the saffron for about 1 minute, stirring to prevent burning. Let cool and then crumble over the pan with dry fingers. Add the warm water and set aside.

2. In a large heavy pot, heat the olive oil over medium-low heat and toast the bread until rich golden brown on both sides, 2 to 3 minutes per side. Take care the toast does not burn. Transfer the toast to a plate and set aside.

3. Lay the lamb in a single layer on a work surface and salt it generously on both sides.

4. Add more oil to the pot to measure 4 tablespoons and raise the heat to medium-high. Working in two batches, cook the lamb until deeply browned on at least two sides, 4 to 6 minutes per side. As each batch finishes browning, transfer to a plate.

5. Preheat the oven to 350°F.

6. Let the pot cool slightly and place over medium-low heat. Add the onion and cook, stirring occasionally, until soft but without color, about 5 minutes. Add the wine and simmer gently for 3 minutes. Remove the pot from the heat and set aside.

7. Dip both sides of the toast in the wine until it's no longer crisp. Break the bread into chunks and transfer to the bowl of a food processor fitted with a metal blade. Add 2 ounces of the peppers and the garlic to the food processor and process for less than 30 seconds, just until a coarse paste forms, pausing 3 or 4 times to scrape down the sides of the bowl. Add the paprika, the reserved saffron water, and the 2 cups of water. Process briefly to incorporate.

8. Stir the bread-pepper mixture into the onion. Stir in the parsley, bay leaves, ¾ teaspoon salt, and the lamb and any accumulated juices. Mix well to combine. Bring to a brisk simmer over medium-high heat.

9. Carefully pour the contents of the pot into a 9-by-12-inch earthenware or glass baking dish and distribute evenly so that the lamb is mostly submerged. Cover tightly and bake for 30 minutes. Reduce the oven temperature to 300°F and cook for 1 hour. Uncover the baking dish and cook for 30 minutes more, basting the exposed pieces of meat every so often (these portions will eventually brown).

10. Slice the remaining 8 ounces peppers into 1-inch-long pieces about ½ inch wide.

11. Remove the casserole from the oven and distribute the pepper strips in the casserole, tucking them between the lamb and partly below the surface of the liquid (though still mostly exposed). Return to the oven and bake for 20 to 40 minutes more. When the dish is done it should be very moist but not excessively saucy. The thickened liquid should be reduced to well below the level of the lamb, but it should remain slightly fluid and still cling to the lower portion of the lamb pieces.

12. Let the casserole rest, uncovered, for 5 minutes. Divide among serving plates, spooning the remaining juices over each serving.

# Lamb Stewed in Muscat Wine

*Daube d'Agneau au Muscat de Rivesaltes*

**Serves 4**

This dish from the Rousillon region of France calls for lamb shoulder with some bone. We use the so-called arm chops (also called round-bone chops), cut from the top of the leg where it meets the shoulder, because they have the right ratio of bone to meat for this dish. By contrast, blade chops (see Butcher's Note, page 138) are far bonier. In any event, the bone simply makes this dish more flavorful. The stew also utilizes the region's dessert wine, which while famous throughout France, comes from a part of the country that feels nearly as Spanish as it does French. Along with a few contiguous appellations in the Languedoc to the north, the Rousillon forms the largest wine-growing region in the world, and so it's no surprise that it produced a distinctive dish cooked in equal parts of Muscat and rosé wines. If you have a covered earthenware dish, use it here. Steamed and mashed turnips seasoned with olive oil and salt would make a very complementary side dish.

**Wine Note:** Lamb and Muscat form a richly sweet and aromatic dish that works best with ripe, sun-filled reds that offer gentle power. The almost-roasted, red fruit taste found in the wines of the Collioure *appellation* are delicious, especially those with a few years of age. One of the region's greatest wines, Domaine du Mas Blanc "Jonquets," was our favorite with the lamb stew, though a number of excellent choices can be found throughout the Languedoc-Rousillon (see page 135 for more on these wines). From California, look for the Edmunds St. John California Syrah, which is always plump, supple, and satisfying.

*2 cups deeply colored dry rosé wine such as Corbières*

*2 large sprigs fresh thyme, plus 2 teaspoons chopped thyme*

*2 large sprigs fresh marjoram*

*Kosher salt*

*3 pounds 1-inch-thick lamb arm chops (round-bone chops) cut into 1½- to 2-inch pieces with some bone attached*

*¼ cup extra-virgin olive oil*

*10 large cloves garlic*

*3 carrots, peeled and sliced into ⅜-inch-thick rounds*

*1 yellow onion, finely chopped*

*2 tablespoons all-purpose flour*

*2 cups Muscat de Rivesaltes, Muscat Beaumes de Venise, or other sweet Muscat wine*

*Freshly ground black pepper*

1. In a small saucepan, combine the rosé wine and thyme and marjoram sprigs and simmer over medium heat for 3 minutes. Remove from the heat and set aside to infuse for 15 to 20 minutes.

2. Salt the lamb generously. In a large sauté pan, heat the olive oil over medium-high heat and, working in two batches, deeply brown the lamb pieces on at least two sides, reducing the heat if they threaten to burn. As each batch browns, transfer to a 9-by-12-inch earthenware or glass baking dish.

3. Preheat the oven to 350°F.

4. Reduce the heat to medium-low and cook the garlic, carrots, and onion, stirring occasionally, until the onion is pale gold at the edges, about 10 minutes. Sprinkle with the flour and cook, stirring, for about 1 minute.

5. Remove and discard the herb sprigs from the rosé wine. Pour the infused rosé and the Muscat into the skillet and bring to a simmer, scraping the bottom of the pot to loosen any browned bits. Pour over the lamb and season with a generous grinding of pepper.

6. Cover the dish and braise in the oven for 20 minutes. Reduce the oven temperature to 250°F and cook for 40 minutes longer.

7. Uncover and braise at no more than a bare simmer until the meat is very tender, about 1½ hours, basting the lamb every so often. Add salt to taste. If, after this time, the stew still seems a little liquid, raise the oven temperature slightly and cook a little longer to thicken. Or turn off the oven and let the stew cool in it, during which time the meat will absorb some of the liquid and the dish will tighten. Cover and reheat as necessary.

8. Garnish with the chopped thyme and serve from the baking dish, spooning the sauce over each serving.

# Braised Lamb in Lemon-Egg Sauce with Peas

Agnello Cacio e Uovo con Piselli

**Serves 4**

Variations of this sumptuous Easter classic are found throughout south-central Italy. Artichokes often replace peas, or the green vegetables are omitted altogether. Pecorino cheese is local but may be replaced by Parmesan. Red wine sometimes stands in for white. Pork fat replaces some or all of the olive oil. There also are variations that replace the quicker-cooking leg meat with milk-fed baby lamb *(abbachio)* or braising cuts from the shoulder, as we use here. What all these versions share is the lush lemon-and-egg sauce that binds it. You could say that our version is a composite of recipes, with inspiration from Campania, Abruzzo, Molise, and Lazio.

This is a very easy dish, but exercise judgment as to when it is time to add the egg-lemon mixture. You want the sauce to be abundant and thick enough to cling to the lamb but not gloppy. If it looks like there is less than 2 cups of liquid in the stew pot when it's time to add the lemon-egg mixture, cook the egg mixture only briefly and thin it with water, if necessary, to make up for any deficit. It will continue to thicken considerably as it cools on the plate.

*Wine Note:* Here's another occasion when the often-underrated Montepulciano d'Abruzzo performs beautifully with a sauce that throws a lot of wines for a loop (see pages 46 and 137 for more on these wines). The warm, velvety quality common to many of these wines is just the right pitch for the even more velvety egg-lemon sauce in this dish. Our favorite this time around was the Camillo Montori Montepulciano d'Abruzzo. Or try a white wine. Sauvignon Blanc is almost always good with lamb, and this dish is no exception. One favorite: Grgich Hills Napa Valley Fumé Blanc "Estate."

---

*3½ to 4 pounds 1-inch-thick bone-in lamb blade chops, cut by the butcher into pieces 1½ to 2 inches long (see Butcher's Note, page 138)*

*Kosher salt*

*¼ cup Italian-Style Lard Paste (page 217) or extra-virgin olive oil*

*1 ounce prosciutto di Parma or similar cured ham, finely chopped*

*1 large yellow onion, thinly sliced*

*6 cloves garlic, thinly sliced*

*1 cup dry white wine*

*¼ teaspoon freshly grated nutmeg*

*1¼ cups water*

*1½ cups fresh or frozen green peas*

*4 large egg yolks*

*3 to 4 tablespoons fresh lemon juice*

*2 tablespoons finely chopped fresh flat-leaf parsley*

*2 ounces Parmigiano-Reggiano
or Pecorino Romano cheese, finely grated*

*Freshly ground black pepper*

1. Generously season the lamb with salt. In a heavy stockpot, heat the lard paste over medium-high heat and, working in 2 batches, cook the lamb until deeply browned on at least two sides, 6 to 8 minutes per side, reducing the heat if it threatens to burn. As each batch finishes browning, transfer to a large plate.

2. Reduce the heat to medium and add the ham, onion, and garlic, and cook, stirring occasionally, for about 5 minutes. Add the wine, bring to simmer, and cook for 3 minutes longer, scraping the bottom of the pot to loosen any browned bits. Add the nutmeg and the lamb and any accumulated juices, stirring well to coat the lamb.

3. Stir in the water. When the mixture barely simmers, cover and cook over medium heat until the meat is tender, 2 to 2½ hours. Turn the lamb in the liquid occasionally. Stir in the peas.

4. In a bowl, beat the egg yolks. Gradually whisk in a few ladlefuls of the hot cooking liquid. Stir in 3 tablespoons of lemon juice, the parsley, the cheese, and a very generous grinding of pepper. Add to the lamb, stirring thoroughly and shaking the pan to distribute the egg mixture.

5. Cook very gently over medium-low heat for 2 to 3 minutes, or until slightly thickened. The sauce should cling to the lamb but still be somewhat fluid. To adjust the consistency, stir in a small amount of water or continue to cook very gently a few minutes more to thicken. Add more lemon juice to taste, if desired. Serve the lamb immediately, topping each serving with a generous portion of sauce.

# Stuffed Lamb Breast

*Poitrine d'Agneau Farcie*

**Serves 4**

This sort of stuffing can be modified with whatever ingredients are at hand, so look to this recipe as a starting point. For example, you can change the ratio of meats, eliminate one completely, or add another kind altogether, including lamb kidney and liver, as French home cooks from the southern Rhône Valley and Provence might do when they make this dish. You can use more or less bread crumbs, substitute dried crumbs for fresh, or add cooked rice instead of the bread crumbs. Vary the herbs and spices to suit your tastes and to utilize what's fresh and available in the garden. Lamb breast is a surprisingly inexpensive cut that's short on meat but long on flavor, a perfect vehicle for stuffing. The stuffed breast reheats well too; wrap tightly and warm in a 325°F oven for thirty to forty minutes. This is also delicious cold with a tart salad or chilled green beans dressed with a vinaigrette.

**Butcher's Note:** We find that many home cooks haven't heard of lamb breast, although fifty years ago it was frequently the only cut European immigrants seeking lamb could afford. Today, you may have to special order it. It's a small, thin cut that, if possible, needs to be left to the butcher to cut a pocket in for stuffing and to crack the rib bones for easy serving. One length of lamb breast, which is actually a half breast, weighs between 2 and 4 pounds when trimmed. If you can't find a single piece that weighs about 3 pounds after trimming, as called for in the recipe, make the dish with two pieces, each weighing 1½ to 2 pounds after trimming. Ask the butcher to cut a pocket in each, and divide the stuffing between them.

**Wine Note:** A lighter-styled Gigondas or Châteauneuf-du-Pape that has had a little time to mellow, say, at least five years, proves a good choice here. One of our favorites was Mas de Collines Gigondas, which is a little more delicate than most of its peers. If an aged wine proves tough to find, a lighter, easy-going Côtes du Rhône is just as good, although the effect will be different. We loved the lively spiced red-fruit savor of Les Fils de Joseph Sabon Côtes du Rhône, though any good wine merchant will have his or her favorite, and you'd do well to put yourself in their hands. From California, look for refined but still gulpable Qupé "Los Olivos Cuvée" from Santa Barbara County, a wine inspired by this part of France.

---

*3 tablespoons olive oil, plus more for rubbing*

*1 small yellow onion, finely chopped*

*12 large cloves garlic, 4 finely chopped, 8 left whole and unpeeled*

*⅓ pound ground lamb*

*⅓ pound ground pork*

*1 cup water*

*Kosher salt*

*One 1-inch-thick slice country-style bread, crust removed*

*2 teaspoons finely chopped fresh thyme or savory (or a combination), plus 8 large sprigs*

*4 tablespoons finely chopped fresh flat-leaf parsley*

*2 generous tablespoons pine nuts*

*¾ ounce Parmigiano-Reggiano or similar cheese, finely grated*

*1 large egg, beaten*

*1 bone-in breast of lamb, trimmed of all but ¼ inch of fat (about 3 pounds after trimming) and cut by the butcher to create a pocket the dimensions of the whole breast (see Butcher's Note)*

*Freshly ground black pepper*

*2 cups dry white wine*

*Quick Tomato Sauce for serving (optional; recipe follows)*

---

1. In a skillet, heat the olive oil over medium heat and cook the onion and chopped garlic, stirring occasionally, for 3 minutes. Raise the heat to medium-high and add the ground lamb and pork, breaking it up with a wooden spoon. Cook until the meat is lightly browned, 4 to 8 minutes, depending on how much moisture the meat gives off. Stir occasionally. Add the water and ½ teaspoon salt and simmer until the liquid almost evaporates, scraping the bottom of the skillet to loosen any browned bits. Transfer to a large bowl and let cool slightly.

2. In a bowl, soak the bread in water until soft. Break into pieces and knead to form a coarse paste. Squeeze until partly dry and crumble into the bowl with the meat. Add the chopped thyme, 2 tablespoons parsley, the pine nuts, cheese, and egg and combine thoroughly to make the stuffing. Set aside.

3. Fill the pocket in the lamb breast, spreading the stuffing evenly and into the corners. Don't pack too firmly. Either sew up the opening using a trussing needle with kitchen string or tie the breast as for a roast, spacing the loops between each rib and pulling each loop fairly firmly to keep the filling in place until it firms up during cooking.

4. Preheat the oven to 450°F.

5. Generously salt and pepper the lamb breast and rub with olive oil to coat. Put the lamb, bone side down, in a roasting pan or baking dish just large enough to contain it (15 by 10 inches is about right) and roast for 20 minutes. Reduce the oven temperature to 350°F and cook the lamb for 45 minutes longer.

6. Meanwhile, in a small saucepan, bring the wine to a boil and keep warm over very low heat.

7. Carefully pour off the fat from the roasting pan. Add the whole garlic cloves, thyme sprigs, and 1 cup of the warm wine and baste the lamb. Cook for 1 hour longer, basting the lamb every 15 minutes or so. Pour off the fat a second time and add the remaining 1 cup warm wine. Roast for 30 minutes longer, basting regularly. Turn off the oven and let the lamb rest for 15 to 30 minutes in the warm oven to firm up the stuffing before slicing.

8. Transfer the lamb to a cutting board. Snip and remove the strings and, using a sharp knife, carefully cut the breast into slices between the ribs, taking care to cut through the filling and pressing firmly to cut through the breastbone. Divide among serving plates.

9. If using the optional tomato sauce, gently reheat it, if necessary, and spoon a generous amount over each serving. Garnish with the remaining parsley and serve.

## Quick Tomato Sauce

**Makes about 3½ cups**

*¼ cup extra-virgin olive oil*

*4 large cloves garlic, chopped*

*One 28-ounce can peeled whole tomatoes, drained with ⅓ cup juice reserved, coarsely chopped*

*½ teaspoon kosher salt*

1. In a skillet, heat the olive oil over medium heat. Add the garlic and cook, stirring occasionally, until the garlic softens but doesn't brown, about 3 minutes.

2. Add the tomatoes, the reserved juice, and the salt and cook at a gentle simmer over medium-low heat, stirring occasionally, until slightly thickened but still a bit fluid, 15 to 20 minutes.

-Chapter 7-

# CHICKEN AND RABBIT

# The Royal Mistress's Chicken

Pollo Bela Rosin

**Serves 4**

Bela Rosin was King Victor Emmanuelle II's much-loved mistress when he ruled the kingdom of Savoy and Sardinia in the mid-nineteenth century (he later became king of a newly unified Italy in 1861). This dish is credited with coming from the Piedmont region of the kingdom, and whether it actually was prepared by her for trysts with the king or was created by other cooks in her honor, though a matter of curiosity, is relatively unimportant. What is important is how this quick, easy, and savory dish marries the flirty flavors of anchovy, Cognac, white wine, and butter in a sauce that lightly coats pan-crisped pieces of chicken.

If you have a very large skillet, you can cook all the chicken pieces together, but if not, work in two batches and transfer the first batch to a very low (200°F) oven, uncovered, while you cook the rest. The goal is to get the chicken very crispy by browning it on its skin side for an extended time over medium heat, which cooks it about two-thirds of the way through. The chicken softens a little when coated with the sauce but still retains its crunch if properly cooked. Serve with spinach sautéed with olive oil, a crushed garlic clove, and salt.

**Wine Note:** We found three wines from the elite of Piedmont's old-guard producers that we loved to drink with the Royal Mistress's Chicken. Our favorite was the Barbera d'Alba from the traditionalist winery Giacomo Conterno. This wine's rustic, mouthwatering licorice and black fruit flavors made us feel like we'd stepped back in time to a place where local food and wine were consumed without fuss and everything tasted good together. Other favorites for this surprisingly wine-friendly dish included the Produttori del Barbaresco Barbaresco (quite easy going for a Nebbiolo-based wine) and, for white wine drinkers, Bruno Giacosa's Arneis, made from the indigenous variety of the same name (*arneis* means "rascal" in local dialect). From California, look for two nicely made Italianate wines, one red and one white: Renwood Barbera from Amador County and the Babcock Pinot Grigio from Santa Barbara.

---

*Kosher salt*

*One 4- to 5-pound chicken, cut into 8 serving pieces (see Butcher's Note, page 156)*

*¼ cup extra-virgin olive oil*

*¼ cup Cognac or similar brandy*

*½ cup dry white wine*

*4 anchovy fillets, drained and mashed to a paste*

*1 cup Chicken Stock (page 215) or canned low-sodium chicken broth*

*⅛ teaspoon freshly grated nutmeg*

*2 tablespoons unsalted butter*

*1 tablespoon all-purpose flour*

*2 tablespoons finely chopped fresh flat-leaf parsley*

---

1. Generously salt the chicken pieces. In a large skillet, heat the olive oil over medium-high heat until just smoking. Reduce the heat to medium and, working in two batches if necessary, brown the chicken, skin side down, until rich golden brown and very crisp on the skin side and about two-thirds cooked through, 12 to 14 minutes. Turn the pieces and cook until just cooked through, about 8 minutes for thick breast pieces and about 12 minutes for legs and thighs (cooking times for thinner breast pieces will be shorter). Transfer to a plate and set aside.

2. Drain off most of the fat in the skillet and place over medium heat. Add the Cognac and cook until only 1 tablespoon remains. Add the wine and anchovies and scrape the bottom of the skillet to loosen any browned bits. Break up the anchovy paste with the back of a spatula or spoon so it mostly dissolves. Simmer until the wine reduces by half, 2 to 3 minutes. Add the stock, nutmeg, and ¼ teaspoon salt. Bring to a simmer and reduce by half again, about 5 minutes longer.

3. In a small bowl, mash the butter with the flour to make a paste. Reduce the heat to low and whisk the butter paste into the skillet. Stir regularly until the sauce thickens so that it lightly coats the back of a spoon, 2 to 3 minutes.

4. Whisk in any accumulated juices from the plate holding the chicken. Add the chicken and cook for 30 seconds to 1 minute, turning the pieces to warm through them through and then coat with the sauce. Don't let the pieces sit too long in the sauce or their crispy skins will soften completely.

5. Divide the chicken among plates, drizzle with any remaining sauce, garnish with the parsley, and serve.

# Chicken with Vinegar Sauce

Fricassée de Poulet au Vinaigre de Vin Rouge

**Serves 4**

This fricassee, popular all over France, traces its roots to the Loire Valley, where vinegar has long been a significant industry. The story goes that hundreds of years ago, boats laden with wine occasionally ran aground when navigating the silty, often shallow stretches of the Loire River near the busy port city of Orléans. This was the precise point where the overland passage to Paris was the shortest, and so once aground, the shipments destined for Paris were delayed. The wine soon turned to vinegar, and an industry sprung up based on the spoiled wine found in and around the city.

Obviously, it is important to use top-quality red wine vinegar in a dish like this. Producers such as Martin Pouret, still based in Orléans, make exceptional traditional wine vinegars that are worth seeking out. Serve the chicken with braised and browned pearl onions and thinly sliced fried potatoes.

**Wine Note:** Both the lighter and richer styles of the Cabernet Franc–based wines of the region work well with this dish because their naturally high acidity is able to withstand, and even complement, the quantity of vinegar. This is all the more amazing when you recall the common refrain, "Don't drink wine with salad because the vinegar in the dressing will ruin the taste of the wine." The incredible flexibility of these wines (and many others from the Loire Valley) makes mincemeat of that bit of advice. We had two favorites in this tasting: the Domaine de la Chanteleuserie Bourgueil "Cuvée Alouettes"—made in a medium-weight style—and the Domaine de Nerleux "Clos de Châtains" Saumur-Champigny, which is a bit richer. This flexibility was demonstrated among

our Loire Valley whites, too. Especially good with the Chicken with Vinegar Sauce was one of the world's great white wines, Domaine de Baumard Savennières "Trie Spéciale," a Chenin Blanc—based wine often too full of its own bracing, mineral richness and intensity to accompany food. It's not always easy to locate, but if you do, it's worth a try with this dish.

Dishes like this can be tough on New World red wines, whose generally lower levels of acidity and higher levels of alcohol sometimes clash with a strong vinegary element. For that reason, we like to stick with whites from these places, especially crisper Sauvignon Blanc, such as the St. Clair Sauvignon Blanc from Marlborough, New Zealand.

---

*Kosher salt*

*One 3½- to 4-pound chicken, cut into 8 serving pieces (see Butcher's Note, page 156)*

*2 tablespoons vegetable oil*

*2 tablespoons unsalted butter*

*Liver reserved from the chicken or about 2 ounces purchased chicken liver (optional)*

*½ cup finely chopped shallots*

*4 large cloves garlic, minced*

*¾ cup off-dry white wine such as Vouvray demi-sec*

*¾ cup high-quality red wine vinegar*

*1 tablespoon tomato paste*

*1 cup Beef Stock (page 212) or canned low-sodium beef broth*

*Freshly ground black pepper*

---

1. Generously salt the chicken on all sides. In a large flameproof casserole, heat the oil and butter over medium-high heat until the butter melts. Working in two batches if necessary, cook the chicken until rich golden brown all over, 10 to 12 minutes per batch, reducing the heat if it threatens to burn. (To avoid overcooking them, remove any thinner breast pieces just before they're cooked through.) Meanwhile, in a small skillet, cook the chicken liver, if using, for 3 to 4 minutes until lightly browned and just cooked through. Transfer the chicken and the liver to a plate, tent loosely with aluminum foil, and set aside.

2. Pour off all but about 4 tablespoons of the fat and place the casserole over medium-low heat. Add the shallots and garlic and cook, stirring occasionally, until translucent, 3 to 4 minutes. Raise the heat to medium-high and add the wine and vinegar. Gently boil until reduced by one third, 4 to 5 minutes. Scrape the bottom of the casserole to loosen any browned bits.

3. Transfer a ladleful of the hot wine-vinegar mixture to a small bowl and whisk in the tomato paste until dissolved. Add it to the casserole along with the stock and ½ teaspoon salt.

4. Return the chicken legs and thighs to the casserole. Partly cover and cook at a bare simmer until the meat is tender, about 45 minutes. Turn the pieces over once or twice during cooking.

5. Add the reserved breast pieces and any accumulated juices and cover the casserole. Gently simmer until the breasts are cooked through, 6 to 8 minutes.

6. Lift the chicken pieces from the casserole and arrange, skin side up, on a baking sheet lined with aluminum foil. If using the chicken liver, chop it into small pieces and set aside.

7. Preheat the broiler.

8. Bring the cooking liquid to a boil over medium-high heat and reduce to about 1½ cups, 3 to 4 minutes.

9. Using a paper towel, blot the chicken skin to remove excess moisture. Broil for a few minutes until the skin is crispy and even blackened in a few spots, but don't let it burn. Divide the chicken among deep serving plates or wide, shallow bowls. Stir the liver into the casserole, if using, along with a few grindings of pepper. Ladle the vinegar sauce around the chicken and serve.

# Chicken in Creamy Riesling Sauce

## Coq au Riesling

**Serves 4**

This dish is really nothing more than a simple, creamy variant on coq au vin, and it's truly spectacular. This classic is from France's Alsace region and is traditionally served with egg noodles or spaetzle.

**Butcher's Note:** We recommend you cut up a whole chicken to get the 8 pieces called for here—2 semi-boneless breast halves, each cut in half to make 4 pieces; 2 thighs; and 2 drumsticks. With the bird breast-side up, slit the skin between the thighs and breast, pull the thighs away, and cut through the exposed ball-and-socket joint. Then, cut each leg in half through the joint between the thigh and drumstick. Next, remove the first two wing joints attached to the breast (reserve these and the carcass for stock). To remove the breast halves, cut straight down along one side of the breastbone—its entire length—until the knife meets the rib cage. Then, begin drawing the knife toward you in long strokes where the breast meat meets the ribs, gradually separating the breast meat from the curve of the ribs and "peeling" the breast away from the ribs with your free hand as you cut (righties should use their left hand to hold the flesh and first remove the left breast half; lefties the opposite). Spin the bird around 180 degrees and repeat with the second breast half. Cut each half in half again crosswise to make 4 pieces of breast meat.

**Wine Note:** Here, a dry Riesling is used in the pot, where its floral qualities help to make the dish distinctive. In mountainous Alsace, it is typical to drink the same wine at the table, a sensible match. That said, this dish illustrates that the obvious move of serving the same wine used in preparing the dish isn't always advisable. Among the wines of the region, Alsatian Riesling is nothing if not elegant, and yet elegance is not what you need to accompany a dish finished with crème frâiche and egg yolks. It's not that Riesling is a bad match, but in our tasting, a crisp, medium-bodied, uncomplicated basic Riesling (the kind produced by almost every winery in the region and used in this dish) felt just too lean and wimpy next to the sauce. On the other hand, a more complicated, textured, and costly *grand cru* seemed too refined in its concentration and too tightly wound (like driving a Ferrari in a construction zone). The place for these wines is alongside rich, refined roasted or braised dishes. Our favorite here was all-purpose, four-wheel-drive Pinot Blanc, the workhorse grape of Alsace. There's no need for the fanciest ones; go for good-quality, basic bottlings such as Domaine Paul Blanck Pinot Blanc, a gentle yet crisp wine whose medium-weight creaminess is just the right mate for the sauce.

From California, look for the mild-mannered and flexible Saddleback Pinot Blanc from the Napa Valley.

2 tablespoons vegetable oil

2 tablespoons unsalted butter

One 3 ½- to 4-pound chicken, cut into 8 serving pieces (see Butcher's Note), or 8 chicken thighs or legs or a combination (about 2 ½ pounds total)

Kosher salt

1 yellow onion, finely chopped

½ cup finely chopped shallots

2 tablespoons all-purpose flour

1 ½ cups Alsatian or other dry Riesling

1 cup Chicken Stock (page 215) or canned low-sodium chicken broth

¼ teaspoon freshly grated nutmeg

1 large sprig fresh thyme

1 bay leaf

¼ cup crème fraîche

2 large egg yolks

1. In a large pot, heat the oil and butter over medium-high heat until the butter melts. Season the chicken generously with salt on all sides. Working in batches if necessary, add the chicken to the pot and cook until rich golden brown all over, reducing the heat if it threatens to burn, 10 to 12 minutes per batch (to avoid overcooking any thinner breast pieces, remove them just before they're cooked through). Transfer to a plate. Pour off all but about 4 tablespoons of the fat.

2. Reduce the heat to medium and add the onion and shallots. Cook, stirring occasionally, until pale gold at the edges, about 10 minutes. Sprinkle the flour over the vegetables and cook for 1 minute longer, stirring. Add the wine, stock, nutmeg, thyme, bay leaf, and ½ teaspoon salt, scraping the bottom of the pot to loosen any browned bits. Bring to a simmer and cook for 3 minutes.

3. Return the thighs and legs and any accumulated juices to the pot. When the liquid reaches a low simmer, cover the pot and cook until tender, about 50 minutes. Check the pot occasionally to ensure that it's simmering gently.

4. Add the breast pieces and any accumulated juices and re-cover the pot. Gently simmer until the breasts are cooked through, 6 to 8 minutes. Transfer the chicken to a plate, cover with aluminum foil, and keep warm in a low (200°F) oven. Reduce the heat to very low and whisk the crème fraîche into the sauce.

5. In a small bowl, beat the egg yolks and gradually whisk in a few ladlefuls of the hot sauce. Whisk the mixture back into the pot and cook, stirring, until the sauce thickens noticeably, 2 to 3 minutes. Do not let the sauce simmer or it may curdle.

6. Return the chicken to the pot and cook below a simmer until the sauce easily clings to the chicken, 1 to 3 minutes.

7. To serve, transfer the chicken to serving plates and spoon the sauce over.

# Classic Chicken in Red Wine

## Coq au Vin

**Serves 6**

*Coq au vin* is arguably the best-known braised poultry dish in the world, and for good reason. It comes from Burgundy, where the local wine was put to good use tenderizing a tough old farmyard *coq* no longer able to rule the roost. Our recipe put a few twists on most traditional ones, with a few ideas taken from Madeleine Kamman in her cookbook *The Making of a Cook*. First, we use only chicken legs and thighs, which remain far more tender during extended cooking than breasts and thus absorb the flavors of the wine and other ingredients more satisfactorily. Second, we cook the wine and stock for about twenty minutes to reduce it and concentrate the flavors before adding it to the chicken. Finally, we thicken the sauce with beurre manié, a paste made of butter and flour, which is a common French technique.

**Wine Note:** Elsewhere in the book, we've declared that red Burgundy is a truly flexible wine with food, so you'd think that region's world-famous Pinot Noir–based wines would be delightful accompaniments to its most famous dish. We'd convinced ourselves still further of the potential goodness of this match because we have even used bottles of good Burgundy in the pot with the chicken. To our surprise, these wines tasted none too good next to our coq au vin. After tasting a range of red Burgundies in different styles, we nearly gave up. The hero of this story came from the fridge: a three-day-old bottle of cheap California Pinot Noir. Tasting it with our coq au vin, the dynamic changed: The harsh clash was replaced by a smooth companionship; the wine tasted of itself and in turn served to elevate the dish. Had we followed our own advice set out in the first chapter, we might have seen this coming.

Because of the large quantity of onions and carrots, the reduced wine and stock, and the finishing swirl of butter to help thicken it, our version of coq au vin, while not a sweet dish per se, gives a certain impression of sweetness. As we've discussed, when serving a red wine alongside a dish with a slight sweetness, those that work best display what we've come to call a "fruitiness" (see page 24). Pinot Noir–based wines from the New World wine regions typically have far more of this fruitiness than do red Burgundies and therefore have a greater chance of tasting really good with a lightly sweet dish. From our tastings, we learned that red Burgundy—one of the world's most precious wine treats—is certainly able to complement a wide range of foods, but some thought must be given to what you plan to serve it with. Avoid dishes that might compete too much with the wine itself, because among a fine red Burgundy's greatest traits are its delicacy, its detail, and what has been called its "transparency of flavor." Red Burgundy can beautifully pair with beef, veal, pork, lamb, chicken, rabbit, duck, quail, squab, and venison with equal ease. But it's probably good advice to focus on baked, roasted, pan-fried, and grilled versions of these meats when serving them. And with coq au vin? Try almost any New World Pinot Noir—the simpler and juicier versions as well as the more sculpted and fancy. One favorite from California (in the former style) is the Au Bon Climat Santa Barbara County Pinot Noir. If you want to serve something French, pour a good bottle of *cru* Beaujolais like the Pascal Granger Juliénas "Grande Cuvée," a great coq au vin partner that, thanks to the ever-mysterious food and wine genies, comes from the southernmost portion of Burgundy itself.

6 ounces fatty, skinless salt pork, cut into strips
about 1 inch long and ¼ inch thick

2 tablespoons vegetable oil

Kosher salt

6 chicken thighs and 6 chicken legs
(3½ to 4 pounds total)

2 yellow onions, chopped

2 large carrots, peeled and chopped

3 large cloves garlic, lightly crushed

1 cup chopped shallots

1 tablespoon tomato paste

1 bottle (750 ml) good-quality Pinot Noir
(see page 32 for notes on cooking with Pinot Noir)

3 cups Chicken Stock (page 215)
or canned low-sodium chicken broth

2 large sprigs fresh thyme

2 large sprigs fresh flat-leaf parsley,
plus 3 tablespoons finely chopped leaves

1 bay leaf

5 black peppercorns

9 to 10 tablespoons unsalted butter,
at room temperature

40 fresh pearl onions, peeled (see Note, page 83),
or thawed frozen pearl onions

10 ounces medium white mushrooms, quartered

3 to 4 tablespoons all-purpose flour

Sliced toasted country-style bread, lightly rubbed
with a cut garlic clove, for serving (optional)

1. In a small saucepan of boiling water, blanch the salt pork for 2 minutes. Drain well and transfer to a large flameproof casserole or Dutch oven. Add the oil and cook the salt pork over medium heat, stirring regularly, until pale gold and crisp, 10 to 12 minutes. Transfer to a small plate with a slotted spoon, leaving the fat in the pot, and set aside. Keep the pot on the stove, off the heat.

2. Salt the chicken pieces generously on all sides. Place the casserole over medium-high heat. Working in two batches, cook the chicken until rich golden brown all over, 10 to 12 minutes per batch, reducing the heat if it threatens to burn. Transfer to a plate and set aside.

3. Pour off all but 4 tablespoons of the fat and return the casserole to medium-high heat. Add the yellow onions, carrots, garlic, and shallots and cook, stirring occasionally, until pale gold at the edges, 8 to 10 minutes. Stir in the tomato paste and cook for 1 minute longer. Add the wine and stock and bring to a boil. Lower the heat to medium and simmer briskly until reduced by one-third, 20 to 25 minutes, scraping the bottom of the casserole to loosen up any browned bits. Add the thyme, parsley sprigs, bay leaf, peppercorns, and ½ teaspoon salt.

4. Return the chicken and any accumulated juices to the casserole and cover, leaving the lid about ¾ inch ajar. Reduce the heat to low and cook at a bare simmer until the meat is very tender, about 1¼ hours, turning the pieces over once or twice during this time. Adjust the heat as needed to maintain a bare simmer.

5. Meanwhile, in a large skillet, melt 3 tablespoons of the butter over medium heat and cook the pearl onions, tossing them regularly, until tender and light gold all over, 15 to 20 minutes. Set aside.

6. Wipe out the skillet and return to medium-high heat. Melt 3 more tablespoons of the butter and cook the mushrooms, tossing them regularly, until lightly browned at the edges, 6 to 8 minutes. Add a few generous pinches of salt; toss well and set aside with the pearl onions.

7. When the chicken is done, transfer the pieces to a plate. Strain the cooking liquid through a colander lined with a double thickness of cheesecloth or through a fine-mesh strainer set over a bowl, pushing hard to extract the flavorful liquid from the vegetables. Skim some or all of the fat from the liquid.

8. Measure the strained and skimmed cooking liquid and return it to the casserole over low heat. For each cup of liquid, measure 1 tablespoon of the remaining butter and 1 tablespoon of the flour and mash together to form a paste. Whisk this paste into the casserole until dissolved and bring to a bare simmer.

9. Return the chicken to the casserole, stir in the pearl onions and mushrooms, and cook, uncovered, at a bare simmer for 5 minutes to heat everything through and to thicken the sauce slightly. Add salt to taste.

10. Divide the chicken, vegetables, and abundant sauce among shallow bowls and garnish each with the salt pork and chopped parsley. Serve immediately, with the toast, if desired.

# Alsatian-Style Chicken with Crayfish

Le Poulet aux Écrevisses

**Serves 4 to 6**

The sauce for this creamy chicken uses shellfish stock and so is not as thick as the sauce in Chicken in Creamy Riesling Sauce on page 156, but otherwise they are similar. Of course, the addition of crayfish sets it firmly apart. We know it's tricky to get fresh crayfish in many parts of the United States, and so we suggest frozen crayfish tails, unless you can find fresh. Serve over egg noodles or spaetzle.

🔖

**Wine Note:** This was an interesting tasting. Because the dishes are made in an almost identical way, you would think that the wines that worked so well with the Chicken in Creamy Riesling Sauce would be great with this dish, too. Not quite, as we found out. Because the sauce has a shellfish base and is less obviously creamy in texture than the other dish, it called for a change in wine. This sort of fine-tuning may seem a little over the top, we know. But the proof was in the tasting, illustrating how much of a crapshoot wine and food pairing can sometimes be (and why you—or even a professional wine steward—shouldn't feel bad when things go a little wrong). What happened? Our best guess is that the medium-weight creaminess that helped the Pinot Blanc mate so nicely with the other dish, while pretty good here, came off as too big and fruity with seafood. The fancy *grand cru* Rieslings here again proved too intense. It turned out that the wine that best blended with the dish and gave the crisp refreshment it needed was a simple, basic Riesling (in this case, the Trimbach Riesling)—the same wine that tasted so shrill and wimpy with the other dish. It's a perfect complement and contrast. Go figure.

---

*Kosher salt*

*8 whole chicken thighs or legs, or a combination
(about 2½ pounds total)*

*2 tablespoons vegetable oil*

*2 tablespoons unsalted butter*

*1 leek, white and pale green parts only, well rinsed
and finely chopped (about 1 cup)*

*½ cup finely chopped shallots*

*¾ cups dry Alsatian Riesling wine*

*2 cups Shellfish Stock (page 215)*

*5 tablespoons crème fraîche*

*2 large egg yolks*

*1 pound cooked and peeled
or thawed frozen crayfish tails*

*2 tablespoons finely chopped fresh chives*

---

1. Generously salt the chicken on all sides. In a large pot, warm the oil and butter over medium-high heat until the butter melts. Cook until rich golden brown all over, 10 to 12 minutes, reducing the heat if it threatens to burn. Transfer to a plate. Pour off all but about 4 tablespoons of the fat in the pot.

2. Reduce the heat to medium and add the leek and shallots. Cook, stirring occasionally, until pale gold at the edges, 10 to 12 minutes. Add the wine, stock, and ½ teaspoon salt, scraping the bottom of the pot to loosen any browned bits. Bring to a simmer and cook for 3 minutes.

3. Return the chicken and any accumulated juices to the pot and return to a bare simmer. Cover the pot and cook until the chicken is tender, about 1 hour. Check occasionally to ensure that it's simmering gently.

4. Transfer the chicken to a plate, tent loosely with aluminum foil, and keep warm in a very low (200°F) oven.

5. Reduce the heat to very low and whisk the crème fraîche into the sauce.

6. In a small bowl, beat the egg yolks and gradually whisk in a few ladlefuls of the hot sauce. Whisk the mixture back into the sauce, stirring until the sauce thickens slightly, 1 to 2 minutes. Stir in the chicken and crayfish and cook very gently to heat them through, but don't let the sauce return to a simmer or it may curdle.

7. Divide the chicken and crayfish among serving plates, topping each serving with a generous portion of the sauce. Garnish with the chives and serve.

# Chicken Gratin with Onion Sauce and Gruyère

### Le Poulet Gaston Gérard

**Serves 4**

The people of Dijon, the capital of the Burgundy region of France, like to commemorate past mayors with food and drink. One of them, Canon Kir, left his name attached to the white wine and cassis aperitif of his invention. And another, the radical, civic-minded Gaston Gérard, inaugurated the Gastronomic Fair of Dijon just after World War I. This easy and satisfying dish emerged from that event. Serve with rice pilaf.

**Wine Note:** Cheese and cream can be tough on wines, especially reds, and so it surprised us to find that the level of a red wine was dropping quickly in our glasses alongside the chicken gratin (more proof, if any were needed, that even the few wine "rules" you think are worth abiding by can crumble right before you). Our favorite among a range of wines was a ready-to-drink medium-weight red Burgundy with a gentle core of earthy, red fruit flavors: the Bouchard Père et Fils Santenay. A Pinot Noir from Oregon like the Adelsheim Pinot Noir from the Willamette Valley would be a kindred choice from the United States.

*Kosher salt*

*One 3 ½- to 4-pound chicken, cut into 8 serving pieces (see Butcher's Note, page 156)*

*2 tablespoons vegetable oil*

*2 tablespoons unsalted butter*

*2 yellow onions, finely chopped*

*¾ cup finely chopped shallots*

*1 ¼ cup dry white wine such as Bourgogne blanc*

*½ cup crème fraîche*

*4 tablespoons Dijon mustard*

*5 ounces Gruyère cheese, coarsely grated*

1. Generously salt the chicken on all sides. In a large sauté pan, heat the oil and butter over medium-high heat until the butter melts. Working in two batches if necessary, cook the chicken until rich golden brown all over, 10 to 12 minutes per batch, reducing the heat if it threatens to burn. (To avoid overcooking them, remove any thinner breast pieces just before they're cooked through.) Transfer to a plate, tent loosely with aluminum foil, and place in a very low (200°F) oven.

2. Pour off all but about 4 tablespoons of the fat and place the pan over medium heat. Add the onions and shallots and cook, stirring occasionally, until pale gold at the edges, 8 to 10 minutes. Raise the heat to medium-high and add the wine. Simmer for 2 minutes, scraping the bottom of the pan to loosen any browned bits.

3. Return the legs and thighs to the skillet along with any accumulated juices. Cook at a bare simmer for 10 minutes, turning the pieces after about 5 minutes. Add the breast pieces and cook for 5 minutes longer. Check to make sure all the chicken is just cooked through. Transfer the chicken to a plate.

4. Whisk the crème fraîche, mustard, and 1 teaspoon of salt into the pan juices until well mixed.

5. Preheat the broiler.

6. Evenly distribute half the cheese over the bottom of an earthenware or glass baking dish just large enough to hold the chicken in a single layer. Arrange the chicken on top of the cheese. Pour all the onion sauce evenly over the chicken and top with the rest of the cheese.

7. Broil until bubbly and just a little golden in spots. Serve immediately from the baking dish, spooning additional onion sauce over each portion.

# Portuguese-Style Jugged Chicken

Frango na Pucara

**Serves 4**

This dish gets most of its salt from the ham and mustard, so the chicken should be just lightly salted. We use only chicken thighs here, as they are the most flavorful part of the chicken. The Portuguese would most likely serve with this French fries, a very good combination indeed.

**Wine Note:** White and red wines are equally good with this dish. For the white wine, try the light, bright, and lemony refreshment of the Quinta da Romeira Bucelas made from Portugal's Arinto grape. We also liked Vinícola de Nelas Dão Escanção, a softly tangy and warmly flavored red. From beyond Portugal, you might try a white like the Dashwood Sauvignon Blanc from Marlborough, New Zealand. For a red, pour a Pinot Noir like the Vavasour Pinot Noir, also from Marlborough.

*Kosher salt and freshly ground black pepper*

*8 chicken thighs*

*4 to 5 tablespoons olive oil*

*24 fresh pearl onions, peeled (see Note, page 83), or thawed frozen pearl onions*

*¼ pound sliced Portuguese presunto, Spanish serrano, prosciutto di Parma, or similar cured ham, finely chopped*

*6 large cloves garlic, crushed*

*6 medium canned tomatoes, drained with ¼ cup juice reserved, coarsely chopped*

*3 bay leaves*

*1 cup dry white wine*

*½ cup tawny Port*

*3 tablespoons Portuguese aguardiente, Italian grappa, or similar brandy*

*½ cup Chicken Stock (page 215), canned low-sodium chicken broth, or water*

*1 tablespoon Dijon mustard*

*2 tablespoons finely chopped fresh flat-leaf parsley*

1. Lightly but evenly salt and generously pepper the chicken thighs on both sides. Set aside in a large bowl.

2. Preheat the oven to 350°F.

3. In a 6- to 8-quart flameproof casserole with a tight-fitting lid, heat 3 tablespoons of the olive oil and cook the pearl onions, ham, and garlic for 3 minutes, stirring occasionally. Stir in the tomatoes, reserved juice, and the bay leaves, bring to a simmer, and cook for 3 minutes. Add the wine, Port, and brandy and simmer gently for 5 minutes longer.

4. Toss the chicken with the remaining olive oil to coat and set aside.

5. Stir the stock and mustard into the casserole and add the chicken, turning it in the sauce to coat. Turn the chicken thighs skin side up and cover the casserole tightly.

6. Bake for 20 minutes. Reduce the oven temperature to 250°F and bake the chicken until tender, about 1 hour and 10 minutes more. Adjust the oven temperature as needed to maintain a bare simmer.

7. Transfer the casserole to the stove top and transfer the chicken to a baking sheet lined with aluminum foil. Arrange the chicken skin side up and cover tightly with more foil. Set aside.

8. Bring the cooking liquid to a brisk simmer over medium-high heat and cook until it becomes a flavorful, slightly thickened but still fluid sauce, 10 to 12 minutes. Stir in the parsley, cover, and keep warm over the lowest possible heat.

9. Preheat the broiler and position the broiling rack so it is 6 inches from the heat source.

10. Uncover the chicken and pour any accumulated juices into the casserole. Broil the chicken until well browned (almost blackened) and crisp, 3 to 5 minutes.

11. Divide the chicken among serving plates and divide the sauce among the plates, spooning a little over the chicken and most of it on the plate.

# Chicken with Roasted Tomatoes, Fennel, and Artichokes

Le Poulet à la Provençal

**Serves 4**

Although decidedly not a traditional dish, this is a composite of the irresistible flavors of Provence, paired with chicken. Be sure to roast the tomatoes as early as a day ahead of time.

**Wine Note:** If you want to make the point that regional food flavors complement regional wines in a synergistic way, you couldn't do much better than drink a well-made, medium-full-bodied Provençal red alongside this dish. Provence is vast, and the diversity of its wine zones resists a homogenous view, yet there are certain flavors and textures shared by its many wines. These distinctive features are not often found in the expensive blockbuster wines produced here, although they can be. They rarely appear in the watery (often pink) plonk knocked back by tourists, either. But between these two extremes there exist wines that are good examples of high-quality, everyday Provençal reds. This is what to look for with this dish.

You want wines of medium- to medium-full body that are richly flavored but not heavy—like a good Côtes du Rhône but with an infusion of something extra. This "something extra" in those we tasted seemed connected to their savory fruit flavors, which—remarkably—smell and taste as though they'd been filtered through a big pile of woody, aromatic herbs. These flavors could have come from nowhere else, and they really sing with the chicken, vegetables, and herbs in this dish. A widely available favorite: the Mas de Gourgonnier from Les Baux de Provence. From California, try the Ojai Vineyard Central Coast Syrah.

---

*One 3½- to 4-pound chicken, cut into 8 serving pieces (see Butcher's Note, page 156)*

*Kosher salt and freshly ground black pepper*

*¼ cup extra-virgin olive oil, or as needed, plus more for drizzling*

*½ large yellow onion, cut lengthwise into ¼-inch-thick slices*

*1 head fennel, trimmed, halved, and cut lengthwise into ⅜-inch wedges*

*10 large cloves garlic*

*2 large artichokes, cleaned (see page 129) and cut into wedges ⅜ inch thick at their widest point*

*¾ cup dry white wine*

*⅔ cup Chicken Stock (page 215) or canned low-sodium chicken broth, plus more as needed*

*1 teaspoon finely chopped fresh thyme*

*½ teaspoon finely chopped fresh rosemary*

*2 bay leaves*

*12 Roasted Tomatoes (page 76)*

*12 to 16 good-quality small black olives such as Gaeta or Niçoise*

*10 to 12 large fresh basil leaves, roughly torn or chopped*

---

1. Preheat the oven to 425°F. Generously sprinkle the chicken pieces with salt and pepper.

2. In a large skillet, heat the olive oil over medium-high heat. Working in two batches if necessary, cook the chicken until rich golden brown all over and cooked about two-thirds through, reducing the heat if it threatens to burn, 10 to 12 minutes for thighs, legs, and large breast pieces and less time for thinner breast pieces. Transfer the breasts to a plate and set aside. Transfer the thighs and legs to an earthenware or glass baking dish, skin side up, and set aside.

3. Stir the onion, fennel, and garlic into the skillet and cook, stirring occasionally, over medium-high heat until pale gold at the edges, 5 to 7 minutes. Sprinkle generously with salt, toss to combine, and distribute the vegetables in the baking dish around the chicken thighs and legs. Reserve as much fat in the skillet as possible.

4. Return the skillet to medium-high heat, add more olive oil if necessary, and add the artichokes. Sprinkle with salt, reduce the heat to medium, and cook until golden brown at the edges but still firm, 5 to 7 minutes. Combine the artichokes with the vegetables and chicken in the baking dish.

5. Return the skillet to medium heat and add the wine. Simmer until reduced to ¼ cup, scraping the bottom of the pan to loosen any browned bits. Stir in the stock, thyme, rosemary, bay leaves, and ¼ teaspoon salt and bring to a boil. Carefully pour the contents of the skillet around the chicken in the baking dish, transfer to the oven, and bake, uncovered, for 15 minutes. Add the reserved chicken breasts and any accumulated juices to the dish. Add ¼ to ½ cup of stock to the casserole if it looks dry. The goal is to have about ½ cup of flavorful liquid at the end of cooking.

6. Distribute the tomatoes and olives in the dish and bake for 12 to 15 minutes longer, or until the breasts are just cooked through.

7. When all the chicken is just cooked through, remove from the oven and let rest for a few minutes.

8. Divide the chicken pieces among serving plates, putting them in the center of the plates. Toss the vegetables in the cooking juices until well coated and divide among the plates. Pour any remaining cooking juices over each serving and drizzle with more olive oil. Scatter the basil leaves over each and serve.

# Roast Chicken with Lemon Sauce

Pollo al Limone

**Serves 4**

A traditional dish from Italy's Campania region, where lemons are much beloved in cooking, this has become a specialty of Rao's Restaurant in New York City. This recipe, inspired by both the authentic version and Rao's, results in a completely addictive dish with lovely flavor tones and crispy textures.

**Wine Note:** While chicken can usually handle all but the biggest reds, it's the lemon sauce here that should shape your choices. We found that medium-weight whites with good acidity and prominent but not excessive fruit flavors allowed the lemon to shine through. The Campanian white variety Falanghina showed well in our tasting here, this time in the form of Falerno del Massico, a *denominazione* from along the region's northern coastline. Our choice was the Villa Matilde Falerno del Massico Bianco. Wines from neighboring regions showed well, too, such as the Regillo Frascati from outside Rome and, from the Marche, the excellent Villa Bucci Verdicchio Classico. We didn't find red wines as enjoyable as whites with this dish, but if you'd like to drink red, because of the lemon bear in mind more strongly than ever our little mantra, "good levels of acidity in wines make for good matches with food." Every soft and fruity wine we tried crashed into the tangy lemony-ness of the dish, and so we recommend you stick with medium-bodied, tart, and not-too-fruity reds, like good basic Chianti, Valpolicella, and the like. Outside of Italy you'd do best to pour crisp, medium-light Sauvignon Blanc–based wines like the Sterling Sauvignon Blanc from California.

*One 3- to 3 ½-pound chicken*

*Kosher salt*

*¾ cup extra-virgin olive oil*

*1 cup dry white wine*

*1 cup Chicken Stock (page 215)
or canned low-sodium chicken broth,
plus more as needed*

*½ cup fresh lemon juice*

*1 large clove garlic, minced*

*½ teaspoon finely chopped fresh rosemary*

*Freshly ground black pepper*

*Pinch of crushed red pepper flakes (optional)*

1. Preheat the oven to 425°F.

2. Let the chicken stand at room temperature for 20 minutes before roasting. Generously salt it inside and out. Using your fingers, rub the chicken all over with ¼ cup of the olive oil.

3. Set the chicken, breast up, on a rack in a roasting pan. Pour the wine and stock around the chicken. Roast for 20 minutes.

4. Reduce the oven temperature to 375°F and roast for another 35 to 45 minutes, or until just cooked through. Add a little more stock, wine, or water if the liquid evaporates beneath the chicken.

5. In a bowl, whisk together the lemon juice, garlic, rosemary, ½ teaspoon salt, a generous grinding of black pepper, and the red pepper flakes, if using. Whisk in the remaining ½ cup of olive oil and set aside.

6. Transfer the chicken to a cutting board designed to catch the juices and let it rest for 5 to 10 minutes. Stir the lemon juice mixture into the roasting pan.

7. Preheat the broiler.

8. Using a very sharp knife, cut the chicken into 10 to 12 pieces: 2 legs, 2 thighs, 2 wings, and 4 to 6 small breast pieces. (It's easiest to work with the breast if you separate it from the back of the bird; discard the back.) While working, try to keep the skin intact. Return the chicken and all the accumulated juices to the roasting pan and gently toss the pieces to coat with the sauce. Turn the pieces skin side up.

9. Broil the chicken until the skin is crispy and blackened in spots, 3 to 5 minutes. Serve with the lemon sauce poured over and around the chicken.

# Roast Chicken with Umbrian-Style Game Sauce

Pollo con Salsa Ghiotta

**Serves 4**

This dish usually is made in Umbria with richly flavored guinea hen, pheasant, quail, and squab, but it's also excellent with milder chicken, as this adaptation attests. Chicken is easier to buy, of course, and if you can find free-range or pasture-raised birds, their flavor will be better than mass-produced chicken, and it will make this dish closer in spirit to the original. By all means, if you want to make this with a game bird, seek them out. You can just as easily adapt this recipe for upland game because the savory sauce is made separately from the bird. Collect the juices from your cutting board and return them to the sauce for good flavor, and if livers or kidneys are included with any of these birds, substitute them for a portion of the chicken livers in the recipe.

**Wine Note:** With chicken or with a game bird such as guinea hen, the earthy-tasting *salsa Ghiotta* is best with medium- to medium-full-bodied whites that are fresh but not too fruity or polished with sweet oak flavor (which clashed with the delicious earthiness of the sauce). A favorite was the Bisci Verdicchio di Matelica from the neighboring Marches region. As for reds, Sagrantino di Montefalco, the terrifically rich Umbrian specialty, is too big for this dish (unless you have made this with squab), but look for its baby brother, Montefalco Rosso. One favorite is the Paolo Bea Montefalco Rosso. A top-quality Chianti like the Castello della Paneretta Chianti Classico is also a good choice and perhaps easier to find. Outside of Italy, pour an American Pinot Noir such as the very good Foxen Vinyard Pinot Noir from Santa Barbara County.

---

One 3- to 3 ½- pound chicken

Kosher salt

2 tablespoons Italian-Style Lard Paste (page 217) or extra-virgin olive oil

⅓ pound chicken livers

1 heaping tablespoon capers, drained

3 large anchovy fillets

½ cup extra-virgin olive oil

2 ½ ounces prosciutto di Parma or similar cured ham, finely chopped

5 large cloves garlic, minced

5 large sage leaves, finely chopped

3 juniper berries, crushed

¼ teaspoon finely chopped fresh rosemary

Pinch of cayenne pepper

1 cup dry white wine

1 cup dry red wine

---

1. Preheat the oven to 425°F.

2. Let the chicken stand at room temperature for 20 minutes before roasting. Generously salt it inside and out. Using your fingers, rub the chicken all over with the lard paste.

3. Set the chicken, breast up, on a rack in a roasting pan. Roast for 20 minutes.

4. Reduce the oven temperature to 375°F and roast for another 35 to 45 minutes, or until just cooked through. As it roasts, baste the chicken a few times with the fat in the pan or additional fat, if necessary.

5. Meanwhile, chop the chicken livers very finely (they will appear loose and watery, but continue chopping so they are thoroughly broken up). Set aside.

6. Chop the capers and anchovies together until they resemble a paste. Set aside.

7. In a skillet, warm 2 tablespoons of the olive oil over medium-high heat and cook the livers, spread in the pan in a thin layer, until browned on one side. Turn and brown the other side. Break the livers up with the back of a wooden spoon and stir in the caper-anchovy paste, the ham, garlic, sage, juniper berries, rosemary, and cayenne.

8. Add the wines and bring to a simmer, scraping the bottom of the skillet to loosen any browned bits. Reduce the heat and simmer very gently until the wine has reduced by two-thirds, 15 to 20 minutes. Remove from the heat and stir in the remaining olive oil. Season to taste with salt and set aside.

9. Transfer the chicken to a cutting board designed to catch the juices and let it rest for 5 to 10 minutes. Remove a leg and thigh and cut into 2 pieces at the joint. Repeat with the other leg and thigh. Cut down on 1 side of the breastbone and then, following the curve of the carcass, cut beneath the breast half to remove the meat in one piece. Repeat with the other side of the breast. Cutting crosswise, slice each breast half on the diagonal into 4 pieces.

10. Divide the chicken among 4 serving plates. Add the juices on the cutting board to the sauce and reheat gently. Spoon the sauce over the chicken and serve.

# Rabbit with Saffron and Black Olives

### Coniglio allo Zafferano

**Serves 4**

In Medieval and Renaissance Tuscany, saffron was cultivated on the slopes of San Gimignano, a tradition that survives today, albeit on a much smaller scale. Much of saffron's prestige was tied to its ability to turn all it touched to gold, a trait beautifully seen in this old Florentine specialty. If you don't like or can't find rabbit, substitute chicken legs to enjoy this special dish. And be sure to buy the best-quality olives you can find (be sure to warn your guests about pits). This is good with dark green vegetables such as spinach or chard.

**Butcher's Note:** Sweet and delicately flavored rabbit should always be purchased fresh and never frozen for the best flavor and texture (you're also more likely to receive the delicious liver and kidneys when you buy it fresh). We suggest ordering it in advance so your butcher can find good rabbit for you. He can also cut it for you as needed for the recipe. But if you'd like to butcher it yourself, it's no more difficult than a chicken.

To cut up a rabbit into pieces, first remove the liver and kidneys from inside the rabbit and reserve, if called for in the recipe. Using a sharp knife, remove the hind legs at the socket joint where they meet the torso. Cut each whole leg into two pieces at the joint between the leg and thigh, as you would for a chicken, so that you have four pieces. Next, remove the two front legs by cutting them where they meet the torso; cut close to the torso so as to include as much meat as possible on the legs. You now have six pieces. What remains is the torso, which, from one end to the other, consists of a short bony neck section, the larger rib section, a

large and meaty saddle section (with its two belly flaps), and a short bony tail section.

Once the legs have been removed and the rear legs are cut in two, separate the central saddle section from the bony sections on either end of it (a cleaver helps): Make one cut across the backbone just below the rib cage where it meets the saddle and then a second cut across the backbone to remove the short tail section from the saddle. Cut the saddle itself in half across the backbone and through the belly flaps; now you have eight larger meaty pieces including the legs.

For the rabbit stock in step 1, chop the remaining torso bones (neck, ribs, and tail) into 1- to 2-inch pieces. Cut away the belly flaps from the saddle to include in the stock.

For the Braised Rabbit with Serrano Ham and Almond Sauce (page 174), proceed as described above to cut the rabbit into eight pieces, and omit the last two (stock) steps. Cut the torso bones—neck, ribs, and tail—into four to six larger pieces and include them in the casserole with the meatier leg and saddle pieces to be eaten (their bones add flavor and they're great to gnaw on). Instead of removing the tougher belly flaps, wrap them around the exposed meat of the saddle pieces (the loins) and secure the flaps with toothpicks. (This helps keep the delicate loins moist during cooking.)

For Rabbit with Sherry and Garlic (page 176), we proceed as described for the Braised Rabbit with Serrano Ham and Almond Sauce, but add a few more cuts to yield large bite-size pieces: First, once you have separated the thighs from the rear legs, cut each one in half, for a total of six rear leg pieces. Cut the front legs in half. Next, rather than cutting the saddle into two large pieces, cut it into four smaller pieces (no need to secure the belly flaps with toothpicks here). Finally, with one crosswise and one longwise cut, cut the large rib cage section into four pieces. Cut the remaining neck and tail pieces to about the same size as the others, if neces-sary. You should have eighteen to twenty pieces or there-abouts. Remove any stray shards of bone with your fingers or tweezers.

**Wine Note:** Once famously known as Vernage in the fifteenth century, today's Vernaccia di San Gimignano is a firm, dry, medium-bodied white wine that pairs nicely with this full-flavored dish. It's not a particularly expressive or aromatic wine, which has led some producers to beef it up with small amounts of permitted grapes (such as Chardonnay) other than the namesake Vernaccia to fill it out. Another method aimed at enhancing Vernaccia is aging in new oak barrels, which to us seems to do nothing but smother or distract from whatever freshness the wine might have had. With this dish, avoid these more costly oak-aged renditions and stick to the less fancy *normale* bottlings issued by a number of producers. One favorite is the Falchini Vernaccia di San Gimignano. For a red wine, a lively young Chianti like the Cecchi Chianti suits the dish beautifully. From outside Tuscany, pour a not-too-heavy, easy-drinking white like the Columbia Crest Semillon-Chardonnay from Washington State or a juicy, lighter-styled red like Bethel Heights Vineyard Willamette Valley (Oregon) Pinot Noir.

*One 3-pound rabbit, cut into 8 serving pieces
(see Butcher's Note), torso bones, liver,
and kidneys reserved*

*1⅔ cups Chicken Stock (page 215)
or canned low-sodium chicken broth*

*1⅔ cups water*

*2 pinches of saffron threads (½ gram)*

*3 tablespoons extra-virgin olive oil*

*3 tablespoons unsalted butter*

*2 yellow onions, very finely chopped*

*6 cloves garlic, minced*

*Kosher salt*

*1 cup white dry wine*

*1 cup black olives such as Gaeta, Niçoise,
or Kalamata, preferably pitted*

1. In a skillet, combine the chopped torso bones with the chicken stock and water and bring to a boil over high heat. Reduce the heat and simmer gently for 45 minutes. Strain the rabbit stock and set aside.

2. Place the saffron in a small, dry skillet over medium heat. Toast the threads for about 1 minute, moving them about to avoid burning. Let cool and then crumble with your fingertips. Set aside.

3. In a large, heavy skillet, heat 2 tablespoons of the olive oil and 2 tablespoons of the butter over medium heat. When the butter melts, add the onions and cook gently for 15 minutes without browning. Add the garlic and cook for 15 minutes more, stirring occasionally. Transfer the onion mixture to a dish, leaving as much of the fat in the skillet as possible, and set aside.

4. Salt the rabbit pieces evenly and on all sides.

5. Reheat the fat in the skillet over medium-high heat and add the remaining 1 tablespoon olive oil and 1 tablespoon butter. Add the rabbit pieces and cook until both sides are lightly browned, 3 to 4 minutes per side. Transfer to a plate. In the same skillet, cook the liver and kidneys until lightly browned and almost cooked through, 3 to 4 minutes. Transfer to a cutting board, chop to a paste, and set aside.

6. Add the wine to the skillet and cook over medium heat until reduced by half, scraping the bottom of the skillet to loosen any browned bits. Stir in half of the saffron, the rabbit stock, and the onion mixture. Add the rabbit pieces and any accumulated juices. Bring just to a simmer, loosely cover with parchment paper, and cover the skillet. Cook until the legs are very tender, about 1½ hours. Adjust the heat as needed to maintain a bare simmer. Transfer the rabbit pieces to a plate and cover to keep warm.

7. Place the cooking liquid over medium-high heat and cook until it just begins to thicken, or until reduced to about 1½ cups. Stir in the remaining saffron followed by the liver paste, the rabbit pieces and any accumulated juices, and the olives. Add salt, if necessary. Gently simmer to concentrate the sauce, turning the rabbit pieces to coat them. The thickened sauce should cling to the rabbit but still be slightly fluid. Divide the rabbit, olives, and sauce among serving plates and serve.

# Braised Rabbit with Serrano Ham and Almond Sauce

### Conejo como en Alfambra

**Serves 4**

This is how they make rabbit in Alfambra, a town within the province of Teruel (after the city of the same name), which is itself part of the northeastern Spanish region of Aragon. It's no secret that Spaniards are crazy for both cured ham and rabbits, and many parts of the country are well known for the quality of their hams. The ham from Teruel is among the country's best and is put to good use in a number of local dishes. Here, an egg yolk–assisted *picada* (a thickener and flavor enhancer added toward the end of cooking) unites a sauce that bathes the rabbit pieces with the flavors of cured ham, almonds, garlic, and parsley. In addition to the leg and loin portions, the meaty carcass pieces often used for stock are included in the dish, both to add flavor and to provide delicious bits to gnaw on. Make sure each plate gets a piece or two.

**Wine Note:** This dish flatters lots of different wine styles except for the most explosively fruity types. Among whites, we loved gentle, medium-weight white Riojas, such as the Palacio y Hermanos Blanco. More dramatic were the full-bodied, barrel-fermented Burgundy-style whites we tasted, issued by just a handful of producers, that exhibit creamy, rich fruit and oak flavors and that, in spite of their sometimes high alcohol levels, make compelling matches for this dish. One of the best was the Remelluri blanco, made by that well-known red Rioja producer. Some rosé wines, which are sometimes clunky with main courses, were delicious here, too. Try the brisk, mouth-filling Muga Rosado, also from Rioja. While looking for reds, we first tried a few wines from the *denominaciónes* Calatayud and Cariñena in Aragon (the home of this dish), which, while deeply delicious (and great values), proved too powerfully fruity for the rabbit. So we turned to neighboring Rioja and, once again, found the kind of red wine that we felt best suited the dish. One widely available favorite: Marqués de Riscal Reserva.

---

*¼ cup olive oil, or as needed*

*One 3-pound rabbit, cut into 8 serving pieces, loin flaps secured with toothpicks, meaty torso bones (neck, ribs, and tail) cut into large chunks, liver and kidneys reserved (see Butcher's Note, page 170)*

*Kosher salt*

*All-purpose flour for dredging*

*1 medium yellow onion, finely chopped*

*6 cloves garlic, minced, plus ½ clove*

*2 ounces serrano or similar cured ham, sliced ⅛ inch thick and finely chopped*

*1¼ cups dry white wine*

*1¼ cups Chicken Stock (page 215) or canned low-sodium broth*

*One ½-inch-thick slice of country bread, crust removed, fried in extra-virgin olive oil until golden on both sides*

*12 blanched almonds, toasted (see Note)*

*2 large egg yolks*

*¼ cup finely chopped fresh flat-leaf parsley, plus more for garnish*

---

1. Preheat the oven to 325°F.

2. In a large skillet, heat the olive oil over medium-high heat. Season the rabbit pieces, including the meaty torso bone pieces, with salt on all sides. Coat with flour and shake off any excess. Working in two batches, cook until golden brown, about 4 minutes per side, adding more oil as needed. Transfer the rabbit to a low-sided earthenware casserole or glass baking dish just large enough to hold the pieces in a single layer. In the same skillet, cook the liver and kidneys until lightly browned and almost cooked through, 3 to 4 minutes. Transfer to a cutting board, mince very finely, and set aside.

3. Add the onion, minced garlic, and ham to the skillet and cook over medium heat for 10 minutes, stirring occasionally. Add the wine and stock and bring just to a boil. Simmer for 3 minutes, scraping the bottom of the skillet to loosen any browned bits. Pour the onion mixture over and around the rabbit. Cover tightly and bake for 35 minutes. Uncover and bake for 15 minutes longer.

4. Remove the casserole from the oven. Transfer the rabbit pieces to a plate and cover with aluminum foil to keep warm. Leave the oven on.

5. In the bowl of a food processor fitted with the metal blade, process the toasted bread, the almonds, the ½ clove garlic, ¼ teaspoon salt, and ¾ cup of the cooking liquid from the casserole until fairly smooth. Add the egg yolks and process a few seconds more. Add to the remaining liquid in the casserole and stir in the ¼ cup parsley and the minced liver and kidneys until thoroughly combined.

6. Return the rabbit to the casserole, turning the pieces to coat with the sauce. Return the casserole to the oven and cook, uncovered, for about 15 minutes, turning the rabbit over in the sauce and basting once. After 15 minutes the sauce should be noticeably thickened but still fluid. Cook for 5 minutes longer if necessary; the sauce will continue to thicken once served.

7. Remove the toothpicks from the loin pieces and divide the rabbit among serving plates. Top with the sauce and garnish with parsley.

**Note:** To toast almonds, spread them in a single layer in a dry skillet or shallow baking pan. Place over medium heat or in a preheated 350°F oven and toast, shaking the pan or stirring the almonds 2 or 3 times until golden and fragrant, 10 to 15 minutes. Transfer to another baking sheet or plate to cool.

# Rabbit with Sherry and Garlic

### Conejo al Jerez

**Serves 4**

While some variation of this dish is popular in many parts of Spain, the sherry suggests Andalucia is its home. We toss the rabbit with the garlic-sherry sauce before baking it and then again when it comes out of the oven, just before serving. For the best flavor, the small pieces of meat should be rolled in the sauce as much as possible.

🍴

**Wine Note:** You can drink white wine with this dish, but it's a great reason to indulge in some of the world's truly distinctive wines, the bracing and mysterious flavors of the palest, lightest, and driest members of the sherry family, fino and manzanilla. Among the driest wines in the world, they have a pretty high alcohol content (about 15 percent) and display a small amount of heat when taken with almost any food, which is one reason they are always served chilled. We found that the flavors and textures of these wines alongside the garlicky rabbit were just so deliciously suited, the slight heat bothered not at all. One of our favorites was the Hidalgo Manzanilla "La Gitana," although many other producers make good fino and manzanilla. There is the widely available Tío Pepe, a fino sherry from González-Byass, and a variety of both types from the house of Emilio Lustau, all excellent. Other producers include Pedro Domecq (their La Iña fino Sherry is excellent) and Barbadillo. Whatever fino or manzanilla sherry you buy, understand that it is only worth drinking when it is very fresh or as young as possible (after a couple years, these wines loose their vibrancy). Since there are usually no vintage dates on these wines, this isn't always easy to determine. But with the exception of a few producers who stamp a production date on the label (the aforementioned "La Gitana" is the best example), your best ally is an honest retailer with a high turnover.

---

*Kosher salt*

*One 3-pound rabbit, cut into 18 to 20 small pieces (see Butcher's Note, page 170), rinsed and blotted dry*

*All-purpose flour for dredging*

*6 tablespoons extra-virgin olive oil, plus more as needed*

*Cloves of 1 large head garlic, thinly sliced*

*2 large sprigs fresh thyme, plus more sprigs for garnish*

*1 cup fino or manzanilla sherry*

---

1. Generously salt the rabbit pieces and coat them with flour, shaking off any excess.

2. In a large skillet, heat the olive oil over medium-high heat and cook the rabbit pieces until golden on all sides (even the larger end surfaces), 3 to 4 minutes per side, adding more oil if needed. Transfer to a plate and set aside.

3. Preheat the oven to 350°F.

4. Let the skillet cool slightly and then pour out all but 4 tablespoons of the oil. Place over low heat. (If any flour in the skillet has blackened excessively, pour off the oil, scrape off any black spots, and add 4 tablespoons of fresh oil. Heat over medium-low heat for a minute or so and then reduce the heat to low.) Stir in the garlic and

thyme and cook gently, stirring occasionally, until the garlic is pale gold at the edges, 1 to 3 minutes.

5. Add the sherry and bring to a simmer over medium heat. Reduce the heat to medium-low and simmer gently for 3 minutes, scraping the bottom of the skillet to loosen any browned bits.

6. Return the rabbit to the skillet along with any accumulated juices and toss it thoroughly to coat with the garlic-sherry mixture. Transfer to a flameproof earthenware or glass baking dish just large enough to contain the rabbit in a single layer, cover tightly, and bake for 20 minutes. Uncover and transfer to the stove top over low heat. Turn the rabbit pieces over in the gently simmering sauce to coat the pieces and to slightly concentrate the flavors of the sauce, 1 to 3 minutes. There may not be a lot of sauce, but it should be flavorful and cling mostly to the pieces of rabbit, with only a small amount of sauce remaining in the bottom of the dish. Reduce futher, if necessary.

7. Remove the thyme sprigs. Divide the rabbit among serving plates and spoon any sauce remaining in the baking dish over the meat. Garnish each plate with a small cluster of fresh thyme sprigs and serve right away.

-Chapter 8-

# GAME BIRDS AND OTHER GAME

# Duck Breasts with Shallots

*Les Magrets à l'Èchalote*

**Serves 4**

This is a recipe that comes from Gascony in the southwest of France, where the duck breasts commonly used come from the local Moulard duck. These duck breasts are thicker than those of the white Pekin ducks, also referred to as Long Island duck, most common in our markets, which is why we call for them here. Moulards—the ducks are a cross between male Muscovys and female white Pekins—are now also widely available in the United States, in part because they are a by-product of foie gras production, which relies on them almost exclusively. Speaking of foie gras, if you like it, it makes a delectable addition to these duck breasts and their tangy shallot sauce: Just prior to slicing the duck in step 4 of this recipe, sear four slices of duck foie gras following the quantities and directions in Braised Duck with Red Wine and Prunes (facing page) and serve it alongside the duck breasts.

**Wine Note:** For these succulent Gascon duck breasts, we looked for the dark, plump, and softly tannic red wines that are abundant in southwest France. In this tasting, our favorites came from Gascony's neighbor to the east, the region of Languedoc-Roussillon. One favorite was the rich, cassis-flavored Château d'Oupia Minervois "Cuvée des Barons." We also loved a California ringer we tossed into our tasting: the Ridge Vineyards Geyserville, a deeply satisfying proprietary red wine made mostly from Zinfandel fruit.

*2 Moulard or Muscovy duck breast halves (about 2 pounds total)*

*Kosher salt*

*2 cups finely chopped shallots*

*1 tablespoon chopped fresh thyme, plus whole leaves for garnish*

*Freshly ground black pepper*

*⅓ cup dry red wine*

*3 tablespoons red wine vinegar*

*2 tablespoons honey*

1. Using a very sharp knife, score the fat covering each breast in a crosshatch pattern at about ½-inch intervals, drawing the knife all the way through the fat but without cutting into the flesh. Salt the breasts generously on both sides.

2. In a heavy skillet, arrange the duck breast halves skin side down and place over medium-low heat. Cook gently until the skin is deeply browned and crispy, like cracklings, and much of the fat has rendered, 10 to 12 minutes. Turn the breasts, raise the heat to medium-high, and cook for 5 to 7 minutes longer for medium-rare. Transfer to a baking pan and keep the duck warm, uncovered, in a very low (200°F) oven.

3. Pour off all but about 3 tablespoons of the duck fat in the skillet (reserve the poured-off fat for another use) and place over medium heat. Add the shallots and cook, stirring occasionally, until translucent, 4 to 5 minutes. Add the chopped thyme, a few grindings of pepper, the wine, vinegar, honey, and ½ teaspoon salt. Stir well and let the liquid reduce until it has almost evaporated. Taste and adjust the seasonings with salt, vinegar, and/or honey, to make the shallots sweet-tart to your taste.

4. When the liquid has almost finished reducing, transfer the duck to a carving board designed to capture the juices. Slice the duck against the grain and on a slight diagonal into slices about ⅜ inch thick. Set aside.

5. Stir any duck juices on the carving board into the shallot reduction and keep cooking until nearly evaporated. Spoon some of the shallot mixture onto the center of each serving plate. Neatly fan the duck slices around the shallots and garnish with the whole thyme leaves. Serve immediately.

# Braised Duck with Red Wine and Prunes

## Le Canard aux Pruneaux

**Serves 4**

Duck with prunes, red wine, and Armagnac is a classic combination from southwest France wherein the sweet warmth of prunes acts as a rich, fruity complement to the braised duck. In this recipe, we offer an optional garnish made of red wine vinegar, honey, and another regional specialty, seared foie gras, for a sweet-and-sour counterpoint to the richness of the duck and prunes. The liver adds a sublime fourth dimension that makes this a perfect dish for a special occasion.

**Butcher's Note:** While both goose and duck foie gras are common in France (some of which is exported), you're more likely to find domestic duck livers in America, where, in upstate New York and in Sonoma County, California, exceptional foie gras is produced. Duck or goose liver, domestic or imported: they are largely interchangeable. What's most important is that you buy from a purveyor you trust, because freshness and quality in foie gras are crucial.

When you buy foie gras, always ask for fresh foie gras. Otherwise, you may get foie gras pâté or terrine, which are cooked products. And always buy grade A livers, the highest grade, which are easier to clean, slice more nicely, and contain fewer bruises. The liver is formed of two lobes, one slightly smaller than the other, and will usually weigh about 1½ pounds (so for this recipe you'll have some left over for another use). The foie gras should be firm and evenly colored (usually a pale beige) and used within a day or so of purchase. If it's packed in Cryovac (an oxygen-free, heavy plastic packaging), it will keep in the refrigerator for up to a week, although it should be used as soon as possible. Before use, simply rinse the foie gras and pat it dry (for use in pâtés and terrines, foie gras requires a more elaborate deveining procedure that is unnecessary here), then let it sit at room temperature for twenty minutes to let it warm slightly, which makes it easier to work with. For this dish, you may want to separate the two lobes lengthwise and cut the slices called for in the recipe just from the larger lobe; wrap and refrigerate the smaller lobe for another use. Handle the liver carefully so that it doesn't crack or tear.

To slice foie gras, put it on a clean kitchen towel to prevent it from sliding on your work surface. Then, using a sharp knife that's been run under hot water to warm it, gently slice the lobe crosswise into thick slices, as called for in the recipe. The lobes can be presliced a few hours ahead, covered tightly in plastic wrap, and kept in the refrigerator.

**Wine Note:** The inky dark and buoyantly fruit-filled red wines common in much of southwest France are just the thing alongside this dish, with or without the foie gras garnish. One favorite in our tasting was a wine from the Domaine Gautier in the Fitou *appellation* of the Languedoc-Roussillon. From outside of France, pour a roundly rich and satisfying Shiraz (Syrah)-based wine from Australia such as d'Arenberg "d'Arry's Original" Shiraz-Grenache from McLaren Vale.

*2 tablespoons vegetable oil*

*3 ounces ventrèche, pancetta, or other unsmoked bacon, cut into ¼-inch dice*

*Kosher salt*

*6 whole duck legs (3 to 3 ½ pounds total), cut in half at the leg joint*

*1 small yellow onion, finely chopped*

*1 small carrot, peeled and finely chopped*

*Cloves of 1 head garlic, crushed*

*⅓ cup Armagnac or Cognac*

*1½ cups full-bodied dry red wine*

*Two 3-by-½-inch strips orange zest (see Note, page 62)*

*1 large sprig fresh thyme*

*1 bay leaf*

*⅔ pound pitted prunes*

**Foie gras garnish (optional)**

*About 1 tablespoon red wine vinegar*

*2 to 3 teaspoons honey*

*¾ pound fresh foie gras, cut crosswise into four ⅝-inch-thick slices (see Butcher's Note)*

*Kosher salt*

1. In a large, heavy pot with a tight-fitting lid, heat the oil over medium heat and cook the ventrèche, stirring occasionally, until crisp. Remove with a slotted spoon and set aside to drain on paper towels.

2. Generously salt the duck pieces all over.

3. Raise the heat to medium-high and, working in two batches, cook the duck until deep golden brown all over, about 15 minutes. Reduce the heat if it threatens to burn. Transfer the duck to a plate and set aside.

4. Pour off all but about 3 tablespoons of the fat and reduce the heat to medium. Add the onion, carrot, and garlic and cook gently, stirring occasionally, for 5 minutes. Add the Armagnac and simmer until almost evaporated. Add the wine and simmer for 3 minutes longer, scraping the bottom of the pot to loosen any browned bits. Stir in the orange zest, thyme sprig, bay leaf, a pinch of salt, and the ventrèche.

5. Nestle the duck in the pot, pour in any accumulated juices from the plate holding the duck, cover tightly, and bring to a bare simmer over very low heat. Cook for 1½ hours, adjusting the heat as needed to maintain a bare simmer. Turn the duck pieces over after 45 minutes.

6. Nestle the prunes between the duck pieces, cover, and simmer gently for 30 minutes longer. Divide the duck among warmed plates. Remove the orange zest, thyme sprig, and bay leaf. Stir the sauce and prunes for a few moments, and, if necessary, reduce the sauce slightly to concentrate the flavor. Then spoon over the duck.

7. For the optional foie gras garnish, before dividing the duck among the plates, heat a dry heavy skillet over high heat.

8. Meanwhile, stir the vinegar and honey, a little at a time, into the wine and prune sauce. Taste the sauce as you go. The finished sauce should be just slightly sweet and sour, but shouldn't taste strongly of either honey or vinegar. Add more of each until you like the balance of flavors. Spoon the sauce and prunes over the duck and keep warm.

9. When the skillet is very hot and beginning to smoke, lightly salt the foie gras and sear it until deeply golden brown, 1 to 1½ minutes per side. Garnish each serving of duck with a slice of foie gras and serve immediately.

# Squab with Sweet Tuscan Wine Sauce

Picchione al Vin Santo

**Serves 2**

Squab, rarely weighing more than 1 pound, are truly a luscious delicacy with a distinctive, full flavor. Italians love them, and so we turned to them for inspiration. The butterflied squab here are marinated, later to be cooked in a skillet beneath the weight of a brick and then surrounded by a simple sauce made from Tuscany's sweet Vin Santo wine and squab scraps. All but the cooking itself can be done ahead of time. The rest comes together in about twenty minutes, when it's time to cook the squab and finish the sauce. In typical French fashion, the latter is accomplished by whisking a beurre manié (kneaded butter and flour mixture) into the pan. It's not a common French Tuscan technique, but it works nicely in this dish. Serve the little birds with stewed white beans and a mildly bitter green, such as chicory, or a rich nutty one, such as Tuscan kale, drizzled with extra-virgin olive oil.

**Butcher's Note:** To butterfly squab, cut along either side of their backbone with poultry shears or a sharp chef's knife (remove and reserve the backbones and wingtips for stock). Lay each bird, breast side up, on a work surface and push firmly on the breastbone with the palm of your hand to lightly crack the backbone and flatten the bird.

**Wine Note:** We found that all kinds of Sangiovese-based Tuscan wines worked well with squab—all, that is, but the most meager or (as usual) the most towering in scale. For example, a slightly nervy but balanced Chianti was a nice counterpoint to the rich squab meat, but so was the more stately warmth and weight of a Brunello di Montalcino, whose rich textures wrapped around the bird without crushing it. A favorite among the Chiantis was La Massa Chianti Classico; among *Brunelli*, the Podere Scopetone Brunello di Montalcino; and from around the beautiful city of Montepulciano at Tuscany's southern limits, the Dei Vino Nobile di Montepulciano. A fine choice from California would be one of the state's better Merlots. A particular favorite is the Shafer Merlot from Napa Valley's Stags Leap District.

### Marinade

*3 tablespoons extra-virgin olive oil*

*1 large clove garlic, finely chopped*

*1 tablespoon finely chopped fresh thyme*

*1 tablespoon finely chopped fresh sage*

*1 teaspoon coarsely ground black pepper*

*2 squab (about 1 pound each), butterflied (see Butcher's Note), scraps reserved*

*Kosher salt*

### Vin Santo sauce

*2 tablespoons olive or vegetable oil*

*Reserved squab carcass scraps, cut into pieces*

*¾ cup Vin Santo or similar sweet wine*

*1½ cups Chicken Stock (page 215) or canned low-sodium chicken broth*

*½ teaspoon kosher salt*

*2 tablespoons unsalted butter, at room temperature, mashed with 1 teaspoon all-purpose flour*

*Kosher salt*

*Extra-virgin olive oil*

---

1. To make the marinade, in a small nonreactive bowl, stir together the olive oil, garlic, thyme, sage, and pepper.

2. Thoroughly rub the marinade into the squab, front and back. Lay the squab on a plate, cover with plastic wrap, and set aside.

3. To begin the sauce, in a saucepan, heat the olive oil over medium-high heat. When hot, add the squab carcass scraps and cook until deeply browned on both sides, 10 to 12 minutes, reducing the heat if they threaten to burn.

4. Add the Vin Santo and bring to a simmer, scraping the bottom of the pan to loosen any browned bits. Reduce the heat and gently simmer until reduced by half, about 4 minutes. Add the stock and salt and bring to a simmer. Cover the saucepan partially and simmer very gently for 45 minutes.

5. Pass the sauce through a fine-mesh strainer, pressing hard on the solids to extract all the flavorful juices. Skim the fat, if you like, and return the sauce to the pan. You should have about ⅔ cup; simmer to reduce the liquid or add a little more stock, as necessary. Set the sauce aside.

6. Generously salt the marinated squab.

7. Preheat one large or two small skillets big enough to fit the butterflied squab in a single layer over medium-high heat. Add enough olive oil to the skillet(s) for a thick film. When the oil begins to smoke, add the birds, breast side down, and weight each with an aluminum foil–wrapped brick or a foil-covered skillet. Top these with weights such as large cans of tomatoes.

8. Reduce the heat to medium and cook the squab until deeply golden brown, 6 to 7 minutes. Turn and weight the squabs on the other side. Cook for about 5 minutes longer. Turn and weight the squabs once more to re-crisp the breast side, about another minute. The squabs should be medium-rare. Cook a few minutes longer, if necessary. Transfer the squab to a cutting board and let rest for about 3 minutes.

9. Meanwhile, finish the sauce: Bring to a simmer, reduce the heat to very low, and whisk in the butter-and-flour mixture. Switch to a rubber spatula and stir until the sauce thickens enough to coat the back of a spoon but is still fluid, about 2 minutes.

10. When ready to serve, cut each squab in half between the breasts, directly through the breastbone. In the center of each warmed serving plate, place half a squab, cut side down. Lean the second half of each squab attractively against the first. Spoon the sauce around each portion and serve.

# Quail with Grapes and Almonds

Les Cailles aux Raisins et Amandes

**Serves 2**

Tiny quail are a treat many can't resist. While there is a long tradition of pairing them with grapes in many of Europe's wine regions, this particular dish has its roots in Alsace, France. While peeling the grapes is not absolutely necessary, it does improve the texture of the dish. Blanch the grapes in boiling water for thirty seconds to make peeling easier, and then flick the skins off with the tip of a sharp paring knife. This is an easy recipe to double if you use two casseroles.

**Butcher's Note:** Quail are available whole or partially boned with their wings and legs intact. You may have to special order them regardless of how they are prepared. Use either whole or partially boned quail here. Either way, use poultry shears or a small knife to clip the bony first two joints on the ends of the wings, if you like, though this is not crucial to the dish's success.

**Wine Note:** This is a great dish for some of the fuller-bodied styles of Alsatian whites, especially Riesling *grand crus* from the region's top vineyards. One favorite: the Domaine Weinbach Riesling "Schlossberg Cuvée Ste. Catherine." Another delicious route is to cook with and then drink an Alsatian Pinot Gris alongside the quail, a good way to utilize this richly textured, sometimes-too-strong white from the region. A favorite at our tasting was the Domaine Pierre Frick Pinot Gris "Rot Murle" (if you like, use a less costly Pinot Gris to cook with). Among American wine regions, Oregon has made a specialty of Pinot Gris, and these wines deserve to be better known, not only because of their quality, but also because—in contrast to their French counterparts—they are extremely flexible with food. One favorite is the Rex Hill Vineyards Pinot Gris "Jacob Hart Vineyard" from the Willamette Valley.

3 tablespoons unsalted butter

½ cup blanched slivered almonds

Kosher salt and freshly ground black pepper

Four 4- to 5-ounce quails (see Butcher's Note)

All-purpose flour for dredging

2 tablespoons vegetable oil

2 tablespoons finely chopped shallot

1 large sprig fresh thyme

½ cup dry Alsatian white wine such as Riesling

½ cup Chicken Stock (page 215)
or canned low-sodium chicken broth

2 teaspoons fresh lemon juice

28 seedless red or white grapes, peeled

3 ounces fresh foie gras, cut into ¾-inch dice
(optional) (see Butcher's Note, page 181)

2 small bunches watercress for garnish

1. In a flameproof casserole or Dutch oven, melt 1 tablespoon of the butter over medium heat and cook the almonds, stirring, until golden. Transfer the nuts to a plate and set aside. Wipe out the casserole.

2. Salt and pepper the quail thoroughly inside and out and coat with flour, shaking off the excess.

3. Melt the remaining butter with the oil in the casserole over medium-high heat. For bone-in quail, when the fat is hot, cook the quail on 1 side until golden, 2 to 3 minutes. Turn and cook for 2 to 3 minutes. Turn the quail breast side down and cook for about 2 minutes longer (prop them against the sides of the pot if necessary). For semi-boneless quail (which are more flat than rounded), cook breast side down for 3 minutes, turn, and cook for 3 minutes longer. Reduce the heat if the quail threaten to burn.

4. Add the shallot and thyme and cook, stirring, for 1 minute. Add the wine and stock and simmer for 2 minutes, scraping the bottom of the pot to loosen any browned bits. Stir in the lemon juice and the grapes and turn the quail breast side up. Reduce the heat to very low, cover the casserole, and gently braise until the quail are cooked to your liking, 12 to 15 minutes for medium-rare and 17 to 20 minutes for medium-well. Transfer the

quail to serving plates and cover with aluminum foil to keep warm.

5. Raise the heat to medium and simmer the cooking liquid until thickened slightly and reduced to about ½ cup. Add salt to taste. If using the foie gras, stir it in and cook just to heat it through, about 30 seconds. Do not let it melt. Pour the sauce over the quail and scatter the grapes on top. Sprinkle with the almonds, garnish with the watercress, and serve.

# Roasted Rack of Venison with Port and Red Currant Sauce

Venison with Cumberland Sauce

**Serves 4**

This is a classic from England, where the autumn hunt has always been taken very seriously. Nowadays, unless you hunt, most of us eat farm-raised venison, which is not as gamy as some might expect yet still retains a pleasing, full flavor and tends to be nice and lean. Though it is traditionally served as a cold sauce alongside cold meat, our adaptation of Cumberland sauce is served hot with chops from a simple, elegant roasted rack of venison. This dish is great for entertaining; an eight-rib rack serves four perfectly. The goal with the lemon and orange zest is to cut matchsticks that will provide texture and flavor to the finished sauce. Use a small knife, vegetable peeler, or a specially designed citrus zester. In winter, serve the venison chops with blanched Brussels sprouts sautéed in butter and finished with bacon. In the summertime, the chops are delicious with buttered string and wax beans.

**Butcher's Note:** Because racks of any animal are, by nature, lopsided, you have to be a bit crafty in order to brown them thoroughly. As they cook, lean the racks against the sides of the skillet or against one another to help you brown those areas that resist contact with the bottom of the pan. If you don't own a pair of kitchen tongs, here's a perfect excuse to buy some; you will find them one of the most useful utensils in the kitchen. As with all racks, start browning with the meaty side down and then work around the circumference of the rack until nicely browned (a rack really has three or four "surfaces"). When you get to the side of the rack that exposes the cut-off rib bones, brown for a few minutes less than others and then put the skillet in the oven to roast (with this side still facing down). In this way, this less-browned side will continue browning as the meat finishes cooking in the oven.

**Wine Note:** With a classic British dish before us, we were, for the first time in this book, without a regional wine tradition to frame our tasting. So, when selecting wines to sample with our venison and Cumberland sauce, we behaved as a nineteenth-century British aristocrat might have: On our table was a selection of top-flight red Bordeaux and Burgundy. This fantasy, it turned out, was a mistake.

Because farm-raised venison is really quite lean and mild, to our taste, it's best enjoyed with wines that don't overpower it. Nevertheless, it goes just fine with big, "important" Bordeaux and Burgundy . . . when the meat is all by itself. The problem at our table was the sauce. This delicious, fruity-sweet Port and red currant sauce really knocks the stuffing out of most wines. After a number of tries, we knew we needed fruity, fairly full-bodied, and decidedly food-friendly wine. To us that means a bigger-boned California or Oregon Pinot Noir. One favorite is St. Innocent Pinot Noir "Villages Cuvée" from the Willamette Valley. Long after the tasting, we had another thought. We realized that the best companion to

this dish and that pesky sauce might be an altogether differ-ent wine, so we returned and tried another historical British favorite, a white. This top-flight German Riesling knocked the ball out of the park. The wine? The Robert Weil Kiedrich Gräfenberg Riesling Spätlese from the Rheingau.

---

*1 small lemon, washed*

*1 small orange, washed*

*¾ cup good-quality Port*

*1½ tablespoons minced shallot*

*5 tablespoons red currant preserves or jelly*

*½ teaspoon ground ginger*

*½ teaspoon dry mustard*

*Kosher salt*

*Two 4-rib racks of venison or one 8-rib rack, halved (about 2½ pounds), frenched, and trimmed of all fat and silver skin*

*¼ cup vegetable oil*

*2 cloves garlic, halved*

*6 sprigs fresh thyme*

*6 tablespoons unsalted butter, cut into tablespoon pieces*

*3 tablespoons Beef Stock (page 212) or canned low-sodium beef broth*

---

1. Using a vegetable peeler or small, sharp knife, remove the colored part, or zest, of all the lemon and half the orange skins, working in strips from top to bottom and taking care not to include the white pith underneath (if some pith remains attached, cut it away with a paring knife). Cut the zest lengthwise into the thinnest possible matchsticks. Put in a small metal sieve.

2. Bring a saucepan of water to a boil over medium-high heat. Submerge the zest in the sieve in the water for 1 minute. Remove and rinse under cool running water. Repeat twice more. Pat the zest dry and set aside.

3. Cut and squeeze the lemon to yield 1 tablespoon of juice. Cut and squeeze the orange to yield 6 tablespoons of juice. Set the juice aside.

4. In a small sauté pan, bring the Port and shallot to a boil over high heat. Reduce the heat to medium-low and simmer until reduced by half, about 3 minutes. Add the red currant preserves, ginger, mustard, and a pinch of salt, whisking until the preserves begin to bubble. Add the citrus zests and whisk in the citrus juices. Simmer over low heat until the sauce thickens a bit and is lightly syrupy, 5 to 6 minutes longer. Remove from the heat and set aside.

5. Preheat the oven to 400°F.

6. Blot the venison dry and generously salt all over. In a large ovenproof skillet, heat the oil over medium-high heat until very hot. Cook the venison racks, turning them with tongs, until deeply browned around their circumference, 8 to 10 minutes (see Butcher's Note).

7. Transfer the skillet to the oven and roast to the desired doneness, 15 to 18 minutes for medium-rare, or when an instant-read thermometer registers 125°F. After 12 minutes, carefully transfer the skillet to the stove top and add the garlic, thyme sprigs, and 4 tablespoons of the butter, tilting the pan to let the ingredients mingle. Baste the meat with the butter for 30 seconds. Turn the racks over, baste again, and return to the oven to finish roasting. When done, baste the meat once more and transfer the venison to a cutting board. Tent loosely with aluminum foil and let rest for 5 minutes.

8. Return the sauce to a simmer and whisk in the stock and the remaining 2 tablespoons butter. Remove from the heat and keep warm on the stove top (it will thicken a bit as it cools).

9. Cut the venison into 8 equal chops. Place 2 chops attractively on each serving plate, spoon the sauce over each, and serve.

**Make-Ahead Tip:** The sauce can be made up to 6 hours ahead and refrigerated or kept at room temperature. Thin with stock or water as necessary.

# Venison Stew with Grappa-Herb Cream

Capriolo alla Valdostana

**Serves 4**

This heady stew comes from the Valle d'Aosta in the Alps of northwest Italy. The Italian-Style Lard Paste provides a distinct richness to the stew, but you can omit it and use extra-virgin olive oil instead (see Note). While you don't need to spend a fortune for the best grappa available, it's worth it to buy a good one; in addition to using it to add its unique flavor to the dish, you can enjoy drinking the rest of the bottle, which you may not with harsh, cheaper grappa. If you don't have access to venison, substitute beef chuck. Serve this with cheese-laced polenta, either soft or cut into rectangles and pan-fried until crisp. Small potatoes, prepared as you like them, are good, too.

**Butcher's Note:** Our preference is for farm-raised venison, which has good flavor but a softer texture than wild venison. We know a lot of people have a freezer full of wild venison come fall, and you can use either in our recipes. When you buy farm-raised venison from us, other butchers, or the Internet, it will almost certainly be packed in Cryovac, a specially sealed heavy plastic that keeps the meat fresh during transport.

**Wine Note:** When it comes to wine, cream is a strange thing—and this dish has a goodly amount of it. Wines with too much tannin, too much acidity, and too much body clash with the soft richness of this creamy stew. This is a question of degree because a lightly tannic, lightly acidic, and moderately rich wine works just fine with this great venison stew. Three wines emerged as our favorites, listed here in typical ascending order of familiarity and availability. The first is a local specialty from the Valle d'Aosta itself, and although it's available in the United States, it is tough to find. Produced high up in the Alpine village of Chambave and made mostly from the indigenous Petite Rouge grape, Ezio Voyat's Rosso "Le Muraglie" is a medium-weight wine that's brightly flavored, thoughtfully rustic in style, and free of obvious tannin—not unlike a less acidic but brightly flavored Barbera. It tastes great with the venison stew. (Interestingly, two nicely made Barbera wines tasted just okay with the dish.)

Our second choice comes from the ferociously windy "entrance" to the Valle d'Aosta, just over the administrative boundary in Piedmont, where lie the vineyards of Carema. There delicate and age-worthy Nebbiolo-based wines, issued by the few remaining producers who bother with the difficult growing conditions, are fascinating. With six to ten years of age or more, they display a lacy, autumnal side of the Nebbiolo grape that is more delicate than its cousins to the south, Barolo and Barbaresco. This delicate style of Nebbiolo is surprisingly delicious with the creamy venison. It's surprising because Nebbiolo is not only regarded as a tannic variety but an acidic one, too (wine and food, we're reminded, is a funny thing). The goodness of the match seemed to be driven by something else in the wine, something that involves the relationship between aged wines and creamy sauces. While aged white wines of various types have been more commonly considered as partners for creamy things—the well-aged, traditional white Rioja wine is a supreme example—certain traits develop in some aged red wines that make them appealing, too. In any event, the wines of the finest maker of Carema are available in the United States, often with five years of age or more. Try the Luigi Ferrando Carema (their so-called white label).

If you can't find either of these, try our third choice, Dolcetto from the Langhe in Piedmont, home of Barolo and Barbaresco. The best of these *dolcetti* are gentle, a bit juicy, medium bodied, and suave in style with no super-extracted fruit and no obvious flavor of new oak. One such wine is the Aldo Conterno Dolcetto d'Alba.

For both cooking and drinking, we recommend the glycerin-rich, full-flavored regular and reserve grappas from Nardini.

---

*1 cup all-purpose flour*

*2 tablespoons kosher salt*

*Freshly ground black pepper*

*1¾ pounds trimmed venison shoulder,
cut into 2-inch chunks,
any juices in the packaging reserved*

*6 tablespoons olive oil or vegetable oil,
or as needed*

*5 tablespoons Italian-Style Lard Paste (page 217)
(see Note)*

*2 large leeks, white and pale green parts only,
well rinsed and chopped*

*1 stalk celery, coarsely chopped*

*1 carrot, peeled and chopped*

*4 large cloves garlic, crushed*

*2 tablespoons tomato paste*

*2½ cups rich dry red wine*

*2 large sprigs fresh thyme*

*6 juniper berries*

*4 whole cloves*

*⅛ teaspoon ground cinnamon*

*1 cup Chicken Stock (page 215),
canned low-sodium chicken broth, or water,
plus more as needed*

### Grappa-herb cream

*1 tablespoon unsalted butter*

*3 tablespoons finely chopped shallot*

*½ cup good-quality grappa*

*1½ cups heavy cream*

*½ teaspoon finely chopped fresh rosemary*

*¾ teaspoon finely chopped fresh sage*

*¾ teaspoon finely chopped fresh thyme*

*1 tablespoon finely chopped fresh flat-leaf parsley*

*⅛ teaspoon kosher salt*

*2 large leeks, white and pale green parts only,
well rinsed and sliced into ¼-inch rounds*

*3 carrots, peeled and sliced into ¼-inch rounds*

*1 tablespoon finely chopped
fresh flat-leaf parsley for garnish*

---

1. In a large mixing bowl, mix the flour with the salt and a generous grinding of pepper. Coat the venison pieces with the flour and shake off any excess.

2. In a large skillet, heat the olive oil over medium-high heat. Working in two batches, cook the venison pieces until deeply browned on at least two sides, about 5 minutes per side, adding more oil if needed for the second batch. Transfer to a deep heatproof bowl large enough to hold the meat, wine, and vegetables. Set aside.

3. Wipe out the skillet. Reduce the heat to medium-low and melt the lard paste. Cook the chopped leeks, celery, carrot, and garlic, stirring occasionally, until the vegetables are softened but without color, 6 to 8 minutes. Stir in the tomato paste and cook for 1 minute.

4. Add the wine, thyme sprigs, juniper berries, cloves, and cinnamon, and any juices reserved from the venison packaging and simmer until the wine is reduced by one-third, about 5 minutes, scraping the bottom of the pan to loosen any browned bits. Pour the hot mixture over the meat, making sure the meat is submerged. If not, add a little water, wine, or a mixture of the two. Let cool to room temperature, cover, and refrigerate for at least 6 hours or up to overnight. Turn the meat once during this time.

5. Preheat the oven to 350°F.

6. Transfer the meat and marinade to a 10-quart flame-proof casserole or Dutch oven with a tight-fitting lid, and slowly warm over very low heat. Stir in the stock, raise the heat to medium-high, and bring to a simmer.

7. Cover the casserole tightly and bake for 20 minutes. Reduce the oven temperature to 250°F and continue baking until the meat is very tender, about 4 hours. Adjust the oven temperature as needed to maintain a bare simmer. If the stew begins to stick to the bottom of the pot, add ¼ to ½ cup of stock or water, as needed. When the meat is tender, the liquid surrounding it should be thickened, concentrated, and saucelike, but still fluid.

8. Meanwhile, make the grappa-herb cream: In a skillet or saucepan, melt the butter over medium-low heat. Stir in the shallot and cook until softened, but without color, about 5 minutes. Add the grappa and simmer gently until reduced to 2 or 3 tablespoons, about 4 minutes. Stir in the cream, rosemary, sage, thyme, parsley, and salt and continue to simmer gently until reduced by one-third, about 4 minutes. Remove from the heat and set aside.

9. To finish the stew, in a saucepan, bring 10 cups of water and 2 tablespoons salt to a rolling boil. Put a metal bowl filled with ice and water near the stove.

10. Cook the leek and carrot slices until the carrots are crisp-tender, 4 to 5 minutes. Drain the vegetables and transfer to the ice bath. Let cool for 1 minute. Using a slotted spoon, gently lift the vegetables from the water and blot dry. Set aside.

11. When the venison is tender, transfer the casserole to the stove top. Remove the thyme sprigs and thoroughly stir in the grappa-herb cream and then the leek and carrot slices. The stew should be rich and creamy and still somewhat fluid. If it needs to be thicker and more concentrated, simmer, uncovered, a few minutes more. If it needs to be thinned, stir in a little stock or water. Add salt to taste. Serve immediately, garnished with the parsley.

**Note:** If you decide to omit the lard paste, use extra-virgin olive oil instead of regular olive or vegetable oil to brown the venison. Rather than discard this oil, leave it in the skillet and add enough additional oil to equal five tablespoons. Proceed with the recipe, leaving out the lard paste but adding a generous pinch each of salt, chopped fresh rosemary, and fresh sage in place of the herbs found in the paste.

# Wild Boar Stew with Porcini Mushrooms and Blueberries

Cinghale ai Frutti di Bosco

**Serves 4 to 6**

This fascinating dish from Piedmont, Italy, is adapted from a standard in that region. Frutti di Bosco literally means "fruits of the forest" and accordingly features porcini mushrooms (presumably either fresh or the dried ones we use here) and *mirtilli,* a native berry for which we've substituted blueberries with great results. They both go into the same pot with wild boar, another denizen of the forest and a very traditional local source of protein. The flavors of the earthy porcini and softly tangy blueberries make a great foil for the rich meat, and the effect of the blueberries is deliciously unexpected as they release little explosions of fruit flavor with each bite. More and more, specialty stores are beginning to sell wild boar, and you can order it from us at Lobels.com. Try to buy the shoulder rather than the slightly drier leg meat.

**Wine Note:** Two wines, one expressing youth and the other a bit of age, suit this rich and gently fruity stew. The youthful choice was a warm and tangy Barbera, again showing its value and versatility as one of the most food-friendly of wines. One favorite is DeForville Barbera d'Alba. The more mature selection in our tasting was a mellow and earthy-flavored ten-year-old bottle of Oddero Barolo. A good California choice would be the Acacia "Carnernos" Pinot Noir.

---

*1 cup all-purpose flour*

*Kosher salt and freshly ground black pepper*

*1¾ pounds trimmed wild boar shoulder, cut into large chunks 3 to 4 inches long by about 1 inch thick, any juices in the packaging reserved*

*6 tablespoons extra-virgin olive oil, or as needed*

*1 yellow onion, coarsely chopped*

*1 stalk celery, coarsely chopped*

*1 carrot, peeled and coarsely chopped*

*4 large cloves garlic, 2 thinly sliced, 2 crushed*

*2½ cups rich dry red wine*

*One 3-inch sprig fresh rosemary*

*4 large fresh sage leaves*

*2 large fresh thyme sprigs*

*6 juniper berries*

*2 cloves*

*4 ounces dried porcini mushrooms*

*4 tablespoons unsalted butter*

*3 cups blueberries*

---

1. In a large bowl, mix the flour with 2 tablespoons salt and a generous grinding of pepper. Coat the boar chunks with the flour and shake off any excess.

2. In a deep skillet or flameproof casserole, heat the olive oil over medium-high heat. Working in two batches, cook the boar until deeply browned on both sides, about 5 minutes per side, adding more oil if needed for the second batch. Transfer to a heatproof bowl large enough to contain the meat, wine, and vegetables. Set aside.

3. Scrape or blot up any burned bits in skillet. Reduce the heat to medium-low and cook the onion, celery, carrot, and sliced garlic, stirring occasionally, until the vegetables are pale gold at the edges, 8 to 10 minutes. Add the wine, rosemary, sage, thyme, juniper berries, cloves, and any juices reserved from the boar packaging and simmer until the wine is reduced by one-third, about 5 minutes, scraping the bottom of the skillet to loosen any browned bits. Pour the hot mixture over the reserved meat, making sure the meat is submerged. If not, add a little water, wine, or a mixture of the two. Let cool to room temperature, cover, and refrigerate for at least 6 hours or up to overnight.

4. Transfer the meat and marinade to a 10-quart casserole or Dutch oven with a tight-fitting lid. Cover and slowly warm over very low heat.

5. Meanwhile, rinse the dried mushrooms in two changes of water, draining each time. Transfer to a deep bowl and cover with 3 cups of very warm tap water. Soak until soft, 20 to 30 minutes. If the meat has warmed through during this time, turn off the heat and set aside, covered.

6. Lightly squeeze some (but not all) of the liquid absorbed by the mushrooms from them and let it drip back into the soaking bowl. Transfer the mushrooms to another bowl and set aside. Strain the soaking liquid through a fine-mesh strainer. Measure 2½ cups and set aside. Reserve the additional liquid separately.

7. Preheat the oven to 350°F.

8. Uncover the casserole, raise the heat to medium, and stir in the reserved 2½ cups of mushroom-soaking liquid and ¾ teaspoon salt. Bring to a simmer, re-cover the casserole tightly, and bake for 20 minutes. Reduce the oven temperature to 250°F and continue to bake until the meat is very tender, about 4 hours. Adjust the oven temperature as needed to maintain a bare simmer.

9. Meanwhile, in a large skillet, melt the butter with the crushed garlic over medium heat. Add the mushrooms and toss to coat with the butter. Season generously with salt and cook, stirring constantly, until golden brown at the edges, 6 to 8 minutes. If the mushrooms seem dry, stir in a few tablespoons of the reserved soaking liquid. Set aside.

10. When the meat is very tender, remove the herb sprigs and sage leaves from the casserole and stir in the blueberries and mushroom-garlic mixture. Lightly push on the meat with a wooden spoon to partly collapse the chunks, allowing them to absorb more of the sauce, but do not shred them.

11. Cover and simmer gently over low heat for 15 minutes to combine the flavors. Taste the stew; it should be fluid, but the liquid should be concentrated and flavorful. If you think the stew is too thick and/or dry, add some of the remaining mushroom liquid or water and simmer, covered, for 15 minutes more. If you think the stew should be thicker and more concentrated in flavor, uncover and gently simmer for about 15 minutes longer, stirring occasionally. Stir in salt to taste and serve.

# -Chapter 9-

# ORGAN AND MIXED MEATS

# Tuscan-Style Meat Loaf with White Wine—Vegetable Sauce

### Polpettone

**Serves 4**

Anyone who has traveled and eaten in Tuscany knows that meat loaves in all their glory are a big deal. Tuscan cooks usually made loaves with finely ground leftover braised or roasted meats. While many of Tuscany's offerings still are made from cooked meats, others, such as this time-honored loaf, are made from ground raw meat. Try to find a butcher who will grind the meat right in front of you or who at least grinds his own meat. If you buy it prepackaged at the supermarket, we suggest a market with good turnover and meat that has not been previously frozen and looks fresh, evenly colored, and moist. This meat loaf is great hot or cold. Serve on a platter ringed with roasted or boiled potatoes and other vegetables, if you like.

**Wine Note:** Medium-bodied white wines go well with this, especially if the meat loaf is served cold. We loved a bottle of the Palazzone Orvieto Classico "Campo del Guardiano" (from Tuscany's neighbor Umbria) alongside the cool meat. Young, fresh, light, and medium-bodied reds such as young Chianti or Morellino di Scansano (chilled or not) work well, too. One favorite: Le Pupille Morellino di Scansano, a delicious, berry-filled Sangiovese-based wine from western Tuscany. For an American choice, look for the Le Ferme Martin Merlot, the easy-drinking second label from the Wolffer Estate on Long Island.

One 1½-inch-thick slice country-style bread, crust removed

3 to 4 tablespoons milk

½ pound ground pork

½ pound ground veal

½ pound ground beef

¼ pound mortadella, preferably Italian, thinly sliced and very finely chopped

1 ounce Parmigiano-Reggiano or other grana-type cheese, finely grated

¼ teaspoon freshly grated nutmeg

Kosher salt

3 large eggs

7 tablespoons extra-virgin olive oil

1 yellow onion, finely chopped

1 small carrot, peeled and finely chopped

1 stalk celery, finely chopped

2 large cloves garlic, finely chopped

2 tablespoons finely chopped fresh flat-leaf parsley

3 large fresh sage leaves, finely chopped

1 cup dry white wine

½ cup water

Freshly ground black pepper

1. In a large mixing bowl, moisten the bread with the milk and using your hands, repeatedly squeeze and mash the bread until it's almost a paste. Drain off any excess milk and add the pork, veal, beef, mortadella, cheese, nutmeg, and 2 teaspoons of salt.

2. Beat two of the eggs and add to the bowl. Using your hands, work the mixture until all the ingredients are very thoroughly combined.

3. Pass the meat mixture back and forth between your hands to form one big, smooth, round meatball without any seams or air pockets. Next, shape the meat into a smooth loaf about 8 inches long by 5 inches wide and 3 inches high. Transfer to a plate, cover, and refrigerate for at least 1 hour.

4. In a skillet, warm 3 tablespoons of the olive oil over medium heat and cook the onion, carrot, celery, garlic, parsley, and sage, stirring occasionally, until the onion is pale gold at the edges, 8 to 10 minutes. Remove from the heat and set aside.

5. Preheat the oven to 325°F.

6. In a flameproof casserole large enough to hold the loaf easily, heat the remaining 4 tablespoons of olive oil over medium-high heat. Salt the chilled meat loaf on top and, when the oil is quite hot, carefully put it in the casserole, salted side down. Cook, undisturbed, until deeply browned, reducing the heat if it threatens to burn, 5 to 7 minutes (see Notes).

7. Salt the side of the meat loaf now facing up and, using a thin metal spatula, very carefully release the meat from the bottom of the casserole. With the help of a second spatula, turn the loaf over. Add the wine and bring to a simmer. Adjust the heat so the wine simmers gently and cook until reduced by one-third, 3 to 4 minutes. Stir in the water. Add the vegetable mixture, spreading some over the top of the meat loaf itself, and baste the meat generously.

8. Wrap a 15-inch-square piece of parchment paper or aluminum foil over the top and sides of the meat so that the paper or foil presses gently against its exposed surfaces. Let the excess extend over the vegetables. Cover the casserole and bake for 40 to 45 minutes, or until an instant-read thermometer inserted in the center registers 155°F.

9. Let the meat loaf rest for 15 minutes, covered in the casserole. Transfer to a cutting board and keep it covered with the parchment or foil.

10. Meanwhile, rewarm the liquid in the casserole over very low heat. Beat the remaining egg in a small bowl and whisk a ladleful of the warm cooking liquid into the egg to temper it without curdling it. Slowly pour the egg mixture into the casserole, whisking continuously for 1 to 2 minutes until the sauce is creamy and fluid. Do not let it boil. (If the sauce seems overly thick, thin it with a bit of water.) Remove from the heat and keep warm.

11. Spoon about one-third of the sauce on serving plates or a serving platter. Slice the meatloaf into ⅜-inch-thick slices and arrange the slices on the plates or platter, overlapping them. Spoon the remaining sauce over the slices and generously top with freshly ground black pepper. Serve immediately.

**Notes:** It's important to let the loaf brown well on its first side, undisturbed, before turning; otherwise, it will stick and tear. A thin metal spatula is easy to slip under the loaf to free it before turning. It's easiest to turn the loaf if the casserole is roomy enough to hold it easily. If the casserole is not too deep, it's pretty simple to work with the spatula.

When you thicken the white wine–vegetable sauce with egg, it becomes delightfully creamy. If you prefer a denser and more intensely flavored sauce, purée it in a blender or food processor, with or without the egg. The sauce can be served chilled on chilled meat and, if necessary, thinned with a little broth or water.

When testing for doneness with an instant-read thermometer, don't overdo it. Too much poking releases valuable juices. A remote digital thermometer with a probe is a good alternative, but the best solution is to master the recipe as it cooks in your oven so that you don't have to rely on any sort of thermometer.

# Alsatian-Style Meat Casserole with Muenster Cheese

### Baeckeoffe au Munster

**Serves 4**

This is a favorite among the Alsatians, who named this rustic stew after the *baeckeoffe,* or baker's oven. In days gone by, dishes such as this were cooked in the local baker's large ovens when they were not being used to bake bread. A housewife might marinate a casserole of meats overnight and then leave it with the town baker, who put it in the bread oven once the fires died down.

Our version is prepared very traditionally but is finished in an uncommon but very Alsatian fashion. Muenster, the famous Alsatian cheese, isn't often used in connection with this, but we find that when the dish is finished with crispy bacon and Muenster, it's fantastic. It also becomes a dish that is just great with the region's world-famous (often love-it-or-hate-it) wine, Gewürztraminer. The ingredient list is long, but the process to make this brothy casserole is simple. Eat it with a spoon and, as is traditional, serve it with a big salad. Though the casserole will not be as good, you can shorten the marinating time or eliminate it altogether.

**Wine Note:** If you like Gewürztraminer, this is your dish. Because of its strong personality, it is rarely consumed with a meal and yet tastes great with this casserole. Try any number of fine producers: Rolly Gassman, Domaine Weinbach, "Réserve Particulière," Charles Schleret, or Schlumberger. If you don't like Gewürztraminer, this dish goes very nicely with many of the region's other white wines. The reason this dish is so suited to white wines might be because the meats are not browned before cooking (browning creates a meatier-tasting dish and would perhaps make this more suitable for bigger red wines—yet it is great as is with the lightweight Pinot Noirs of the region). In any event, this dish also goes well with Alsace's other dry white wines with big personalities, such as Riesling, Pinot Gris, the perfumed Muscat, and even the more neutral-tasting Pinot Blanc. In our preferences for a white wine with a pot full of red meats, once again, we found that wine and food don't always behave the way we expect them to.

2½ cups dry Alsatian Gewürztraminer wine

2 tablespoons finely chopped shallot

1 small stalk celery, thinly sliced

1 carrot, peeled and thinly sliced

2 large cloves garlic, finely chopped

2 bay leaves

2 sprigs fresh thyme

2 cloves

2 juniper berries, lightly crushed

¾ teaspoon ground coriander

Freshly ground black pepper

½ pound boneless pork shoulder,
cut into 1¼-inch cubes

½ pound boneless lamb shoulder,
cut into 1¼-inch cubes

½ pound boneless beef chuck,
cut into 1¼-inch cubes

2 ounces fatty, skinless salt pork, cut into strips
about ¼ inch thick and 1 inch long (optional)

2 tablespoons vegetable oil, lard, or goose fat

2 pounds large waxy potatoes such as Yukon Gold,
peeled and sliced ⅛ inch thick

Kosher salt

1 yellow onion, chopped

1 large leek, white and pale green parts only,
well rinsed and chopped

1 cup Chicken Stock (page 215)
or canned low-sodium chicken broth

½ pound thick-sliced bacon

½ pound Alsatian Muenster cheese,
cut into ¼-inch-thick slices

1.  In a saucepan, bring the wine to a simmer over medium-high heat. Reduce the heat and simmer gently until reduced to 2 cups, 4 to 5 minutes. Transfer to a large heatproof glass, ceramic, or other nonreactive bowl and let the wine cool for a few minutes.

2.  Add the shallot, celery, carrot, garlic, bay leaves, thyme sprigs, cloves, juniper berries, coriander, and a few generous grindings of pepper to the wine. When completely cool, add the pork, lamb, beef, and salt pork, if using. Mix well, cover, and refrigerate for at least 6 hours and up to 12 hours.

3.  Preheat the oven to 375°F. Grease the bottom and sides of a 3- to 4-quart heavy flameproof casserole with a tight-fitting lid with the oil.

4.  Lay one-third of the potatoes in an overlapping fashion in the casserole to cover the bottom completely and season with salt. Distribute half of the onion and leek over the potatoes. Remove half the meat and vegetables from the marinade, distribute both evenly over the onion and leek, and sprinkle with salt. Arrange another one-third of the potatoes on top of the meats, season with salt, and then layer on the remaining onion and leek and then the remaining meat and vegetables. Season with salt. Arrange the last third of the potatoes in an attractive pattern over the top.

5.  Pour the marinade remaining in the bowl and the stock over all. Sprinkle again with salt and cover the casserole tightly. (If the casserole lid does not fit tightly, lay a sheet of aluminum foil between the lid and the casserole to help seal it.) Bake for 30 minutes. Reduce

the oven temperature to 250°F and bake for 3½ hours longer. Remove the casserole from the oven and let it rest for 15 to 30 minutes.

6. Meanwhile, cut the bacon into 1-by-½-inch pieces and cook in a skillet over medium heat until crispy. Drain on paper towels and set aside.

7. When ready to finish the dish, preheat the broiler.

8. Distribute the cheese over the entire surface of the potatoes and put the casserole under the broiler until the cheese has melted and is golden in spots. To serve, divide the casserole among shallow bowls and place a large ladleful of the broth in each. Garnish with the reserved bacon and serve immediately.

# Piedmontese Mixed Poached Meats and Vegetables with Parsley Sauce

Bollito Misto con Salsa Verde

**Serves 6**

When serving this classic from the Piedmont and neighboring Emilia-Romagna regions of Italy, use a very sharp or electric carving knife or a serrated bread knife to slice the meats. Although we instruct you to serve this dish in elegant, individual shallow bowls, you could also serve it on a large platter, family style, moistened with a little broth. In addition to forks and knives, set the table with spoons to sip the broth flecked with the salsa verde.

The meats poach to unusual succulence, the broth is rich and restorative, and the addictive salsa verde is a touch of bright green genius that pulls everything together. We love this simple dish, in part because the cooking is largely unsupervised and the final dish keeps and reheats well. Two pieces of advice: First, because of its simplicity, *bollito misto* is greatly improved by the use of homemade chicken stock, so we encourage you to make a batch (see page 215). Second, to help the meats poach to optimum tenderness, let each of them come to room temperature before cooking.

🔨

**Wine Note:** Two special points emerged in our tastings for this dish, both as a result of the direct, spare quality of the meats. One, any wine that displays an impression of new oak, whether modest or bold, interferes with the simplicity of this dish. Even if you love the qualities that new oak brings to wines, you will find yourself reevaluating your affection when the wine is served alongside bollito misto. Two, what these poached meats need is a certain juiciness and tang, the wine in this way performing much like the accompanying salsa verde does, setting off the simple succulence of the meats themselves. Tannin feels strongly out of place here, maybe because there's no browned, roasted, or grilled crust on these meats. Interestingly, higher alcohol levels (14 or 15 percent), which sometimes taste clumsy and hot at the table, don't behave this way here. Again, could this be because there's no crust on the meats? So then, what sort of wine does this need? It needs a wine that is juicy and tangy in taste, low in tannin, solidly alcoholic, and fairly full in body. If you're familiar with the wines of Piedmont, you know the answer: Barbera. With a grand and traditional dish like this, it is fitting that the wine that best washed down this assortment of meats was also grand and traditional. We liked a selection of some of Piedmont's finest producers of Dolcetto, Barbera, and Nebbiolo, old- and new-school alike. But it was the Barbera D'Alba from Giacomo Conterno that everyone agreed most complemented the tastes and textures of the dish.

*1½ pounds beef brisket*
*(see Butcher's Note, page 69)*

*Kosher salt*

*1½ cups dry white wine*

*14 cups Chicken Stock (page 215)*
*or canned low-sodium chicken broth*

*½ pound end piece (scrap) prosciutto di Parma*
*or similar cured ham*

*1 fresh veal tongue (1 to 1½ pounds),*
*trimmed of excess fat*

*1 yellow onion, quartered*

*2 bay leaves*

*1½ pounds veal shoulder roast, tied*

*One 3-pound chicken*

*Bouquet garni: 1 large sprig fresh thyme,*
*1 small sprig fresh rosemary, and 4 sage leaves*

*24 baby turnips, peeled, or 4 medium turnips,*
*peeled and cut into 6 or 8 wedges*

*12 white or red new potatoes (about 1 pound),*
*halved or quartered, if large*

*4 to 5 large carrots, peeled and cut on the*
*diagonal into chunks about 2 inches long*

*3 red onions, cut lengthwise into quarters,*
*with stem end intact, peeled*

*2 cups Parsley Sauce (recipe follows)*

*1½ tablespoons finely chopped*
*fresh flat-leaf parsley*

1. Remove the brisket from the refrigerator about 1 hour before cooking (do so with all the meats as the recipe proceeds). When ready to cook, rub the brisket with 1 rounded tablespoon of salt and set aside.

2. In a very large, deep pot (at least 12-quart capacity), bring the wine to a simmer over medium heat and cook until reduced by half, about 5 minutes. Add the stock, ham, and 2 teaspoons salt and bring to a simmer over high heat. Reduce the heat to a bare simmer and add the beef brisket. Cover the pot and adjust the heat to maintain the barest possible simmer, which should be maintained throughout the entire cooking time and for all of the meats.

3. Meanwhile, in another pot, combine the veal tongue, yellow onion, bay leaves, and 1 tablespoon salt with enough water to cover by 2 inches. Bring to a boil, reduce the heat, and simmer gently for 45 minutes, uncovered. Remove from the heat and let the tongue cool in the cooking liquid until cool enough to handle. Using your fingers or a paring knife, peel the membrane surrounding the tongue. Cut away any remaining gristle and fat and return the tongue to the cooking liquid. Set aside.

4. After the brisket has cooked for 3 hours, rub the veal shoulder with 1½ teaspoons salt and let stand for 5 minutes. Add it to the pot with the brisket. Cover the pot and continue cooking at the barest possible simmer for 1 hour. Add the veal tongue, cover, and cook for 1 hour longer, for a total so far of 5 hours.

5. Generously rub the chicken with salt inside and out and let stand for 5 minutes. To make the bouquet garni, tie the herbs in a square of cheesecloth. Add to the cooking pot along with the chicken; arrange the other meats to accommodate the chicken. Cover and simmer for 25 minutes.

6. Add the turnips, potatoes, carrots, and red onions, nestling them between the meats. Cover and simmer until the vegetables are tender and the chicken is cooked through, about 20 minutes longer. Remove and discard the ham end and bouquet garni.

7. To serve, cut the brisket against the grain into ½-inch-thick slices. Untie the veal shoulder and cut into ½-inch-thick slices. Cut the veal tongue on the diagonal into ⅜-inch-thick slices. Remove the two breast halves from the chicken: Cut along one side of the breastbone and then, following the curve of the rib cage with your knife (or pulling with your fingers), remove the meat in one chunk. Repeat with the other breast half and cut each into ⅜-inch-thick slices. Pull the remaining chicken meat off the bone in chunks or hack the legs and thighs into 8 to 10 pieces. Keep warm under foil.

8. Fill a large sauceboat with the cooking broth, a serving dish with the parsley sauce, and a small dish with coarse salt to pass at the table.

9. Put a few slices of each variety of meat in warmed large, shallow serving bowls or deep plates. Place a piece or two of each vegetable in and around the meats. Moisten each serving with a small ladleful of the cooking broth and sprinkle lightly with the parsley. Cover and keep the remaining meat warm.

10. Serve right away, passing the broth, parsley sauce, and salt at the table.

# Parsley Sauce
Salsa Verde

**Makes about 2 cups**

---

*3 cups lightly packed fresh flat-leaf parsley leaves*

*5 to 6 anchovy fillets*

*4 hard-cooked egg yolks*

*2 heaping tablespoons capers, drained*

*2 tablespoons white wine vinegar*

*1 large garlic clove, sliced*

*½ teaspoon kosher salt*

*Generous pinch of cayenne*

*1 cup extra-virgin olive oil, plus more as needed*

---

1. In the bowl of a food processor fitted with the metal blade, combine all the ingredients except the olive oil and pulse to chop, pausing to scrape down the sides of the bowl as needed.

2. With the motor running, add the olive oil through the feed tube in a steady stream until all is added and the ingredients are finely chopped. The sauce should be flecked with green, thick but slightly runny, and look a little like broken herb mayonnaise. Process briefly with additional oil as needed. Cover and refrigerate for up to 1 day.

# Venetian-Style Calves' Liver

### Fegato alla Veneziana

**Serves 2**

Harry's Bar in Venice is notable for generations of catering to the rich and famous. In its glory days, Orson Welles and Charlie Chaplin could be spied at the bar. And, also famously, it's the birthplace of the Bellini cocktail. Harry's also makes a mean plate of calves' livers. The restaurant's take on this regional specialty is a real treat for avid liver lovers and will delight even those who are not sure they fall into this category. Its appeal is in the very thin, small pieces of liver, seared in a very hot pan until edged with brown, and melded with sweet, long-cooked onions, a splash of white wine, and a finish of butter and parsley.

As simple as this may be, it does require a willingness to sear the liver in a smoking hot pan. Read through the recipe so that you're prepared to execute the last few steps swiftly and thus avoid overcooking the liver, although we've found that this is so tasty that a tendency to overcook does very little harm. While it demands focus, if you want to serve four diners, make another batch at the same time in a second skillet. We like this served over a mound of soft polenta or alongside small slabs of grilled polenta.

**Butcher's Note:** To ready the calf's liver for cooking, peel the tissue from the surface of the meat and trim away any large, gristly tubes. Using a very sharp knife, cut the liver into 2 to 4 roughly equal-sized slabs of any length but each about ¾ inch in height and 1 to 2 inches in width. Working with one slab at a time, cut each into ¼-inch-thick bite-size pieces as uniform in width as possible. If you don't feel up to it (or your knives are dull), any or all of this can be performed by your butcher.

**Wine Note:** As often as not, when Venetians reach for a red wine, Valpolicella is their choice (see page 89 for more information on these wines). Sipping a glass alongside this sweet and savory dish, you can't argue with their good sense. The favorites in our tasting were the Le Salette Valpolicella Classico and Zenato Valpolicella Classico Superiore, both zesty, medium-weight, and just the right foil for the liver. Interestingly, the richer and more extracted bottlings, such as the exceptionally fine Allegrini "Palazzo della Torre," proved just too powerful for the dish among our group. For an American choice, a simple medium-weight Pinot Noir is the play here. One favorite: the Ramsay Pinot Noir from California's North Coast.

---

*5 tablespoons extra-virgin olive oil*

*3 yellow, white, or sweet onions, or a mixture, halved and very thinly sliced*

*Kosher salt*

*¾ pound calf's liver, cut into ¼-inch slices, at room temperature (see Butcher's Note)*

*¼ cup dry white wine*

*2 tablespoons finely chopped fresh flat-leaf parsley*

*Freshly ground black pepper*

*2 tablespoons unsalted butter, cut into 4 pieces*

---

1. In a large skillet, heat the olive oil over medium heat and cook the onions, stirring often, for about 5 minutes. Reduce the heat to medium-low and continue to cook, stirring occasionally, until the onions are softened and lightly golden but not browned, 30 to 40 minutes. Stir in a generous pinch of salt and transfer the onions and oil to a small bowl. Remove all onion bits remaining in the skillet and strain the oil mixed with the onions back into the skillet. Press lightly on the onions to extract as much oil as possible. Set the onions aside.

2. Have all the ingredients close at hand for finishing the dish. Turn on the stove vent if you have one.

3. If needed, add more olive oil to the skillet to measure about 4 tablespoons and heat over high heat. When the oil has smoked for about 30 seconds, quickly and carefully add the liver in a single layer. Sear the liver, undisturbed, for 1½ to 2 minutes, or until deeply browned along the underside edges.

4. Using a metal spatula, scrape the liver from the bottom of the pan and turn over. Sprinkle generously with salt and add the wine, scraping the bottom of the skillet to loosen any browned bits, and cook for about 20 seconds, stirring. Reduce the heat to medium-low and stir in the onions, two-thirds of the parsley, and a few generous grindings of black pepper. Add the butter and stir until the liquid in the skillet thickens slightly, 30 seconds to 1 minute. Add salt to taste.

5. Serve immediately, garnished with the remaining parsley.

# Creamy Chicken Livers with Vin Santo

Cibreo Aretino

**Serves 4 as an appetizer, 2 as a main course**
Here is another old Tuscan favorite with as many variations as there are sun-drenched villas tucked into Tuscany's golden hills. *Cibreo* traditionally includes the gizzards, hearts, and cockscombs from the chicken, as well as the liver. Cockcombs may be making a small comeback in upscale restaurants, but we omitted them in deference to the home cook. With the livers alone, this is truly delicious, but if you feel the desire to include any of the chicken parts we mentioned, feel free. (Both gizzards and hearts should be thinly sliced before browning; cockscombs should be simmered in lightly salted water or broth for 10 minutes and patted dry before browning.) Along with a salad, this makes a great luncheon or a quick dinner. Alone, it makes a lovely first course as part of a more elaborate meal.

**Wine Note:** Though wine gods and taste-meisters may hurl lightning bolts, we found that a glass of chilled, sweet, nutty Vin Santo, Tuscany's distinctive dessert wine, tastes best with this. Yes, a number of Tuscan dry reds and whites are quite good, too, so drink them if the thought of consuming liver with a sweet wine makes you squirm. While very good wine and food matches are common enough throughout the book, overall we find that truly great wine and food matches are rare. It's much more fun to play along when a match like this presents itself, a match that, it should be said, wouldn't have

struck anybody as strange as recently as a hundred years ago when restaurants and dinner hosts frequently matched meat and sweet wine.

Foie gras and Sauternes is a similar tradition that displays the affinity of savory liver and sweet wine. Although chicken livers may lack the sex appeal of foie gras, with a glass of Vin Santo, they blossom. It's nice, too, that once you have used the half cup called for in the sauce, the rest of the bottle (which starts at about $20) won't languish in the pantry. If any is still in the bottle after dinner, keep drinking it straight through dessert. The widely available Lungarotti Vin Santo from neighboring Umbria is affordable and very good. Any number of producers of Chianti, Brunello di Montalcino, and Vino Nobile di Montepulciano make excellent Vin Santo, so ask your wine merchant for help if you want to splurge on a special bottle (most are available in half bottles, too). Although the styles and prices vary somewhat, all but the very sweetest versions of Vin Santo work well with this dish. Be sure to serve them cool but not iced.

---

*1⅔ pounds chicken livers, trimmed of any connective tissue, cut into 1-inch pieces*

*3 tablespoons vegetable or olive oil*

*Kosher salt*

*2 tablespoons unsalted butter*

*1 small yellow onion, finely chopped*

*½ cup Vin Santo or similar sweet wine*

*¾ cup Chicken Stock (page 215) or canned low-sodium chicken broth*

*2 large egg yolks*

*2 teaspoons fresh lemon juice*

*2 teaspoons all-purpose flour*

*Freshly ground black pepper*

*4 thick slices country-style bread, toasted*

*2 tablespoons finely chopped fresh flat-leaf parsley*

---

1. Blot the chicken livers dry and bring to room temperature on a plate lined with paper towels.

2. Turn on the stove vent if you have one. Preheat a large heavy skillet over medium heat for a few minutes. Raise the heat to high, wait about 20 seconds, and add the oil, swirling to coat the skillet. When the oil begins to smoke, quickly and carefully add the chicken livers and cook until nicely browned on the first side, 2 to 3 minutes. Using tongs, turn the pieces over and continue to cook for about 1 minute longer. The livers should be barely pink in the center. Salt them generously and toss to distribute the salt. Transfer to a plate and set aside.

3. Let the skillet cool slightly and place it over medium heat. Melt the butter and cook the onion, stirring occasionally, until softened but not colored, 5 to 6 minutes. Add the Vin Santo and cook until reduced by half, 2 to 3 minutes, scraping the bottom of the skillet to loosen any browned bits. Add the stock and bring just to a simmer.

4. In a small bowl, whisk together the egg yolks, lemon juice, flour, ¼ teaspoon salt, and a few generous grindings of pepper. When the stock mixture is hot, gradually whisk a ladleful into the egg mixture. Reduce the heat to low, pour the egg mixture into the skillet, and stir with a rubber spatula, making sure to run it along the edges of the skillet, until the sauce thickens slightly, 30 seconds to 1 minute.

5. Return the chicken livers and any accumulated juices to the sauce, stirring to coat. Cook over low heat, stirring regularly, until the sauce clings to the pieces of liver but is still fluid, 2 to 3 minutes more. If necessary, cook the sauce a few moments more to thicken or thin with a tablespoon or two of stock or water.

6. Place the toasts on warmed serving plates and spoon the mixture over them. Garnish with the parsley and a generous grinding of pepper. Serve at once.

# Madrid-Style Tripe with Oxtail and Chorizo

Callos a la Madrileña

**Serves 4 to 6**

This dish for tripe lovers tastes richly of Spain. One of its secrets is that the tripe is cooked twice and for a very long time—first, alongside browned oxtails and a pig's foot, and then again with onions, garlic, tomato, serrano ham, chorizo, and smoked paprika. The result is a soft, gelatin-rich broth that bathes the meltingly tender tripe in a rich composite of these flavors and textures. All of the cooking should be done at the barest possible simmer so that the right amount of liquid evaporates and the tripe cooks to the desired texture. When prepared in this way, *callos a la Madrileña* ranks with the elite tripe preparations of western Europe, which include *tripes à la mode de Caen* (tripe cooked with vegetables and apple brandy); *gras-double Lyonnaise* (tripe with lots of onions, wine vinegar, and parsley); *gras-double à la Provençal* (tripe with tomato, garlic, parsley, basil, and cheese); *buseca* (Milanese-style tripe with vegetables, shell beans, turnips, cabbage, and grated cheese); *trippa alla Romana* (tripe with long-cooked meat and tomato sauce, mint, and grated cheese). This dish takes time, but as tripe lovers know, most of the best tripe dishes do.

**Wine Note:** If you've taken the time to prepare callos a la Madrileña, why not seek out a fine ten- to fifteen-year-old Rioja Gran Reserva to serve alongside the mellow but spicy tripe. They are great partners. One standout in our tasting was the La Rioja Alta Gran Reserva "904." For a simpler wine from the New World, look for a soft and silky Pinot Noir like the Alamos Pinot Noir from Nicolás Catena in Mendoza, Argentina.

*3 pounds preblanched honeycomb beef tripe, trimmed (about 2 ½ pounds after trimming)*

*1 pig's foot (about 1 pound), split lengthwise by the butcher*

*Kosher salt*

*2 pounds oxtail, cut crosswise into pieces*

*¼ cup vegetable or olive oil*

*1 ½ cups dry white wine*

*14 cups water*

*2 cloves*

*1 yellow onion, halved*

*1 small carrot, peeled*

*4 large cloves garlic, crushed*

*1 bay leaf*

*2 sprigs fresh thyme*

**Vegetable-paprika sauce**

*¼ cup extra-virgin olive oil*

*4 ounces Spanish chorizo, casing removed, halved lengthwise and sliced ⅛ inch thick*

*1 yellow onion, finely chopped*

*6 cloves garlic, minced*

*3 ounces thinly sliced serrano
or similar cured ham, finely chopped*

*3 canned large plum tomatoes,
drained and chopped*

*2 teaspoons smoked sweet Spanish paprika
such as pimentón de la Vera*

*⅛ teaspoon cayenne pepper*

*2 teaspoons finely chopped fresh thyme*

*2 tablespoons finely chopped fresh flat-leaf parsley*

*Sliced country-style bread, toasted,
for serving (optional)*

---

1. Working in the sink, put the tripe in a large bowl, cover it with cold water, and rinse by agitating and swishing it around in the water for 30 seconds or so and then draining. Repeat until the water runs clear, or nearly so. Drain. Cut off or pull away any excessively fatty deposits. If the tripe has a few areas that are bunched up and much thicker than the rest of it, use a small knife and butterfly these areas by cutting into their thickness and folding them open to make the thickness of the tripe even.

2. Transfer the tripe and the pig's foot to a large heavy pot, cover with cold water by 2 inches, and bring to a boil over high heat. When the water reaches a boil, drain and rinse the meats under cold water. Cut the tripe into rectangles about 2 by 4 inches and set aside the tripe and pig's foot in a large bowl.

3. Generously salt the oxtail pieces on both sides.

4. Wipe out the cooking pot, add the vegetable oil, and heat over medium-high heat. Cook the oxtail until deeply browned on both sides, about 5 minutes per side. As each piece finishes browning, add to the bowl with the meats.

5. Pour off the oil and place the pot over medium heat. Add the wine and simmer for 3 minutes, scraping the bottom of the pot to loosen any browned bits. Add the oxtail, tripe, and pig's foot and cover with the 14 cups water. Bring to a simmer over medium-high heat, thoroughly skimming any foam that rises to the surface.

6. Stick the cloves into the onion halves and add to the pot along with the carrot, garlic, bay leaf, and thyme. Cook, uncovered, at the barest possible simmer (no more than a few bubbles breaking the surface) for 5 hours. Stir occasionally and make sure the tripe is submerged. After 5 hours, drain the meats into a colander lined with cheesecloth set over a large bowl. Let the meats sit until cool enough to handle. Reserve the cooking liquid.

7. While the meats are cooling, make the sauce: Wipe out the pot and heat the olive oil over medium-high heat. Cook the chorizo, tossing regularly, until slightly crisp but still tender, about 1½ minutes. Transfer to a plate with a slotted spoon and set aside until needed.

8. Reduce the heat to medium-low and add the chopped onion, garlic, and ham and cook until the onion is soft but without color, about 5 minutes. Stir in the tomatoes, smoked paprika, cayenne, and thyme and cook 1 minute more. Remove from the heat and set aside.

9. When the meat is cool enough to handle, pick the meat from the oxtail and shred it into a bowl, discarding all fat and bones (you want to collect any loose gelatinous material to help thicken the stew). Repeat with the pig's

foot (there won't be much meat) and add both meats to the reserved vegetable sauce. Discard the remaining vegetables in the colander.

10. One by one, place the tripe rectangles on a cutting board and cut them crosswise into very thin slices about 2 inches long. Add to the vegetable sauce.

11. Measure 6 cups of the reserved cooking liquid (reserving the rest) and stir this into the pot of meats and vegetables. Reheat and cook, uncovered, at a bare simmer, stirring occasionally, until the tripe is very tender and the liquid has thickened to become richly gelatinous but still soupy, 2 to 2½ hours. It should resemble a very dense but still fluid stew. Simmer additionally to thicken or add small amounts of the reserved cooking liquid to thin.

12. Stir in the reserved chorizo and let the stew rest off the heat for 5 minutes. Ladle into wide, shallow bowls and garnish with parsley and toasts, if using. Serve with spoons.

-Chapter 10-

# Stocks
# and
# Seasoning
# pastes

# Beef Stock

### Makes about 7 cups

---

*¼ cup olive or vegetable oil*

*4 pounds meaty beef bones,*
*such as ribs, shin, or tail*

*16 cups cold water*

*1 onion, quartered*

*1 carrot, peeled*

*1 stalk celery*

*2 large cloves garlic, crushed*

*2 sprigs fresh thyme*

*½ teaspoon salt*

---

1.  In a stock pot, heat the oil over medium-high heat and cook the beef bones, in 2 batches if necessary, until very deeply browned on all sides, including the meaty edges of ribs, 6 to 8 minutes per side. Reduce the heat if they threaten to burn. Remove the beef to a plate and pour off the oil in the pot.

2.  Return the pot to medium-high heat and add the water, scraping the bottom of the pot to loosen any browned bits. Return the beef and any accumulated juices and bring to a simmer. As it comes to a simmer, skim off any foam that rises to the surface with a ladle or large spoon. Cook, uncovered, at the barest possible simmer, stirring occasionally, for 2½ hours.

3.  Add the onion, carrot, celery, garlic, thyme, and salt. Cook, uncovered, at the barest possible simmer, stirring occasionally, for 2 hours and 30 minutes.

4.  Remove from the heat and let the stock rest for 15 minutes. Strain through a large fine-mesh strainer or a colander lined with a double layer of damp cheesecloth into a large bowl.

5.  Fill a larger bowl or the sink with ice and water and nest the bowl of stock in it. Stir regularly until the stock has cooled.

6.  Transfer the cooled stock to airtight containers and refrigerate for up to 3 days or freeze for up to 3 months.

# Pork Stock

### Makes about 5 cups

---

*3 tablespoons vegetable oil*

*3 pounds meaty pork spareribs*
*or bone-in country-style ribs, or a combination,*
*cut into individual ribs or large pieces*

*8 cups cold water*

*½ yellow onion, halved again*

*½ carrot, peeled*

*½ stalk celery*

*2 large cloves garlic, crushed*

*2 small sprigs fresh thyme*

*¼ teaspoon salt*

---

1. In a stock pot, heat the oil over medium-high heat and cook the pork in two batches until the meat is very deeply browned on all sides, including the meaty edges, 6 to 8 minutes per side. Reduce the heat if it threatens to burn. Transfer the pork to a plate and pour off the oil in the pot.

2. Return the pot to the medium-high heat and add the water, scraping the bottom of the pot to loosen any browned bits. Return the pork and any accumulated juices to the pot and bring to a simmer. As it comes to a simmer, skim off any foam that rises to the surface with a ladle or large spoon.

3. Add the onion, carrot, celery, garlic, thyme, and salt. Cook, uncovered, at the barest possible simmer, stirring occasionally, for 1 hour and 30 minutes.

4. Remove from the heat and let the stock rest for 15 minutes. Strain through a large fine-mesh strainer or a colander lined with a double layer of damp cheesecloth into a large bowl.

5. Fill a larger bowl or the sink with ice and water and nest the bowl of stock in it. Stir regularly until the stock has cooled.

6. Transfer to airtight containers and refrigerate for up to 3 days or freeze for up to 3 months.

# Veal Stock

### Makes about 8 cups

*¼ cup olive or vegetable oil*

*4 pounds meaty pieces of veal, with bone attached (see Notes)*

*16 cups cold water*

*1 yellow onion, quartered*

*1 carrot, peeled*

*1 stalk celery*

*2 large cloves garlic, crushed*

*2 sprigs fresh thyme*

*2 teaspoons tomato paste (optional; see Notes)*

*½ teaspoon salt*

1. In a stock pot, heat the oil over medium-high heat and cook the veal, in two batches if necessary, until very deeply browned on all sides, including the meaty edges, 6 to 8 minutes per side. Reduce the heat if it threatens to burn. Transfer the veal to a plate and pour off the oil in the pot.

2. Return the pot to medium-high heat and add the water, scraping the bottom of the pot to loosen any browned bits. Return the veal and any accumulated juices to the pot and bring to a simmer. As it comes to a simmer, skim off any foam that rises to the surface with a ladle or large spoon. Note the level of the liquid in the pot. Cook, uncovered, at the barest possible simmer, stirring occasionally, for 2 hours. To compensate for the evaporating liquid, every so often add small amounts of hot water

to keep the liquid at or near the level you noted. As the stock simmers, continue to skim the impurities that rise to the surface occasionally as carefully and thoroughly as you can.

3. Add the onion, carrot, celery, garlic, thyme, tomato paste, if using, and salt. Continue to simmer in the same way for 2 hours longer, skimming occasionally, although this time, do not add any water so that the broth slowly concentrates and reduces in volume.

4. Remove from the heat and let the stock rest for 15 minutes. Strain through a large fine-mesh strainer or a colander lined with a double layer of damp cheesecloth into a large bowl.

5. Fill a larger bowl or the sink with ice and water and nest the bowl of stock in it. Stir regularly until the broth has cooled.

6. Transfer to airtight containers and refrigerate for up to 3 days or freeze for up to 3 months.

**Notes:** Use veal breast cut into individual ribs; veal shoulder, neck, or shank cut into chunks; or any combination of these. If your butcher has veal bones in manageable sizes, add some of those, too.

The tomato paste adds good color, but it is not necessary for this stock to work with any of the recipes in the book.

# Lamb Stock

### Makes about 4 cups

*3 tablespoons vegetable oil*
*3 pounds meaty lamb bones, preferably some from the neck shoulder, cut into large pieces*
*8 cups cold water*
*½ medium onion, halved again*
*½ carrot, peeled*
*½ stalk celery*
*2 large cloves garlic, crushed*
*2 small sprigs fresh thyme*
*¼ teaspoon salt*

1. In a stock pot, heat the oil over medium-high heat and cook the lamb in two batches until the meat is very deeply browned on at least two sides, 6 to 8 minutes per side. Reduce the heat if it threatens to burn. Transfer the lamb to a plate and pour off the oil in the pot.

2. Return the pot to medium-high heat and add the water, scraping the bottom of the pot to loosen any browned bits. Return the lamb and any accumulated juices to the pot and bring to a simmer. As it comes to a simmer, skim off any foam that rises to the surface with a ladle or large spoon.

3. Add the onion, carrot, celery, garlic, thyme, and salt. Cook, uncovered, at the barest possible simmer, stirring occasionally, for 2 hours.

4. Remove from the heat and let the stock rest for 15 minutes. Strain through a large fine-mesh strainer or a colander lined with a double layer of damp cheesecloth into a large bowl.

5. Fill a larger bowl or the sink with ice and water and nest the bowl of stock in it. Stir regularly until the stock has cooled.

6. Transfer to airtight containers and refrigerate for up to 3 days or freeze for up to 3 months.

# Chicken Stock

### Makes about 6 cups

---

*3 pounds chicken wings, cut into 3 or 4 pieces each*

*8 cups cold water*

*½ large onion, halved again*

*½ carrot, peeled and halved*

*½ stalk celery, halved*

*2 large cloves garlic, crushed*

*2 sprigs fresh thyme*

*½ bay leaf*

*¼ teaspoon salt*

---

1. In a stock pot, combine the chicken wings with the water and bring to a simmer over medium-high heat. As it comes to a simmer, skim off any foam that rises to the surface with a ladle or large spoon.

2. Add the onion, carrot, celery, garlic, thyme, bay leaf, and salt. Cook, uncovered, at a gentle simmer, stirring occasionally, for 1 hour.

3. Remove from the heat and let the stock rest for 15 minutes. Strain through a large fine-mesh strainer or a colander lined with a double layer of damp cheesecloth into a large bowl.

4. Fill a larger bowl or the sink with ice and water and nest the bowl of broth in it. Stir regularly until the broth has cooled.

5. Transfer to airtight containers and refrigerate for up to 3 days or freeze for up to 3 months.

# Shellfish Stock

### Makes 2½ to 3 cups

---

*2 tablespoons vegetable oil*

*½ pound shrimp with shells, coarsely chopped*

*1½ cups Chicken Stock (at left)
or canned low-sodium chicken broth*

*1½ cups water*

*1 yellow onion, chopped*

*1 shallot, chopped*

*1 small carrot, peeled and chopped*

*1 stalk celery, chopped*

*1 sprig fresh thyme*

*1 bay leaf*

*4 black peppercorns*

---

1. In a saucepan, heat the oil over high heat until almost smoking. Add the shrimp and cook, stirring occasionally, until the shells turn orange and the exposed meat is pale gold at the edges, about 3 minutes.

2. Add the stock and water, scraping the bottom of the pan to loosen any browned bits. Bring to a simmer and skim any foam that rises to the surface.

3. Add the onion, shallot, carrot, celery, thyme, bay leaf, and peppercorns and return to a simmer. Cover partially and simmer gently over low heat for 45 minutes.

4. Strain the mixture through a fine-mesh strainer into a bowl, pressing firmly and repeatedly on the solids to extract all their flavorful juices.

5. Use immediately, or let cool, transfer to airtight containers, and refrigerate for up to 3 days.

# Portuguese-Style Hot Red Pepper Paste

Massa de Malagueta

**Makes about 1 cup**

---

*½ pound fresh medium-hot red chili peppers
such as fresno, red jalapeño, or serrano*

*1 small garlic clove, sliced*

*1 teaspoon kosher salt*

*¼ cup olive oil*

---

1. Using a paring knife, remove the stem and seeds from the peppers, reserving some of the seeds. Chop the peppers coarsely and transfer to the bowl of a food processor fitted with the metal blade.

2. Add the garlic, salt, and olive oil and process for 30 seconds to 1 minute, pausing occasionally to scrape down the sides of the bowl, until a homogenous paste forms, with some of the bright red bits still showing in the paste. Process briefly with the reserved seeds if you like a hotter paste. Cover and refrigerate until ready to use.

# Portuguese-Style Sweet Red Pepper Paste

Massa de Pimentão

**Makes about 1 cup**

---

*4 large red bell peppers, seeded and cut in half*

*1 large clove garlic, sliced*

*¼ teaspoon kosher salt*

*1 teaspoon sweet paprika*

*Generous pinch of cayenne*

*3 tablespoons olive oil*

---

1. Preheat the oven to 350°F.

2. Lightly oil the surface of a large baking pan. Arrange the peppers, cut side down, in the pan and roast for 1 to 1½ hours, or until their skins have blackened in spots and the peppers are tender. Remove the peppers from the oven and, when cool enough to handle, peel and discard the skins.

3. Put the peppers in the jar of a blender and add the remaining ingredients. Blend at medium speed for 1 to 2 minutes or until a smooth purée forms, pausing occasionally to scrape down the sides of the jar. Transfer the mixture to a small bowl. Cover and refrigerate until ready to use.

**Make-Ahead Tip:** Though it's best made the day of use, this paste can be made a day or two ahead and stored, tightly covered, in the refrigerator.

# Italian-Style Lard Paste

### Makes about ½ cup

*½ clove garlic, peeled*

*Pinch of kosher salt*

*6 ounces fatty, skinless salt pork, rinsed and cut into chunks (see Note)*

*2 teaspoons finely chopped fresh sage*

*1 teaspoon finely chopped fresh rosemary*

*¼ teaspoon freshly ground black pepper*

1. Chop up the garlic and sprinkle with the salt. Work the garlic into a paste by repeatedly smearing it with the broad side of a chef's knife.

2. Transfer the garlic paste to the bowl of a food processor fitted with the metal blade. Add the salt pork, sage, rosemary, and pepper. Process until very smooth, 3 to 4 minutes, pausing regularly to scrape down the sides of the bowl.

3. Pack the lard paste into a ramekin or custard cup, cover tightly with plastic wrap, and refrigerate for up to 1 month.

**Variation:** To make a Spanish-Style Lard Paste, substitute 1 tablespoon of finely chopped fresh thyme for the sage and rosemary.

**Note:** Use salt pork with little or no lean meat. Even after processing, the paste will contain small bits of solids, which can burn over high heat. Because of this, we recommend browning food first in olive oil and, once it's browned, draining off and discarding the oil, then adding the lard paste as called for in the recipe. If you prefer not to bother with this step, watch the lard paste carefully during browning. This paste is traditionally made with fresh pork fatback, which is difficult to find in the United States. But if you do, by all means use it—it yields an even better result than salt pork. Because fatback is less salty than salt pork, just remember to compensate (when making the dishes in this book) by adding a bit more salt than is called for.

# Index

# Table of Equivalents

*The exact equivalents in the following tables have been rounded for convenience.*

LIQUID/DRY MEASURES

| U.S. | Metric |
|---|---|
| ¼ teaspoon | 1.25 milliliters |
| ½ teaspoon | 2.5 milliliters |
| 1 teaspoon | 5 milliliters |
| 1 tablespoon (3 teaspoons) | 15 milliliters |
| 1 fluid ounce (2 tablespoons) | 30 milliliters |
| ¼ cup | 60 milliliters |
| 1/3 cup | 80 milliliters |
| ½ cup | 120 milliliters |
| 1 cup | 240 milliliters |
| 1 pint (2 cups) | 480 milliliters |
| 1 quart (4 cups, 32 ounces) | 960 milliliters |
| 1 gallon (4 quarts) | 3.84 liters |
| 1 ounce (by weight) | 28 grams |
| 1 pound | 454 grams |
| 2.2 pounds | 1 kilogram |

LENGTH

| U.S. | Metric |
|---|---|
| 1/8 inch | 3 millimeters |
| ¼ inch | 6 millimeters |
| ½ inch | 12 millimeters |
| 1 inch | 2.5 centimeters |

OVEN TEMPERATURE

| Fahrenheit | Celsius | Gas |
|---|---|---|
| 250 | 120 | ½ |
| 275 | 140 | 1 |
| 300 | 150 | 2 |
| 325 | 160 | 3 |
| 350 | 180 | 4 |
| 375 | 190 | 5 |
| 400 | 200 | 6 |
| 425 | 220 | 7 |
| 450 | 230 | 8 |
| 475 | 240 | 9 |
| 500 | 260 | 10 |